75TH ANNIVERSARY EDITION

D-DAY

REMEMBERED

6 JUNE 1944

IN PARTNERSHIP WITH
IWM

RICHARD HOLMES

SEVENOAKS

THIS IS A SEVENOAKS BOOK

Text copyright © Richard Holmes 2004, 2014, 2019

Design and map copyright © Carlton Books Ltd 2004, 2019

Imperial War Museums photographs and memorabilia copyright © Imperial War Museums

This edition published in 2019 by SevenOaks, an imprint of the Carlton Publishing Group, 20 Mortimer Street, London W1T 3JW

Material from this book was originally published in *The D-Day Experience* by Richard Holmes in 2004

A CIP catalogue for this book is available from the British Library

ISBN 978 1 78177 947 7

Printed in Dubai

CONTENTS

05	INTRODUCTION
06	INDEX OF MAPS
08	THE PLANNING
16	THE LEADERS
20	GERMAN FORCES & DEFENCES
28	DECEPTION & INTELLIGENCE
36	THE RESISTANCE & SOE
42	PEGASUS BRIDGE
52	BRITISH AIRBORNE ASSAULT
58	US AIRBORNE ASSAULT
68	UTAH BEACH
76	POINTE DU HOC
82	OMAHA BEACH
96	GOLD BEACH
102	JUNO BEACH
112	SWORD BEACH
124	VILLERS-BOCAGE
134	PLUTO & MULBERRY
142	OPERATION EPSOM
148	BOCAGE FIGHTING & CHERBOURG
156	OPERATION CHARNWOOD
162	MEDICS
168	BATTLE FOR ST-LÔ
178	OPERATION GOODWOOD
184	OPERATION COBRA
190	OPERATION LÜTTICH
194	TACTICAL AIR SUPPORT
200	OPERATIONS TOTALIZE & TRACTABLE
206	THE FALAISE POCKET
212	THE LIBERATION OF PARIS
220	TRANSLATIONS / INDEX / CREDITS

INTRODUCTION

IT WAS THE LARGEST-EVER AMPHIBIOUS OPERATION, AND IS ONE OF THOSE EVENTS FOR WHICH THE MUCH-MISUSED PHRASE "TURNING POINT" IS INDEED APPROPRIATE.

Yet there is more to the summer of 1944 than D-Day, crucial though it was. First, we must acknowledge the role played by Russia in eating the heart out of the German army. D-Day is seen in its proper context only if set alongside the Russian Belorussian offensive, which destroyed German Army Group Centre on the Eastern Front that summer.

Second, D-Day was made possible by the Western Allies' efforts elsewhere. Strategic bombing weakened the German industrial base and diverted resources to the defence of the Reich. The long and painful slog up Italy by the men nicknamed "D-Day dodgers" forced the Germans to commit troops who would have been valuable on the Eastern or Western fronts. Nor should we forget that while D-Day was the much-publicized beginning of the end of the war in Europe, in Burma Bill Slim's 14th Army battled on far from the spotlight.

D-Day also relied on naval superiority, so long and so bitterly fought for. Without the Battle of the Atlantic there could have been no D-Day. Though the emphasis of this book is on land operations in France, no historian can be unaware of the part played by the naval plan, Operation Neptune, in enabling the landings to take place in the first instance. Almost 7,000 vessels, from battleships to landing craft, were assigned to Operation Neptune. Most were British, American and Canadian, but it is an indication of the breadth of the coalition that there were French, Norwegian, Dutch, Polish and Greek vessels too.

Last, D-Day's importance all too often obscures the significance of the Normandy campaign as a whole. Getting ashore was only part of the challenge, though challenge it certainly was. The force disembarked in Normandy had to be sustained with food, ammunition and reinforcements along sea lanes kept open by Allied navies, and supported by aircraft from strategic bombers to those ubiquitous Dakotas which helped revolutionize the evacuation of casualties.

RICHARD HOLMES

OPPOSITE *A trio of infantrymen move cautiously forward on a patrol in the Baron and Eterville area south-west of Caen.*

INDEX OF MAPS

13   **Operation Neptune** Naval assault phase: 6 June

24   **German Defences in the West** Divisional deployments: 6 June

57   **British Airborne Assault** 6th Airborne Division: 6 June

61   **US Airborne Assault** 101st and 82nd Airborne Divisions: 6 June

73   **Utah Beach** US landings: 6–8 June

85   **Omaha Beach** US landings: 6–8 June

99   **Gold Beach** British landings: 6 June

108   **Juno Beach** Canadian landings: 6 June

115   **Sword Beach** British landings: 6 June

125   **Villers-Bocage** British 7th Armoured Division: 11–13 June

147   **Operation Epsom** British advance south of Caen: 24–30 June

151   **The Capture of Cherbourg** US advance to Cherbourg: 13–30 June

161   **Operation Charnwood** British & Canadian capture of Caen: 7–9 July

171   **Battle for St-Lô** US advance south: 30 June–24 July

183   **Operation Goodwood** British attempted breakout: 18–21 July

187   **Operation Cobra** US breakout: 25–31 July

183   **Operation Lüttich** German counter-attack: 7–8 August

203   **Operations Totalize & Tractable** British & Canadian offensives: 7–15 August

210   **The Falaise Pocket** German army surrounded: 6–19 August

218   **The Liberation of Paris** Allies cross the Seine: 14–25 August

FRANCE 6 June 1944

NORMANDY LANDINGS 6 June 1944

ALLIED ADVANCES 13 June 1944

ALLIED ADVANCES 19 August 1944

CHERBOURG

MAP p.151: CHERBOURG

les Pieux

30 JUNE

Bricquebec

Carteret   Barneville   St-Sauveur-le-Vicomte

Portbail   30 JUNE   Beuzeville-la-Bas

la Haye-du-Puits   St-Jores

Lessay

Périers

Coutances

Bréhal

Granville

St-Pair-sur-Mer

N

Carolles   Sartilly

Avranches

Baie du Mont-St-Michel

le Mont-St-Michel

0   10 km
0   10 miles

MAP KEY Common symbols used on the maps in this book:

NATIONAL COLOURS

- US
- British
- Canadian
- French
- Polish
- German

MILITARY UNITS / TYPES

- ⊠ Infantry
- ◤ Armoured
- ⊠ Motorized infantry
- ⌒ Airborne
- ◈ Parachute

SIZE OF MILITARY UNITS

- XXXXX Army group
- XXXX Army
- XXX Corps
- XX Division
- X Brigade
- III Regiment
- II Battalion
- Elements of a unit (elts)

MILITARY SYMBOLS

- ♛ Defence battery
- ● German resistance
- ■ Area of strong German resistance
- ⌣ Beach mines
- —XXXX— Army boundary line
- —XX— Divisional boundary line
- ▲ Strategic point
- ◉ Town
- ✴ Site of bombing
- → German movement
- → Allied movement

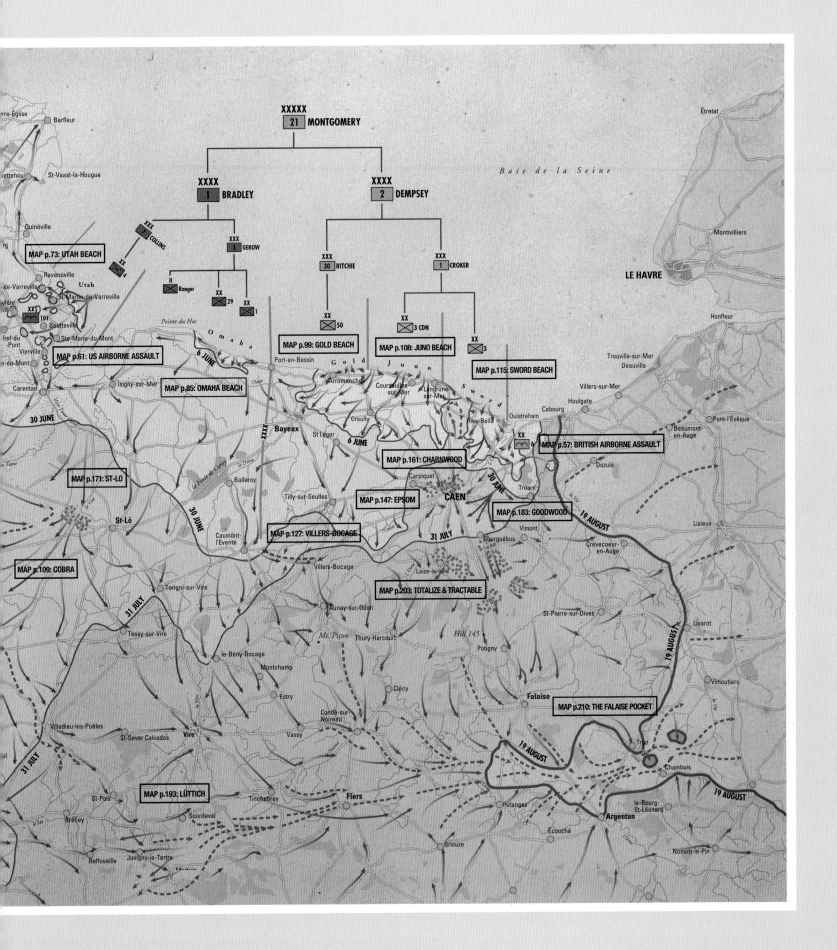

XXXXX
21 MONTGOMERY

XXXX
1 BRADLEY

XXXX
2 DEMPSEY

XXX
7 COLLINS

XXX
5 GEROW

XXX
30 RITCHIE

XXX
1 CROKER

XX
4

II Ranger

XX
29

XX
1

XX
50

XX
3 CDN

XX
3

XX
101

Baie de la Seine

Étretat

Barfleur

St-Vaast-la-Hougue

Quinéville

Montivilliers

LE HAVRE

MAP p.73: UTAH BEACH

Ravenoville

Utah

St-Martin-de-Varreville

Boutteville

Honfleur

Ste-Marie-du-Mont

Vierville

Pointe du Hoc

Omaha

MAP p.61: US AIRBORNE ASSAULT

6 JUNE

Port-en-Bessin

Gold

Juno

Arromanches

Trouville-sur-Mer

Deauville

MAP p.85: OMAHA BEACH

Isigny-sur-Mer

l'Aure

Courseulles-sur-Mer

Langrune-sur-Mer

MAP p.115: SWORD BEACH

Villers-sur-Mer

Carentan

30 JUNE

Bayeux

St Léger

Creully

6 JUNE

Riva-Bella

Sword

Ouistreham

Cabourg

Houlgate

Pont-l'Évêque

Beaumont-en-Auge

l'Orne

MAP p.57: BRITISH AIRBORNE ASSAULT

Dozulé

MAP p.171: ST-LO

La Forêt de Cerisy

la Drôme

Balleroy

MAP p.161: CHARNWOOD

Carpiquet

CAEN

30 JUNE

Troarn

la Vie

Tilly-sur-Seulles

MAP p.147: EPSOM

MAP p.183: GOODWOOD

19 AUGUST

Lisieux

St-Lô

30 JUNE

Caumont-l'Eventé

MAP p.127: VILLERS-BOCAGE

l'Odon

Bourguébus

Vimont

Crèvecoeur-en-Auge

MAP p.109: COBRA

31 JULY

Villers-Bocage

Laize-la-ville

31 JULY

St-Pierre-sur-Dives

Torigni-sur-Vire

MAP p.203: TOTALIZE & TRACTABLE

Dive

Tessy-sur-Vire

Aunay-sur-Odon

l'Orne

Livarot

Mt. Pinçon

Thury-Harcourt

Hill 145

Potigny

le-Bény-Bocage

Montchamp

Vimoutiers

Clécy

Falaise

MAP p.210: THE FALAISE POCKET

la Vire

Estry

Villedieu-les-Poêles

Condé-sur-Noireau

19 AUGUST

St-Sever Calvados

Vire

Vassy

la Vire

l'Orne

Trun

Chambois

31 JULY

MAP p.193: LÜTTICH

Tinchebray

Flers

19 AUGUST

19 AUGUST

St-Pois

le-Bourg-St-Léonard

la Sée

Brécey

Sourdeval

Putanges

Argentan

Écouché

Reffuveille

Juvigny-le-Tertre

Briouze

Nonant-le-Pin

THE PLANNING

ON 12 FEBRUARY 1944 GENERAL DWIGHT D. EISENHOWER, SUPREME COMMANDER, ALLIED EXPEDITIONARY FORCE, WAS DIRECTED TO "ENTER THE CONTINENT OF EUROPE AND, IN CONJUNCTION WITH OTHER UNITED NATIONS, UNDERTAKE OPERATIONS AIMED AT THE HEART OF GERMANY AND THE DESTRUCTION OF HER ARMED FORCES."

It had been clear from December 1941 that the defeat of Germany was the principal Allied war aim, although there were challenges to overcome before an invasion of Europe was possible. War industry had to be developed, and sea and air communications maintained: winning the Battle of the Atlantic against German submarines would be crucial. Germany was worn down by land, air and sea, with her industrial capacity eroded by the growing weight of Allied strategic bombing. The war against Japan forced America and, to a lesser degree, Britain, to devote resources to the Far East, and the

relationship with Russia, whose leader Joseph Stalin repeatedly demanded the opening of a second front, had to be developed.

While the Allies were united in their opposition to Germany, they had practical and cultural differences. The British sometimes struck the Americans as over-cautious and preoccupied with imperial concerns,

BELOW *Band of Brothers? The Allied commanders, 1 February 1944. From left to right: Bradley, Ramsay, Tedder, Eisenhower, Montgomery, Leigh-Mallory, and Eisenhower's chief of staff, Walter Bedell Smith.*

OPPOSITE *Envelope used for circulating SHAEF meeting minutes.*

BLM 106

TOP
SECRET

SHAEF   CONFERENCES.

while the Americans sometimes seemed brash and headstrong. Nevertheless, there were sufficient good working relationships within the alliance, notably that between US President Franklin D. Roosevelt and British Prime Minister Winston Churchill, to ensure that strategy moved inexorably in the right direction.

Operation Bolero saw the concentration of US men and equipment in Britain. After the Allied invasion of North Africa in November 1942, an Allied conference at Casablanca outlined plans for the invasion of Europe in 1944. Although a Supreme Allied Commander was not yet nominated, the British Lieutenant General F. E. Morgan was appointed "Chief of Staff to the Supreme Allied Commander (designate)", Cossac for short. The Washington conference in May 1943 elaborated the forces that he would have at his disposal, and ordered that a draft of the plan for what was now called Operation Overlord should be ready by 1 August. The planners were helped by the fact that much work had already been done on similar projects. The Dieppe raid of August 1942, when a Canadian division had been landed with disastrous results, was amongst the landings from which planners could draw lessons.

The Cossac team considered three invasion areas: the Pas de Calais, Normandy and Brittany. The latter was ruled out by distance, both from Britain and from Allied objectives in Europe, and the Pas de Calais

was too obvious. It was decided that Normandy, with its large port at Cherbourg, was a better choice. The outline plan envisaged an amphibious assault by three divisions, with airborne divisions dropped on both flanks. There were still unanswered questions, notably who would actually command the invasion, and how enough landing craft could be made available. But in December 1943 it was announced that Eisenhower would take command, with Air Chief Marshal Sir Arthur Tedder as his deputy. All three component commanders were British: General Sir Bernard Montgomery would command ground forces, Admiral Sir Bertram Ramsay naval forces, and Air Chief Marshal Sir Trafford Leigh-Mallory air forces. Montgomery recognized that the blow delivered by the Cossac plan was unlikely to be sufficiently heavy, and in early 1944 he expanded it to comprise an amphibious assault by five divisions with drops by three airborne divisions.

OPPOSITE *US War Bonds poster used in the campaign to raise money to meet the cost of the invasion.*

BELOW *After the raid: Dieppe, 19 August 1942, where 2nd Canadian Infantry Division suffered over 3,300 casualties. Fire support was hopelessly inadequate, and planners had not assessed the effect of shingle on tank tracks.*

'I AM VERY UNEASY ABOUT THE WHOLE OPERATION. AT THE BEST IT WILL FALL SO VERY VERY FAR SHORT OF THE EXPECTATIONS OF THE BULK OF THE PEOPLE, NAMELY THOSE WHO KNOW NOTHING OF ITS DIFFICULTIES. AT THE WORST IT MAY WELL BE THE MOST GHASTLY DISASTER OF THE WHOLE WAR. I WISH TO GOD IT WERE SAFELY OVER.

FIELD MARSHAL SIR ALAN BROOKE, CHIEF OF THE IMPERIAL GENERAL STAFF, 5 JUNE 1944

BELOW *A Sicilian beach seen from a British landing craft. Two Allied armies invaded Sicily in July 1943. The amphibious landings went comparatively well, but airborne operations were marred by poor weather.*

6 JUNE 1944

OPERATION NEPTUNE

**NAVAL FORCES ASSIGNED TO OPERATION NEPTUNE
(THE NAVAL ASSAULT PHASE)**

NAVAL COMBATANT VESSELS: 1,213
LANDING SHIPS AND CRAFT: 4,126
ANCILLARY SHIPS AND CRAFT: 736
MERCHANT SHIPS: 864

TOTAL: 6,939

BRITISH/CANADIAN: 9%
US: 16.5%
OTHER ALLIES: 4.5%

133,000 men landed from the sea

ABOVE *The insignia of the Supreme
Headquarters Allied Expeditionary
Forces (SHAEF). The flaming sword
represents avenging Allied forces; the
black, the darkness of Nazism; and the
rainbow, the liberty to come.*

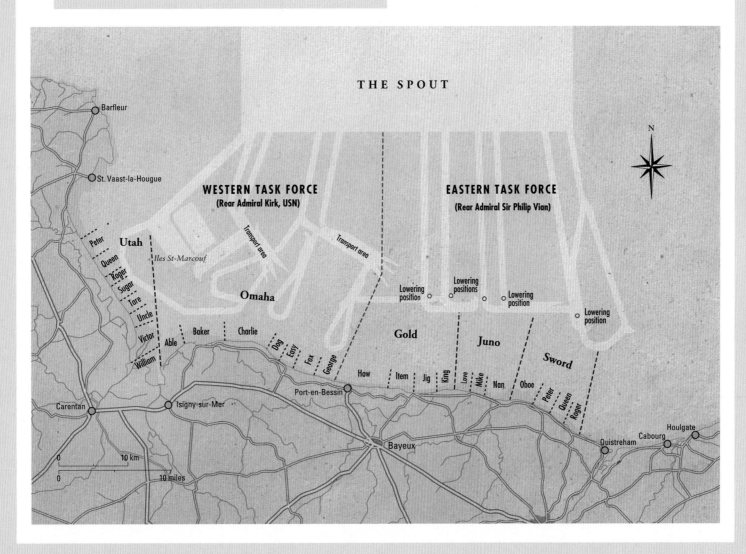

[BLM 72/2]   APPENDIX 'A'.

MOST SECRET.

First Impressions of Operation 'OVERLORD'
made at the request of the Prime Minister
by General MONTGOMERY.

1.   The following must be clearly understood :

(a) Today, 1 January, 1944, is the first time I have
seen the Appreciation and proposed plan or considered
the problem in any way.

(b) I am not as yet in touch with Admiral RAMSAY and
have not been able to consult any Naval expert.

(c) I have not been able to consult the Air C-in-C,
or any experienced air officer.

(d) Therefore these initial comments can have little
value.   They are merely my first impressions after
a brief study of COS(43)416(0).

2.   The initial landing is on too narrow a front and is
confined to too small an area.

By D + 12 a total of 13 Divisions have been landed on
the same beaches as were used for the initial landings.
This would lead to the most appalling confusion on the beaches,
and the smooth development of the land battle would be made
extremely difficult – if not impossible.

Further Divisions come pouring in, all over the same
beaches. By D + 24 a total of 24 Divisions have been landed,
all over the same beaches; control of the beaches and so on
would be very difficult; the confusion, instead of getting
better, would get worse.

My first impression is that the present plan is im-
practicable.

3.   From a purely Army point of view the following points
are essential:

(a) The initial landings must be made on the widest
possible front.

(b) Corps must be able to develop their operations
from their own beaches, and other Corps must NOT
land _through_ those beaches.

(c) British and American areas of landing must be
kept separate. The provisions of (a) above
must apply in each case.

(d) After the initial landings, the operation must be
developed in such a way that a good port is secured
quickly for the British and for American forces.
Each should have its own port or group of ports.

4.   The type of plan required is on the following lines:

(a) One British Army to land on a front of two, or
possibly three, Corps. One American Army similarly.

(b) Follow-up Divisions to come in to the Corps already
on shore.

(c) The available assault craft to be used for the
leading troops. Successive flights to follow
rapidly in any type of unarmoured craft, and to
be poured in.

/The air....2

APEX 'A' (Con't).

- 2 -

(d) The air battle must be won before the operation
is launched. We must then aim at success in the
land battle by the speed and violence of our operations.

5.   It is hardly possible to discuss the broad plan without
Naval and Air discussion. But if such a thing were possible
there would be many advantages in putting armies on shore in
such a way that:

(a) The British effort was directed to securing the
CAEN – CHERBOURG area, with CHERBOURG as the main
British port initially.

(b) The American effort was directed to securing the
area ST. MALO – ST NAZAIRE – BREST, with the main
American ports in the BREST peninsula.

6.   I am disturbed at the limitations of transport aircraft
referred to in para 17 of the Digest.

There are four Airborne Divisions, and four U.S.
Parachute Regts available. All of these will be needed
for the initial effort. We must surely take steps to
ensure that we can lift at one time at least the equivalent
of four Airborne Divisions.

(Sgd) B.L. MONTGOMERY.

MARRAKECH,
1st January, 1944.   General.

TOP SECRET

TOP SECRET

BIGOT   BIGOT [BLM 106/20]

SCAEF 21st MEETING

2nd June, 1944.   5

SUPREME HEADQUARTERS
ALLIED EXPEDITIONARY FORCE
Office of AC of S, G-3

Minutes of Meeting held in the ANCXF Conference Room
at SOUTHWICK HOUSE at 1000 hours, 2nd June, 1944

PRESENT

General Dwight D. Eisenhower
Air Chief Marshal Sir A. Tedder
Admiral Sir B.H. Ramsay
General Sir B.L. Montgomery
Air Chief Marshal Sir T.L. Leigh-Mallory
Lieutenant General W.B. Smith
Lieutenant General Sir H.M. Gale
Rear Admiral J.E. Creasy
Major General H.R. Bull
Major General K.V. Strong   (BLM)
Major General F.W. de Guingand
Air Vice Marshal H.E.P. Wigglesworth
Air Vice Marshal J.M. Robb
Brigadier General A.S. Nevins

I.   WEATHER FORECAST

The agreed weather forecast was presented orally by Group Captain Stagg.
Admiral Ramsay and Air Chief Marshal Leigh-Mallory stated the effect of the
predicted weather conditions from the Naval and Air Force viewpoints,
respectively.   General discussion followed.

The Supreme Commander directed that the sailing of Bombarding Squadrons and
other preparations necessary at this time should proceed.   The next SCAEF
meeting for further critical examination of the weather forecast is to be held
at 2130 hours, 2nd June, in the ANCXF Conference Room at SOUTHWICK HOUSE.

II.   BOMBING ON D DAY AND SUBSEQUENT DAYS

Air Chief Marshal Leigh-Mallory discussed the plan for bombing, on D day and
subsequent days, designated to establish a belt of bombed routes through towns
and villages thereby preventing or impeding the movement of enemy formations
toward the areas seized by our troops.   He inquired as to his freedom to proceed
with the execution of this plan in view of the civilian casualties which would
result.   Air Chief Marshal Tedder stated the necessity of being certain of the
efficacy of this line of action.

The Supreme Commander announced his approval of the planned bombing as an
operational necessity to assist the Army in landing and in securing a firm
foothold.

III. WARNING THE FRENCH

Air Chief Marshal Leigh-Mallory inquired if any additional methods could be
adopted to warn the FRENCH inhabitants of the bombing.   Air Chief Marshal Tedder
advocated the dropping of warning leaflets on D day and subsequent days to
minimize civilian casualties.

-1-

TOP SECRET

TOP SECRET

The AC of S, G-3, was directed to arrange with the PW Division for the
provision of appropriate leaflets to be dropped by the Air Forces within the
lodgement and cover areas on D day and subsequent days.

IV.   NEXT SCAEF MEETING

It was announced that the next SCAEF meeting would be held in the ANCXF
Conference Room at Southwick House at 2130 hours, 2nd June, 1944.

DISTRIBUTION

One copy each officer present
One extra copy to Air Chief Marshal Sir A. Tedder
One copy each to Lieutenant General F.E. Morgan
   and Major General Hoyt Vandenburg
One copy AG Records

TOP SECRET

ABOVE *Minutes of the SHAEF meeting held on 2 June 1944, marked
Top Secret, during which the plan for the bombing on D-Day and
subsequent days was discussed in view of civilian casualties.*

THE LEADERS

THE LEADERS OF THE FORCES THAT CLASHED IN NORMANDY PRESENTED A SHARP CONTRAST.

Dwight Eisenhower, born in 1890, the son of a railway worker, was commissioned in 1913. He saw no action in the First World War, but worked closely with US Army Chief of Staff George C. Marshall and, although decidedly junior, commanded the North African landings in 1942. Eisenhower emerged as a skilful conciliator rather than a flamboyant leader. He had deep reserves of moral courage, and though he can be criticized for spending too long looking up to the military/political level rather than down to the operational/tactical level, his common sense and good nature were invaluable strengths. While Tedder, his British deputy, was devoted to him, the prickly but experienced Montgomery argued that Eisenhower had no real grasp of his task. Ramsay was a hard-working and level-headed naval officer who did much to make Operation Neptune, the naval part of the invasion plan, work well. Leigh-Mallory was an experienced fighter commander, on poor terms with the "bomber barons" whose heavy aircraft froze off the invasion sector. He got on badly with both Coningham, whose Allied Second Tactical Air Force provided air cover in Normandy, and Montgomery, who thought him over-cautious.

The German Commander in Chief West was Field Marshal Gerd von Rundstedt. Born in 1875, Rundstedt served throughout the First World War, retired on age grounds in 1938, but commanded army groups in 1940 and 1941. He was brought back from retirement to be Commander in Chief West in March 1942. Rundstedt was brave, honourable and conventional. He did not enjoy Eisenhower's power, for neither German air nor naval forces in the west (small though both were) answered to him, and his authority was so circumscribed by Hitler that he quipped that the only troops he could move were the sentries at his gates.

Rundstedt clashed with Field Marshal Erwin Rommel, whose Army Group B held the invasion area. Rommel, his reputation made in North Africa, threw his energy into the improvement of beach defences. He argued that the invasion had to be stopped on the beaches, so German armour must be committed early. His experience convinced him that the traditional solution of identifying the main thrust and concentrating to meet it would not work in the face of Allied air power. Hitler imposed a compromise solution, which was to leave the armoured divisions of Panzer Group West too far from the coast, and only a single armoured division, 21st Panzer, came into action on D-Day.

The Allies enjoyed advantages before the first shot was fired. Although there was some friction in their chain of command, the structure was logical, and the supreme commander had the temperament for his task. The German system, in contrast, mirrored the conflicting power blocs of the Third Reich, with the heavy hand of Hitler all too apparent.

ABOVE *Ramsay had retired from the navy before the war, but was the directing brain of the Dunkirk evacuation in 1940. He made a characteristically level-headed contribution to Allied planning in 1944.*

ABOVE Although Eisenhower lacked great operational experience, his engaging manner and easy style made him a natural coalition commander.

ABOVE Early in 1944 Montgomery was given command of 21st Army Group comprising all Allied land forces committed to D-Day.

ABOVE Tedder had commanded the Mediterranean Allied Air Forces before being appointed Eisenhower's deputy. He was a staunch supporter of Ike's, but had little time for Montgomery.

ABOVE Leigh-Mallory, a First World War pilot, played a prominent part in the Battle of Britain, and headed Fighter Command from 1942. His tenure as Eisenhower's air commander was marred by personality clashes.

ABOVE Rundstedt, born in 1875, had actually retired in 1938, but commanded army groups in 1940 and 1941. 0After another spell of retirement he became Commander in Chief West in 1942.

ABOVE Rommel had an outstanding First World War record as an infantry officer, and was a divisional commander in 1940. He shot to prominence as commander of Axis troops in North Africa.

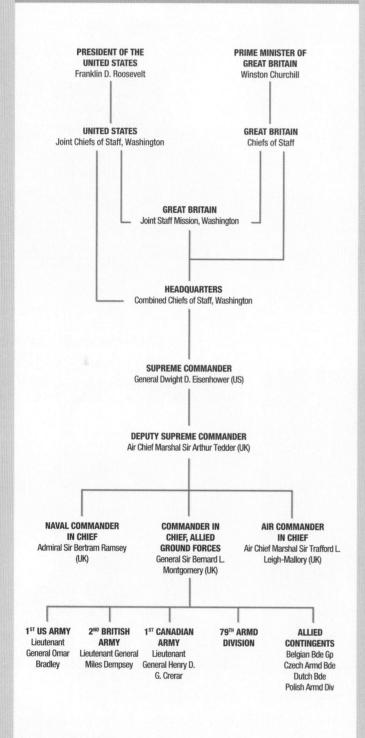

ALLIED CHAIN OF COMMAND NORMANDY

6 JUNE 1944

PRESIDENT OF THE UNITED STATES
Franklin D. Roosevelt

PRIME MINISTER OF GREAT BRITAIN
Winston Churchill

UNITED STATES
Joint Chiefs of Staff, Washington

GREAT BRITAIN
Chiefs of Staff

GREAT BRITAIN
Joint Staff Mission, Washington

HEADQUARTERS
Combined Chiefs of Staff, Washington

SUPREME COMMANDER
General Dwight D. Eisenhower (US)

DEPUTY SUPREME COMMANDER
Air Chief Marshal Sir Arthur Tedder (UK)

NAVAL COMMANDER IN CHIEF
Admiral Sir Bertram Ramsey (UK)

COMMANDER IN CHIEF, ALLIED GROUND FORCES
General Sir Bernard L. Montgomery (UK)

AIR COMMANDER IN CHIEF
Air Chief Marshal Sir Trafford L. Leigh-Mallory (UK)

1ST US ARMY
Lieutenant General Omar Bradley

2ND BRITISH ARMY
Lieutenant General Miles Dempsey

1ST CANADIAN ARMY
Lieutenant General Henry D. G. Crerar

79TH ARMD DIVISION

ALLIED CONTINGENTS
Belgian Bde Gp
Czech Armd Bde
Dutch Bde
Polish Armd Div

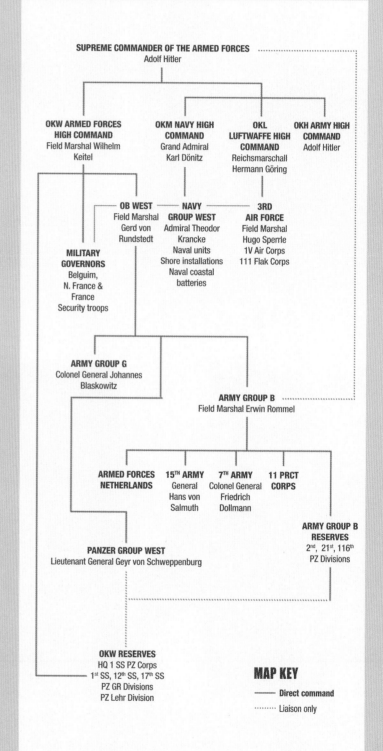

GERMAN CHAIN OF COMMAND NORMANDY

6 JUNE 1944

SUPREME COMMANDER OF THE ARMED FORCES
Adolf Hitler

OKW ARMED FORCES HIGH COMMAND
Field Marshal Wilhelm Keitel

OKM NAVY HIGH COMMAND
Grand Admiral Karl Dönitz

OKL LUFTWAFFE HIGH COMMAND
Reichsmarschall Hermann Göring

OKH ARMY HIGH COMMAND
Adolf Hitler

OB WEST
Field Marshal Gerd von Rundstedt

NAVY GROUP WEST
Admiral Theodor Krancke
Naval units
Shore installations
Naval coastal batteries

3RD AIR FORCE
Field Marshal Hugo Sperrle
1V Air Corps
111 Flak Corps

MILITARY GOVERNORS
Belguim,
N. France &
France
Security troops

ARMY GROUP G
Colonel General Johannes Blaskowitz

ARMY GROUP B
Field Marshal Erwin Rommel

ARMED FORCES NETHERLANDS

15TH ARMY
General Hans von Salmuth

7TH ARMY
Colonel General Friedrich Dollmann

11 PRCT CORPS

ARMY GROUP B RESERVES
2nd, 21st, 116th PZ Divisions

PANZER GROUP WEST
Lieutenant General Geyr von Schweppenburg

OKW RESERVES
HQ 1 SS PZ Corps
1st SS, 12th SS, 17th SS
PZ GR Divisions
PZ Lehr Division

MAP KEY

— Direct command

······· Liaison only

ABOVE *Eisenhower's handwritten note, wrongly dated,*
taking full personal responsibility for the D-Day landings.
This was to have been published if they had failed.

GERMAN FORCES & DEFENCES

FOR THE GERMANS, THE WEST WAS "A POOR MAN'S WAR" OVERSHADOWED BY THE STRUGGLE AGAINST THE RUSSIANS.

Rundstedt was responsible for the whole of France and the Low Countries, with 1st and 19th Armies of Army Group G covering the area south of the Loire, 7th and 15th Armies of Army Group B dealing with the Loire to the Dutch border, and Armed Forces Netherlands holding Holland. He had to do much with little. General Blumentritt, his chief of staff, complained that there was insufficient motor transport: infantry divisions had to rely on horses. Air attacks had reduced the flow of fuel,

ammunition and spares, and many units had to detrain so far back that they were already tired by the time they came into battle. Some formations, like the SS Panzer divisions, were very good indeed, but others had been worn down by combat in the east and had not yet been

BELOW *This propaganda shot shows a fast-firing MG 34 machine gun in a beach bunker. The soldier on the right has two stick grenades to hand.*

fully reconstituted. Coastal divisions had weak artillery and little inherent mobility. Many of their officers and men had already been wounded, and one division was composed entirely of men with stomach ailments. The Germans made wide use of *Osttruppen,* recruited from amongst Russian prisoners of war and comprising a variety of national and ethnic groups: there were no less than 21 "Russian" battalions in the 7th Army alone. Blumentritt identified 25 different types of division which varied in composition, with requirements for spares and ammunition which made them a quartermaster's nightmare.

Although the Germans were certain that the Allies would indeed invade – in November 1943 Hitler issued a directive foreseeing an

FRIEDRICH DOLLMANN

was commissioned into the Bavarian field artillery in 1901 and spent the First World War in regimental and staff appointments. He commanded 7th Army in the 1940 campaign, earning the Knight's Cross and promotion to colonel general. Dollmann remained in the same post, and by 1944 lacked any recent combat experience. Criticized by Hitler for permitting the fall of Cherbourg, Dollmann probably committed suicide at Le Mans on 28 June, though formal records attribute his death to a heart attack.

RIGHT *Identity disk of one of the Organization Todt construction workers. The disk was discovered in 1988 on the site of a POW camp for Germans at Foucarville, behind Utah Beach. In the spring of 1944 Organization Todt, under the direction of Albert Speer, had committed around 18,000 men to Atlantic Wall building duties.*

BELOW *A 1943 German photograph shows the erection of beach defences. These anti-landing obstacles were primitive by the standards of the Atlantic Wall in June 1944.*

RIGHT *A Maschinenpistole 40 (MP 40), a German sub-machine gun developed during the war. These were in limited supply and were issued only to select troops.*

offensive "not later than the spring, perhaps earlier" – they were unsure as to time and place. Most generals, deciding on the basis of traditional military education, thought the Pas de Calais, the most direct route, a more likely objective than Normandy. Hitler, reasoning intuitively, suspected that Normandy was more probable, but General Walter Warlimont admitted that his comrades were "not quite convinced" by this. The Germans were in a state of acute air inferiority, although many generals argued that this had less effect on the outcome of individual battles than it did on movement behind the lines. "It was like pitting a racehorse against a motor car," wrote one.

Yet it was not that simple. The Germans had some first-rate weapons, like the 88mm anti-tank gun, and tanks like the Panther and Tiger. Until defeats in the east and west in mid-1944 struck fatal damage to its replacement system, the German army took more time and trouble to train senior NCOs than the British and Americans took to train junior officers. And if the fighting on the Eastern Front had done terrible damage to the Germans, it had also left them with a hard-forged nucleus of experienced junior commanders, men like Michael Wittmann, who almost single-handedly stopped the British 7th Armoured Division on 14 June, and Hans von Luck, whose determination did so much to thwart British plans in Operation Goodwood the following month. Allied policy of offering Germany only unconditional surrender persuaded many German soldiers, even if they had little sympathy with the Nazis, that failure in Normandy would result in the invasion of their homeland. The defenders of Normandy were certainly not supermen: but this was an army with proud traditions, fighting with its back to the wall against adversaries who enjoyed quantitative superiority but often lacked experience and the sheer killer instinct.

ABOVE *Rommel is briefed at what the original caption calls "his anti-invasion headquarters". He was in fact based at the Duc de la Rochefoucauld's château at La Roche-Guyon, between Rouen and Paris.*

RIGHT *An aerial photograph, taken just before D-Day, shows a variety of beach defences exposed at low water: most were designed to disable landing craft.*

INSET *A sign warning French civilians to stay off the mined beaches.*

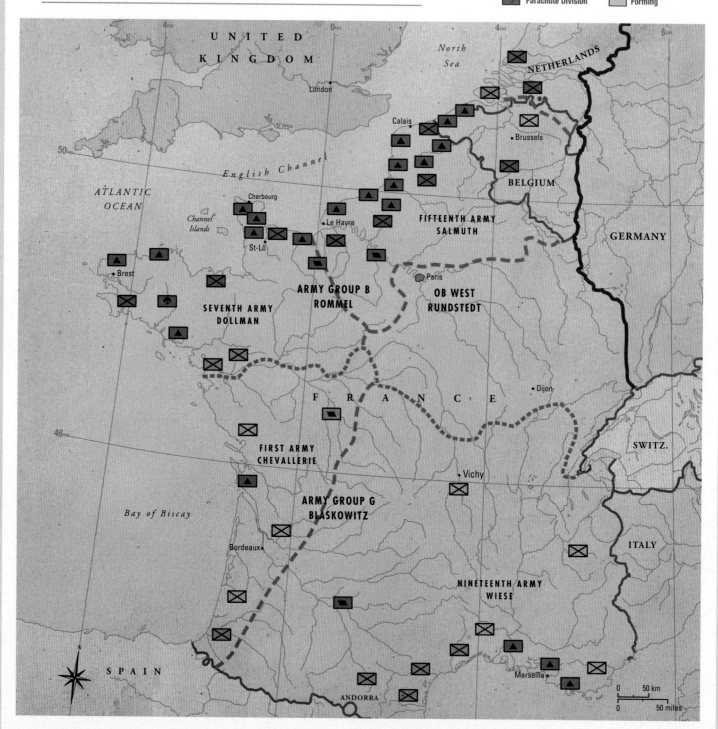

GERMAN DEFENCES IN THE WEST

MAP KEY

- – – – Army boundaries
- · · · · Army Group boundaries
- ——— Rear boundary of the OB West

Divisional deployments

- ⊠ Infantry Division
- ▰ Panzer Division
- ◣ Parachute Division
- ▲ Static Division
- ▰ Refitting
- ▰ Forming

UNITED KINGDOM

London

North Sea

NETHERLANDS

Calais

Brussels

BELGIUM

GERMANY

ATLANTIC OCEAN

English Channel

Cherbourg

Channel Islands

Le Havre

St-Lô

FIFTEENTH ARMY
SALMUTH

Brest

Paris

ARMY GROUP B
ROMMEL

OB WEST
RUNDSTEDT

SEVENTH ARMY
DOLLMAN

F R A N C E

Dijon

SWITZ.

FIRST ARMY
CHEVALLERIE

Vichy

ARMY GROUP G
BLASKOWITZ

Bordeaux

Bay of Biscay

ITALY

NINETEENTH ARMY
WIESE

N

SPAIN

Marseille

ANDORRA

0   50 km
0   50 miles

COPY No. 205

TOP SECRET

O.N.1. APPENDIX VII,

ANNEXE A.

ASSAULT BEACH DEFENCE MAPS.

ABOVE & OVERLEAF *Top-secret Allied documents showing details of German beach defences.*

GERMAN ANTI-TANK OBSTACLES USED AS UNDERWATER OBSTACLES

TETRAHEDRA. I.

2'6 or
4·0 high.

TETRAHEDRA. II

2'6 or
4·0 high

GERMAN STEEL OBSTACLES—HEDGEHOG

5'7"

N.B. Has also been
seen supported on
stakes, making overall
effective height of
8ft.

GERMAN ANTI-TANK OBSTACLES USED AS UNDERWATER OBSTACLES

CURVED RAIL OBSTRUCTIONS

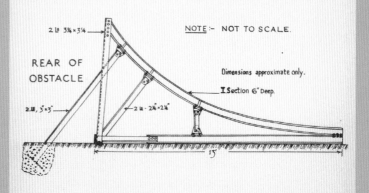

2 Ls 3⅜ × 3¼

NOTE :- NOT TO SCALE.

REAR OF
OBSTACLE

Dimensions approximate only.

I Section 6" Deep.

2 Ls, 5 × 5

2 Ls - 2¾ × 2¼

15'

TYPICAL GERMAN DEFENCE WORKS IN THE WEST
COAST ARTILLERY OBSERVATION POST

TOP SECRET

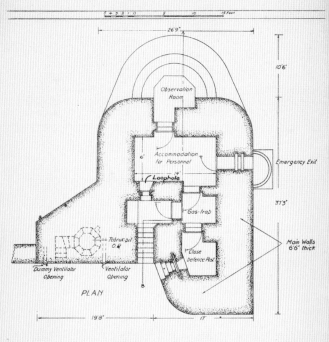

PLAN

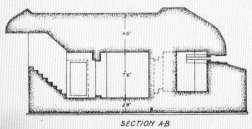

SECTION A·B

K

TYPICAL GERMAN DEFENCE WORKS IN THE WEST

TOP SECRET

PILLBOX WITH 75mm A/TK GUN -

Scale 1:200

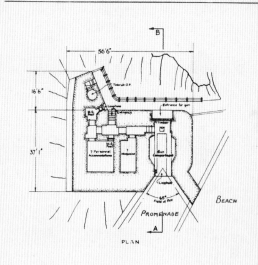

PLAN

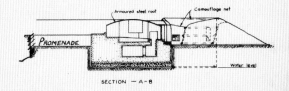

SECTION — A-B

M

DECEPTION & INTELLIGENCE

IF THE GERMANS HAD OBTAINED TIMELY AND ACCURATE INFORMATION, THEY COULD HAVE STOPPED THE INVASION IN ITS TRACKS: INTELLIGENCE AND DECEPTION WERE FUNDAMENTAL TO THE CAMPAIGN'S OUTCOME.

The Allies had to glean information on a wide range of factors, to keep their own preparations secret and to persuade the Germans that the invasion would take place elsewhere.

The British had penetrated German ciphers to produce invaluable signals intelligence known as Ultra (short for Top Secret Ultra). They had also cracked the Japanese diplomatic cipher, so that reports sent from Berlin to Tokyo fell into their hands. And while German agents in Britain had fared badly, the double agent Garbo (a Spaniard called Juan Pujol) fed the Germans a rich diet of misinformation, helping convince them that the Normandy landings were one part of a two-pronged thrust, with the second aimed at the Pas de Calais.

RIGHT *The 25-pound field gun was the workhorse of British artillery. This dummy gun, limber and truck, intended to deceive an observer from 500 to 1,000 yards, were collapsible and folded flat for stowage.*

WINDOW

was the codename for one of the war's simplest but most effective inventions. Strips of aluminium foil were dropped in clouds from aircraft in order to confuse German radar. The technique was first used to create "spoof" bombing raids, diverting defending fighters from real ones. The night before D-Day some of the best crews in Bomber Command flew circuits over the Channel dropping Window in a timed pattern to persuade German radar operators that an invasion fleet was heading for the Pas de Calais.

ABOVE *General Heinz Guderian in his command vehicle watches soldiers sending messages using the Enigma machine. Some of the Enigma codes were regularly read by Allied intelligence from the early stages of the war.*

Operation Fortitude relayed the same message on a larger scale. A fictitious First US Army Group (FUSAG) was "stationed" in south-east England, and fake camps and spurious radio traffic were designed to persuade the Germans that substantial forces were ready for the short hop across the Channel. Fortitude North produced a fictitious 4th Army in Scotland, ready to invade Norway. German intelligence, like the chain of command in Normandy, lacked a single controlling voice, and its various agencies "vied with each other in supplying Hitler with reports".

Allied intelligence on Normandy came from many sources. The BBC appealed for holiday postcards of the whole of France, and relevant ones were collated. The French Resistance produced information on German defences and deployments. Some air photographs revealed the landscape from above, while others, taken from low-flying aircraft, helped create the beach panorama which would be visible from landing craft. Although the Allied air forces softened up objectives in Normandy, more bombs were dropped outside the invasion sector than within it. Experts made night-time landings on Normandy beaches to take sand samples which would help ascertain their load-bearing capacity. By the time D-Day arrived the Allies enjoyed excellent intelligence, while their opponents were shrouded by the fog of war.

RIGHT *When deflated, the dummy Sherman tank fitted into a valise only slightly larger than a sports bag.*

ABOVE *This pneumatic dummy Sherman tank, made by Dunlop Rubber Company, could be blown up like a balloon.*

OPPOSITE *These full-sized dummy Landing Craft, Tanks (LCT), each 160 feet long, were used in harbours in south-east England to suggest that the invasion would be directed at the Pas de Calais.*

'GENFLDM VON RUNSDTEDT AND HIS STAFF EXPECTED THE INVASION ... SOMEWHERE BETWEEN CALAIS AND THE MOUTH OF THE SEINE. THIS WAS THE MOST VULNERABLE AREA FOR THE SHORTEST THRUST THROUGH NORTHERN FRANCE AND BELGIUM INTO GERMANY AND THE RUHR.

GENERAL GUNTHER BLUMENTRITT, CHIEF OF STAFF, COMMANDER IN CHIEF WEST

Bisher bekannt gewordene Abzeichen des brit. Heeres (Stand 15.6.1944)

Geheim! [Ic-Unterlagen West]

Erläuterungen:
ohne Kreuz: Abzeichen auf Grund von Originalunterlagen
ein Kreuz: Abzeichen auf Grund von Zeichnungen
zwei Kreuze: Abzeichen auf Grund von Beschreibungen

Oberkommando Mittl. Osten — engl. H.Gru.21

a) Feldheer

engl. A.O.K. 1 — engl. A.O.K. 2 — engl. A.O.K. 4 — engl. A.O.K. 8 — engl. A.O.K. 9 — engl. A.O.K. 12 — engl. A.O.K. 14 — kanad. A.O.K. 1

I. engl. A.K. — II. engl. A.K. — III. engl. A.K. — IV. engl. A.K. — V. engl. A.K. — VII. engl. A.K. — VIII. engl. A.K. — IX. engl. A.K. — X. engl. A.K. — XII. engl. A.K. — XIII. engl. A.K.

XIV. engl. A.K. — XVI. engl. A.K. — XXX. engl. A.K. — I. kanad. A.K. — II. kanad. A.K. — I. austral. A.K. — I. poln. A.K. — II. poln. A.K.

1. engl. I.D. — 2. engl. I.D. — 3. engl. Pz.Gren.Div. — 4. engl. I.D. — 5. engl. I.D. — 7. engl. I.D. (Besatzungs-Div.Stab) — 8. engl. I.D. (Besatzungs-Div.Stab) — 9. engl. I.D. — 15. engl. I.D. — 32. engl. I.D. — 33. engl. I.D.

34. engl. I.D. — 36. engl. I.D. — 38. engl. I.D. (mot) — 42. engl. I.D. — 43. engl. I.D. (mot) — 45. engl. I.D. — 46. engl. I.D. — 47. engl. I.D. — 48. engl. I.D. — 49. engl. I.D. — 50. engl. I.D. (mot)

51. engl. I.D. — 52. engl. I.D. — 53. engl. I.D. — 54. engl. I.D. — 55. engl. I.D. — 56. engl. I.D. — 57. engl. I.D. — 58. engl. I.D. — 59. engl. I.D. — 61. engl. I.D. — 62. engl. I.D.

70. engl. I.D. — 76. engl. I.D. — 77. engl. I.D. — 78. engl. I.D. — 80. engl. I.D. — 90. engl. I.D. — 1. kanad. I.D. — 2. kanad. I.D. — 3. kanad. I.D. — 6. kanad. I.D. — 7. kanad. I.D.

6. austral. I.D. — 7. austral. I.D. — 9. austral. I.D. — 2. neuseel. I.D. (mot) — 6. neuseel. I.D. — 3. südafrik. I.D. — 4. südafrik. I.D. — 7. südafrik. I.D. — 4. ind. I.D. — 5. ind. I.D. — 6. ind. I.D.

8. ind. I.D. — 10. ind. I.D. — 26. ind. I.D. — 11. afrikan. I.D. — 12. afrikan. I.D. — 1. griech. I.D. — 2. poln. Pz.Gren.Div. — 3. poln. I.D. — 4. poln. I.D. — 5. poln. I.D. — 6. poln. I.D.

7. poln. I.D. — engl. selbst. Inf.Brig. 148 — engl. Inf.Brig. 231 — engl. Garde-Pz.Div. — 1. engl. Pz.Div. — 6. engl. Pz.Div. — 7. engl. Pz.Div. — 8. engl. Pz.Div. — 9. engl. Pz.Div. — 10. engl. Pz.Div. — 11. engl. Pz.Div.

14. engl. Pz.Div. — 15. engl. Pz.Div. — 20. engl. Pz.Div. — 26. engl. Pz.Div. — 42. engl. Pz.Div. — 79. engl. Pz.Div. — 4. kanad. Pz.Div. — 5. kanad. Pz.Div. — 5. südafrikan. Pz.Div. — 6. südafrikan. Pz.Div. — 31. Ind. Pz.Div.

32. ind. Pz.Div. — 43. ind. Pz.Div. — 1. poln. Pz.Div. — 2. poln. Pz.Div. — engl. H.Pz.Brig. 1 — engl. Pz.Brig. 4 — engl. H.Pz.Brig. 21 — engl. Pz.Brig. 23 — engl. H.Pz.Brig. 25 — engl. H.Pz.Brig. 41 — kanad. H.Pz.Brig. 1

kanad. H.Pz.Brig. 2 — engl. Aufkl.Brig.(mot) 1 — engl. Aufkl.Brig.(mot) 2 — engl. Aufkl.Brig.(mot) 3

b) Heimatheer

Oberkommando d. Heimatverteidigung, G.B. — Wehrkreis Süd, Engl. — Wehrkreis Südost, Engl. — Wehrkreis Ost, Engl. — Wehrkreis West, Engl. — Wehrkreis Nord, Engl. — Wehrkreis Schottland — Essex Div.

Geographical Section, General Staff
W.O. 1946
O.R. 6333

BELOW *Garbo's most important message sent shortly after midnight on 9 June 1944, three days after the Normandy landings, warned of a second larger Allied invasion force heading for the Pas de Calais and forced Hitler to keep two Panzer divisions in the Calais area, ensuring the success of the Normandy landings.*

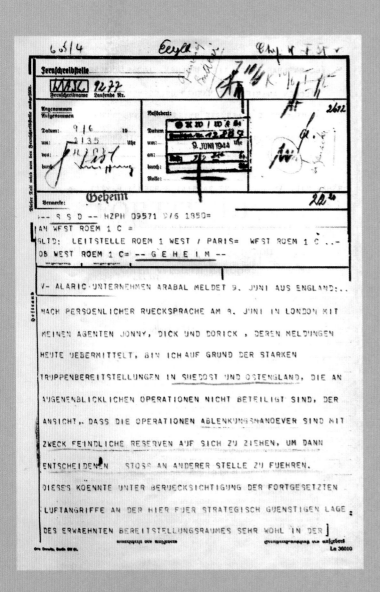

OPPOSITE *A German chart of fasle British unit insignia fed to the Abwehr by Garbo and other double agents.*

RIGHT *German intelligence map issued on 3 July 1944, nearly a month after D-Day, clearly showing the success of Operation Fortitude. The Germans hugely overestimated the number of Allied divisions stationed in Britain, and believed for several weeks after 6 June that the main Allied attack would come via the narrow Dover Straits at the Pas de Calais.*

Frankreich

THE RESISTANCE
& SOE

GERMAN VICTORY IN 1940 DIVIDED FRANCE. THERE WERE THOSE WHO AGREED
WITH MARSHAL PÉTAIN, HEAD OF THE NEW FRENCH STATE BASED AT THE SPA
TOWN OF VICHY, THAT DEFEAT WAS THE OUTCOME OF DECADENCE. AND THERE
WERE OTHERS WHO BELIEVED IN ARMED RESISTANCE.

There were some stirrings early on, and the German invasion of Russia in 1941 brought French Communists into the struggle. However, the Resistance grew gradually, and was marked by the factionalism which mirrored French politics.

In 1940 the Special Operations Executive (SOE) was set up "to co-ordinate all action, by way of subversion and sabotage, against the enemy overseas…." It was divided into "country sections", though France was the responsibility of several sections. Section RF worked with General de Gaulle's Free French in London, but Section F did not, and SOE's historian observes that inter-section jealousies "often raged with virulence". The US equivalent of SOE, the Office of Strategic Services (OSS), also maintained a French section.

LEFT *Resistance groups used weapons parachuted in by the Allies or captured from the Germans. This truck bears the Cross of Lorraine, and FFI for Forces Françaises de l'Intérieur.*

BELOW *Crève-pneus – a box of mines used by the French Resistance for blowing up the tyres of German vehicles. No identifying marks of any kind were used on equipment dropped by the Allies for use by the Resistance.*

ABOVE *Heavy bombers of the US 8th Air Force, based in Britain, dropping weapons and equipment to the Resistance in 1944.*

ABOVE *In an image replete with symbolism, local people inspect a multi-barelled Nebelwerfer (Moaning Minnie to Allied soldiers) captured at Fleury-sur-Orne. The bunker behind sheltered villagers during the subsequent fighting.*

SOE recruited men and women from a cross-section of British and French society. A young peer was killed in Normandy in 1942; a successful sabotage team was led by a fireman and a garage hand. Agents were sent to France by parachute or Westland Lysander light aircraft. They carried out numerous tasks, from sabotage of key installations, through the collection of intelligence to the organization of arms drops. If captured, they could expect no mercy. As their historian wrote: "The best died silent; or if they had to talk, said nothing the enemy wanted to hear."

Resistance groups made a major contribution to the Allied war effort in 1944, by providing intelligence on defences (one bicycle-racer from Bayeux regularly sped along the coast road with plans concealed in his handle-bars) and by the methodical sabotage of rail and telephone communications. In March 1944, de Gaulle decreed that the Resistance would be assimilated into the French army as the Forces Françaises de l'Intérieur, but Communist FTP groups generally declined to obey. Although the importance of the Resistance was later exaggerated, it was important both for its practical work and for the way it kept the soul of France alive.

BELOW RIGHT *Railway-track bomb detonator used by the French Resistance in Normandy. Disruption of the railway network played an important part in reducing the flow of German reinforcements to the invasion area.*

BELOW *The Resistance made a valuable contribution to the "War of the Rails". This railway depot on the German lines of communication was sabotaged in March 1944.*

VIOLETTE SZABO

was the spirited daughter of an English father and French mother, who married a Free French officer in 1940. She joined SOE in 1943, and was parachuted into France on a reconnaissance mission in April 1944. Recovered by a Lysander light aircraft, she was parachuted into Limoges 24 hours after D-Day to help co-ordinate Resistance work with the Allied invasion. However, she encountered a German patrol and was captured when her ammunition ran out. Subsequently shot in Ravensbruck concentration camp, she was awarded a posthumous George Cross, Britain's supreme award for gallantry off the field of battle.

11 Jan 44

Cancels requirements
dated 17 Dec 43.

SECRET

INTELLIGENCE REQUIREMENTS

OPERATION HARDTACK 24

TOPOGRAPHICAL.

Beach

1. Describe nature and firmness of beach where crossed.

2. Recover samples of sand from below and above high water mark.

3. Describe nature and dimensions of runnels on beach.

Wall.

4. Nature and dimensions of wall or bank between high water mark
   and dunes - is it an obstacle to infantry, MT and/or AFVs?

Dunes.

5. How easy is movement through the dunes for infantry, MT and/or AFVs?

6. How easy is it to recognise a given spot or skyline in the dunes
   from seaward?

7. How good is cover for infantry in the dunes?

Floods.

8. Limits of any flooded area met?

9. Exact depth of flooding (state places of measurement)?

10. Extent to which flooded or saturated ground forms obstacle to
    movement.

11. Are roads and tracks across flooding clear of water?
    If so how high, and by how wide and firm a verge?
12. Recover sample of mud from below flood water.
Roads.

13. What are dimensions and conditions of all roads and tracks?
    Are there any signs of prepared road or bridge demolitions?

DEFENCES.

14. Detailed description with measurements of any underwater obstacles,
    including details of apparent condition and method of fixing into
    ground.

15. Details of any wire fences encountered (size, layout, type and
    fixing of pickets); recovery of specimen wire strands and of any
    attached warning devices.

16. Details of any minefields encountered, giving:-

        Type of mine
        spacing
        use of tripwires
        marking and fencing-off.

56   484

Recovery of a specimen mine would be useful but is not essential.

ABOVE *Assignment orders from Operation Hardtack 24
given to Free French Commandos in January 1944 for their
reconnaissance of the invasion area at Utah Beach.*

PEGASUS BRIDGE

THE BRIDGES OVER THE CAEN CANAL AND THE RIVER ORNE – THE FORMER
CODENAMED PEGASUS AND THE LATTER HORSA – PROVIDED A CRUCIAL LINK
BETWEEN INVASION BEACHES AND AIRBORNE LANDINGS. IN BRITISH HANDS,
THEY WOULD ENABLE ARMOUR LANDED BY SEA TO OPERATE EAST OF THE RIVER.

Held by the Germans, they might form a barrier between sea-landed and airborne forces, or enable German tanks to take the landings in the flank.

They would be seized by glider assault by Major John Howard's D Company, 2nd Battalion, The Oxfordshire and Buckinghamshire Light Infantry. Howard had been a regular army NCO before the war, and was an Oxford policeman in 1939. Having rejoined the army, he was commissioned in 1940. He commanded a tough company, and placed special emphasis on night training. Howard had three platoons, and was

BELOW *A Horsa glider is towed into the air by an RAF Albemarle, part of the second airborne drop on the night of 6 June.*

BELOW *Gliders Numbers 1 and 2 within yards of Pegasus Bridge. Behind the line of trees the Café Gondrée, the first French building to be liberated on D-Day, is visible across the Caen Canal.*

reinforced by two more, and a troop of engineers. The force would land in six Horsa gliders, three for each bridge, with Howard leading the assault on Pegasus and Captain Brian Priday that on Horsa. The company had a close relationship with its pilots. When aerial photographs revealed that the Germans were digging holes for anti-glider poles, Staff Sergeant Jim Wallwork, Howard's pilot, told the men that even if the poles were in place they would help by slowing down the overloaded gliders.

Wallwork took off from Tarrant Rushton at 10.56 pm on 5 June, and landed near the eastern end of Pegasus just after midnight. One man was killed in the landing, but within minutes Howard's team had secured the bridge, only Lieutenant Den Brotheridge being killed. Although the troops attacking Horsa landed further from it, their

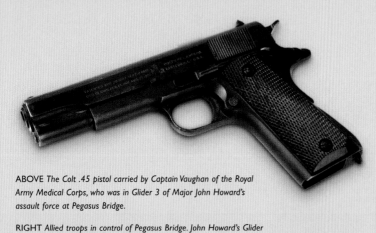

ABOVE *The Colt .45 pistol carried by Captain Vaughan of the Royal Army Medical Corps, who was in Glider 3 of Major John Howard's assault force at Pegasus Bridge.*

RIGHT *Allied troops in control of Pegasus Bridge. John Howard's Glider Number 1 is still visible across the canal.*

JOHN HOWARD

had left the regular army before the war, joining the Oxford police in 1939. Recalled to service, he rose rapidly and received a commission in 1940. His company was specially selected for its D-Day mission, and he was awarded the Distinguished Service Order for his achievement. Slightly wounded, he was more seriously hit later, and was badly injured in a jeep crash that November. A civil servant after the war, he remained a respected figure on veterans' visits to Normandy.

assault was also successful, and Howard ordered his radio operator to send the success signal, "Ham and Jam". There were sporadic German probes during the night and the following morning, but not the armoured counter-attack that the British feared. Howard's men were reinforced by paras during the night and at about 1.00 pm on 6 June they heard bagpipes heralding the approach of Lord Lovat's 1st Special Services Brigade from the beaches. They had taken the bridges as ordered, and held them till relieved.

ABOVE *A universal carrier, manned by British troops, crosses the secured Pegasus Bridge over the Caen canal.*

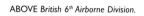

ABOVE *British 6th Airborne Division.*

RIGHT *Major Howard's "Acme Thunderer" whistle, worn round his neck during the assault on Pegasus Bridge, and used to rally his troops in the dark.*

MACHINE GUN
EMPLACEMENT

BARBED WIRE

PILLBOX
(LATER HOWARD'S H.Q.)

N

HORSA BRIDGE →

ANTI-TANK
GUN

CANAL DE CAEN ←

1

PEGASUS BRIDGE

HORSA BRIDGE

GLIDERS

TRENCHES
AND
BUNKERS

2

3

ABOVE *Aerial reconnaissance photograph showing the three Horsa gliders of Major John Howard's Pegasus Bridge assault force. Note the broken fuselage of Glider Number 2, caused by pilot Oliver Boland's last-minute swerve to avoid hitting the lead glider.*

INSET *Aerial reconnaissance photograph showing Pegasus Bridge over the Caen Canal and Horsa Bridge over the Orne River after Major Howard's attack.*

ABOVE *Major John Howard's handwritten glider load weights, crucial to the operations.*

A.M. FORM No. 1479 **TOP** ~~MOST~~ **SECRET** ULTRA

TO BE KEPT UNDER LOCK AND KEY AND NEVER TO BE REMOVED FROM THE OFFICE.
THIS FORM IS TO BE USED FOR AIR INTELLIGENCE MESSAGES ONLY.

NR. No.	GR. No.		OFFICE SERIAL No.
DATE	TIME OF RECEIPT	TIME OF DESPATCH	SYSTEM
TO :			
FROM :			

SENDERS No.

(T.O.O. 0930/6/6/44)   CX/MSS/T207/29(ZTPG/248920,934)

———————————   KV 6611

——————————————————————

W E S T   E U R O P E

————————————————

TIME OF DESPATCH
9.30 am.
6.6.44

COMPILED FROM DOCUMENT DATED 6/6 SEEN BY SOURCE:-

                                      9.30 am

" FIRSTLY. AN R BOAT REPORTED AT ~~0930~~ HOURS 6TH

THE BENOUVILLE BRIDGE OVER CAEN CANAL IN BRITISH

HANDS, AND 2 GLIDERS LANDED. SECONDLY. SEA DEFENCE
                                       9.50 am

COMMANDANT NORMANDY REPORTED AT ~~0950~~ HOURS THE

GATTEVILLE BATTERY ENGAGING LARGE ENEMY UNIT".

                                    1.32 pm

THE ABOVE HAS BEEN PASSED AT ~~1332~~Z/6/6/44. AS

KV 6611/SH/AG/FU/ON/EF/ST/DL/TA.

——————————————————————

BB/AM/WO/ADY   HYD/APTP/VH   1430Z/6/6/44

RD EA

DISTRIBUTION :

DEGREE OF PRIORITY	TIME OF ORIGIN	SIGNATURE OF ORIGINATOR, NOT TO BE TELEPRINTED	OPERATOR'S RECEIPT

ABOVE A German D-Day report, deciphered at Bletchley Park, reporting that British airborne forces had captured a bridge over the Caen Canal and that coastal batteries were engaging a large Allied force. The report is written up to look as if it came from an agent in order to protect the Enigma secret.

BIGOT NEPTUNE.

TOP SECRET
Copy No. 1.
2nd May, 44.

5 Par Bde OO no. 1 Appx A.

Ref Maps. 1/50,000 Sheets 7/F1, 7/F2
1/25,000 Sheet No. 40/16 NW.

To: Maj RJ HOWARD, 2 OXF BUCKS.

INFM

1. **Enemy**

   (a) Static def in area of ops.

   Garrison of the two brs at BENOUVILLE 098748 and RANVILLE 104746 consists of about 50 men, armed with four LAA guns, probably 20 mm, four to six LMG, one AA MG and possibly two A Tk guns of less than 50cm cal. A concrete shelter is under constr, and the br will have been prepared for demolition. See ph enlargement A21.

   (b) Mobile res in area of ops.

   One bn of 736 GR is in the area LEBISEY 0471 - BIEVILLE 0674 with probably 8 to 12 tks under comd. This bn is either wholly or partially carried in MT and will have at least one coy standing by as an anti-airtps picket.

   Bn Hq of the RIGHT coastal bn of 736 GR is in the area 065772. At least one pl will be available in this area as a fighting patrol, ready to move out at once to seek infm.

   (c) State of Alertness.

   The large scale preparations necessary for the invasion of the Continent, the suitability of moon and tide will combine to produce a high state of alertness in the GERMAN def. The br grn may be standing to, and charges will have been laid in the demolition chambers.

   (d) Detailed infm on enemy def and res is available on demand from Div Int Summaries, air phs and models.

2. **Own Tps.**

   (a) 5 Para Bde drops immediately NE of RANVILLE at H minus 4 hrs 30 mins, and moves forthwith to take up a def posn round the two brs.

   (b) 3 Para Bde drops at H minus 4 hrs 30 mins and is denying to the enemy the high wooded ground SOUTH of LE MESNIL 1472.

   (c) 6 Airldg Bde is ldg NE of RANVILLE and WEST of BENOUVILLE at about H plus 12 hrs, and moves thence to a def posn in the area STE HONORINE LA CHARDONNERETTE 0971 - ESCOVILLE 1271.

   (d) 3 Br Div is ldg WEST of OUISTREHAM 1079 at H hr with objective CAEN.

3. **Ground.**

   See available maps, air ph and models.

INTENTION

4. Your task is to seize intact the Brs over R.Orne and canal at BENOUVILLE 098748 and RANVILLE 104746, and to hold them until relief by 7 Para Bn. If the brs are blown, you will est personnel ferries over both water obstacles as soon as possible.

METHOD.

5. **Composition of force.**

---

(2).

5. **Composition of force.**

   (a) Comd Maj RJ HOWARD 2 OXF BUCKS.

   (b) Tps D Coy 2 OXF BUCKS less sp Brens and 3 "M dets.
   two pls B coy 2 OXF BUCKS
   det of 20 Sprs 249 Fd Coy (Airborne)
   det 1 Wing Glider P Regt

6. **Flight plan.**

   (a) HORSA gliders available 6.

   (b) LZ X. triangular fd 099745. 3 gliders.
   LZ Y. rectangular fd 104747. 3 gliders.

   (c) Timing. First ldg H minus 5 hrs.

7. **Gen Outline.**

   (a) The capture of the brs will be a coup de main op depending largely on surprise, speed and dash for success.

   (b) Provided the bulk of your force lands safely, you should have little difficulty in overcoming the known opposition on the brs.

   (c) Your difficulties will arise in holding off an enemy counter-attack on the brs, until you are relieved.

8. **Possible enemy counter-attack.**

   (a) You must expect a counter-attack any time after H minus 4 hrs.

   (b) This attack may take the form of a Battle gp consisting of one coy inf in lorries, up to 8 tks and one or two guns mounted on lorries, or it may be a lorried inf coy alone, or inf on foot.

   (c) The most likely line of approach for this force is down one of the rds leading from the WEST or SW, but a cross-country route cannot be ignored.

9. **Org of def posn.**

   It is vital that the crossing places be held, and to do this you will secure a close brhead on the WEST bank, in addition to guarding the brs. The immediate def of the brs and of the WEST bank of the canal must be held at all costs.

10. **Patrolling.**

    (a) You will harass and delay the deployment of the enemy counter-attack forces of 736 GR by offensive patrols covering all rd approaches from the WEST. Patrols will remain mobile and offensive.

    (b) Up to one third of your effective force may be used in this role. The remaining two thirds will be used for static def and immediate counter-attack.

11. **Emp of RE**

    (a) you will give to your Sprs the following tasks only, in order of priority:-

    Neutralising the demolition mechanisms.
    Removing charges from demolition chambers.
    Establishing personnel ferries.

    (b) In your detailed planning of the op you will consult the CRE or RE comd nominated by him in the carrying out of these tasks by the RE personnel under your comd.

12. **Relief.**

    I estimate that your relief will NOT be completed until H minus 3 hrs, ie, two hrs after your first ldg. One coy 7 Para Bn will, however, be despatched to your assistance with the utmost possible speed after the ldg of the Bn. They should reach your posn by H minus 3 hrs 30 mins, and will come under your comd until arrival of OC 7 Para Bn as in para 13(b).

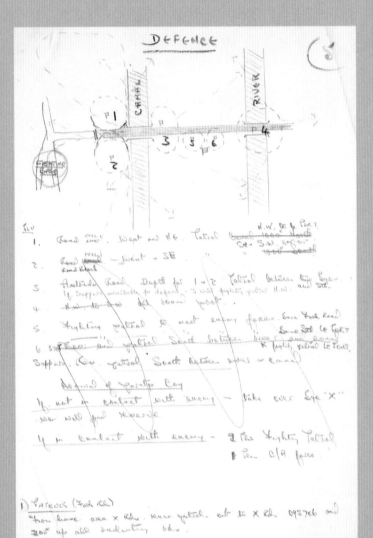

BRITISH AIRBORNE ASSAULT

THE BRITISH 6TH AIRBORNE DIVISION, COMMANDED BY MAJOR GENERAL RICHARD
"WINDY" GALE, WAS DROPPED BETWEEN THE RIVER ORNE AND THE HIGH GROUND OF
THE BOIS DE BAVENT TO SECURE THE EASTERN FLANK OF THE INVASION SECTOR.

Some of its units had special missions: a reinforced glider company, as we have seen, seized Pegasus Bridge. The 9th Parachute Battalion was to take the German coastal battery at Merville. Its plan was disrupted when some attackers were dropped far away, and although the guns (which proved to be smaller-calibre than had been expected) were put out of action, the battery was briefly reoccupied by the Germans. Men of 3rd Parachute Squadron Royal Engineers were to destroy the bridges over the River Bures so as to prevent the Germans using them. They succeeded in destroying those at Troarn, Bures and Robehomme, and with the assistance of 1st Canadian Parachute Battalion, that over

LEFT *This photograph, taken on 5 June, shows Horsa gliders on the runway with the Halifax bombers that will tow them to France standing ready. All aircraft bear the Allied recognition stripes.*

OPPOSITE ABOVE *British paratroopers sit beside an Albermarle towing aircraft before leaving for France.*

OPPOSITE BELOW *Shoulder patch and "wings" worn by British glider pilots.*

OVERLEAF *The main airborne drop was preceded by the arrival of Pathfinders who set up beacons to mark dropping zones. These Path-finders are synchronizing their watches before boarding their aircraft.*

a tributary stream at Varaville. The division's two parachute brigades, 3rd and 5rd, were dropped during the night, and most units were widely scattered. Many soldiers spent a confusing night endeavouring to link up with their comrades in the darkness, colliding with German patrols and securing strongpoints. One estimate suggests that not more than 60 per cent of the 4,800 men of the division who were landed in France on D-Day were actually able to participate in the day's fighting. On the morning of 6 June, 4th Airlanding Brigade began to arrive by glider, and with it came heavy engineer stores, light tanks and jeeps, field and anti-tank guns, putting the division in a much better position to resist any attack by German armour. It is a measure of the risks run by glider pilots that 71 of the 196 who landed became casualties.

Although the eastern flank was now largely secure, it was certainly anything but quiet. The village of Bréville, up on the ridge overlooking the main glider landing zone, was the one hole in the division's perimeter. On the night of 12 June it was attacked by a scratch force based on the much-depleted 12th Parachute Battalion. The two brigadiers involved were wounded, and 12th Parachute Battalion lost 141 of the 160 officers and men who attacked, including the commanding officer. However, by dawn the village was secured, and Major General Gale later declared that its seizure was the turning point in the fight for the Orne bridgehead. It is axiomatic that airborne troops are best used for operations requiring dash, and should be withdrawn as soon as their objectives have been taken. But 6th Airborne Division remained up on the hard shoulder it had created throughout the long and bloody Normandy summer, demonstrating that it could cope with a long attritional slog as well as with the dangerous chaos of an airborne assault.

RIGHT *Two military police NCOs of 6th Airborne Division guard a crossroads near the village of Ranville on 9 July. There is a Horsa glider in the background.*

BELOW *An aerial view of 6th Airlanding Brigade's landing zone near Ranville. The high ground of the Bois de Bavent is at the top of the photograph. The gliders remained in situ for weeks to come.*

RICHARD "WINDY" GALE

commanded 6th Airborne Division in Normandy. Brought up in Australia, he served in the Machine Gun Corps in the First World War, winning the Military Cross, but was only a lieutenant colonel in 1940. Promoted to head Britain's first airborne brigade, he was director of airborne forces at the War Office before taking command of 6th Airborne Division as a major general. After the war he commanded the British Army of the Rhine and served as Deputy Supreme Allied Commander Europe.

MAP KEY

- **W** Intended landing zones
- Actual landing zones
- Bridge captured
- Bridge destroyed
- Battery destroyed
- German strong points
- German resistance points

6 JUNE 1944

BRITISH 6TH AIRBORNE DIVISION

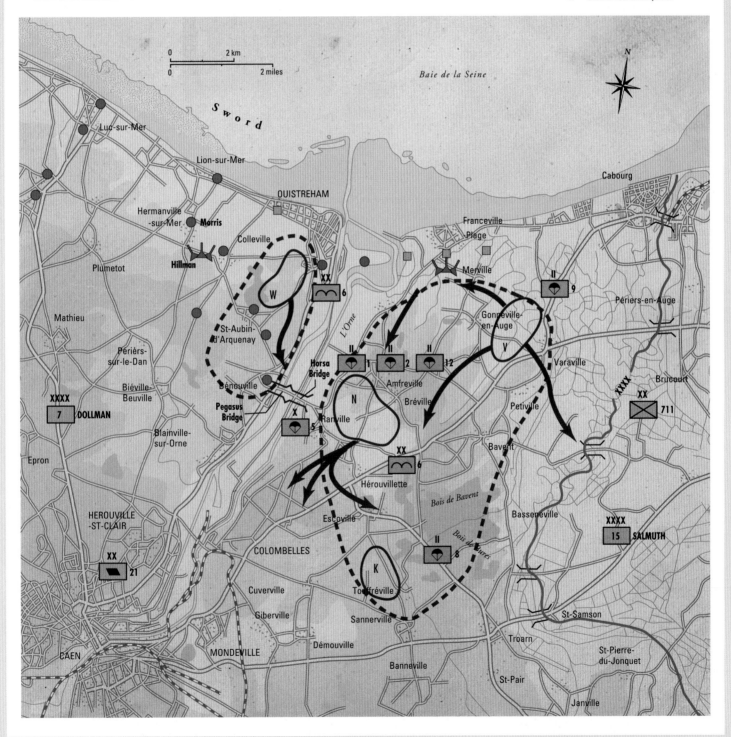

US AIRBORNE ASSAULT

TWO US AIRBORNE DIVISIONS, MAJOR GENERAL MATTHEW B. RIDGWAY'S 82ND AND MAJOR GENERAL MAXWELL TAYLOR'S 101ST, WERE TO LAND AT THE BASE OF THE COTENTIN PENINSULA ON THE WESTERN FLANK OF THE INVASION BEACHES.

Each had two three-battalion parachute infantry regiments and one glider infantry regiment, with supporting artillery and engineers. Some planners favoured a bolder project, the establishment of an airhead in the area of Evreux and Dreux to threaten the Seine crossings and Paris, but Eisenhower, arguing that the force would be vulnerable once it had landed, favoured a more conservative option. However, some argued that the Cotentin plan was risky enough as it stood. Leigh-Mallory called it "a very speculative operation", and had it modified so that many of the gliders would arrive on the evening of D-Day.

BELOW *Eisenhower had an easy style with soldiers. Here he talks to paratroopers of the 101st Airborne Division at Greenham Common airfield on 5 June 1944. The censor has obscured their divisional flashes.*

It was eventually decided that 101st Airborne Division would be dropped behind Utah Beach, to secure the beach exits and be prepared to exploit through Carentan. 82nd Airborne Division was to land further north-west, astride the River Merderet, to capture the crossings over the river, seize the little town of Ste-Mère-Eglise, on the main Cherbourg-Bayeux road, and be prepared to exploit westwards. The Germans had flooded the valleys, turning the area into a patchwork of inundated fields laced with deeper watercourses and dotted with solidly built Norman villages and farms.

ABOVE *A stick of parachutists ready to jump above the Cotentin early on 6 June. The heavily laden men have hooked their static lines, which will open their chutes, onto the cable above them.*

The first wave of parachutists, some 13,000 men, was to be dropped from 822 C-47 aircraft. Many pilots lacked experience for their demanding task, and in the early hours of 6 June this became even more difficult as a bank of thick cloud confronted them as they flew in from the east. A mixture of poor visibility and ground fire scattered the aircraft and, with them, the parachutists they dropped. Some were

MAXWELL D. TAYLOR

was commissioned from West Point in 1922 but was only a major when war broke out. Quickly promoted, he commanded the artillery of 82nd Airborne Division, and in 1943 carried out a dangerous mission behind the lines in Italy. He led 101st Airborne Division in Normandy and in Operation Market Garden in September. He later served as Chief of Staff of the US Army, Chairman of the Joint Chiefs, and US Ambassador to Vietnam.

BELOW *US 101st Airborne Division.*

MATTHEW B. RIDGWAY

joined the infantry from West Point in 1917. In 1939 he accompanied US Army Chief of Staff George C. Marshall on a mission to South America. Ridgway commanded 82nd Infantry Division in 1942, supervising its conversion to an airborne formation. After leading his division in Normandy he commanded XVIII Airborne Corps. In 1950 he succeeded Douglas MacArthur at the head of the US Eighth Army in Korea, and was US Army Chief of Staff 1953–56.

released too late and fell into the sea, or drowned in flooded rivers: others hit trees or roofs. Most who landed safely were hopelessly lost, and spent the night searching for other Americans, bumping into German patrols, with losses on both sides, or simply sleeping.

Much of 505th Parachute Infantry Regiment of 82nd Airborne Division was dropped close to Ste-Mère-Eglise: one soldier landed with his parachute hooked onto the town church's steeple and survived, but others were less lucky, and fell among the garrison, alerted by Allied bombing of the village. The place was secured early on, and the vital road was blocked after a spirited action at Neuville. By the end of the day, 82nd Airborne was strongly posted around Ste-Mère-Eglise, but was in contact neither with the troops coming ashore at Utah Beach nor with the 101st. It had lost over 1,200 men, over half of them missing. Maxwell Taylor's men were more fortunate. Although only about 2,500 of the 6,600 men dropped had assembled by the evening

of D-Day, they seized many of their objectives, and secured the exits from Utah Beach and some of the bridges near Carentan.

The inaccuracy of the drops helped to confuse the Germans, whose senior commanders spent the early hours of 6 June confronted by reports which gave no clear pointer to Allied intentions. Many were away at a war game at Rennes, and one divisional commander, Lieutenant General Wilhelm Falley, was killed when he encountered a party of parachutists. Like the British drop, the American airborne assault did not go according to plan, but it too fulfilled its task.

BELOW LEFT *One of the "crickets" carried by US airborne troops on their D-Day jump. They were used to distinguish friend from foe in the dark: one click was to be answered by two.*

BELOW *This aerial view of the area round Ste-Mère-Eglise, gives a good impression of the difficult country into which the two US airborne divisions were dropped.*

6 JUNE 1944

US 101ST & 82ND AIRBORNE DIVISIONS

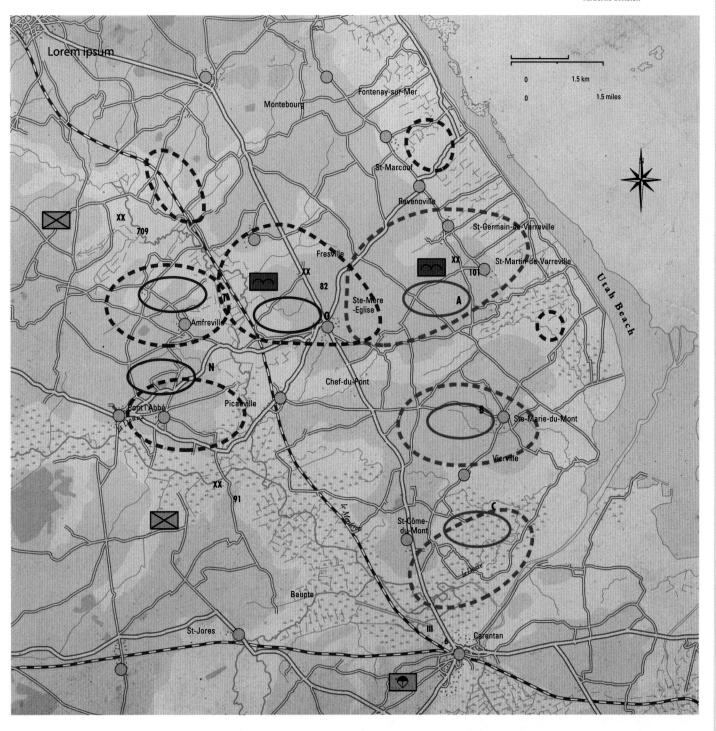

Lorem ipsum

Montebourg

Fontenay-sur-Mer

St-Marcouf

Ravenoville

St-Germain-de-Varreville

XX
709

Fresville

St-Martin-de-Varreville

XX
82

XX
101

Ste-Mère
-Eglise

A

Amfreville

N

Chef-du-Pont

Pont l'Abbé

Picauville

B

Ste-Marie-du-Mont

Vierville

XX
91

St-Côme-
du-Mont

C

Baupte

St-Jores

III

Carentan

Utah Beach

0   1.5 km

0   1.5 miles

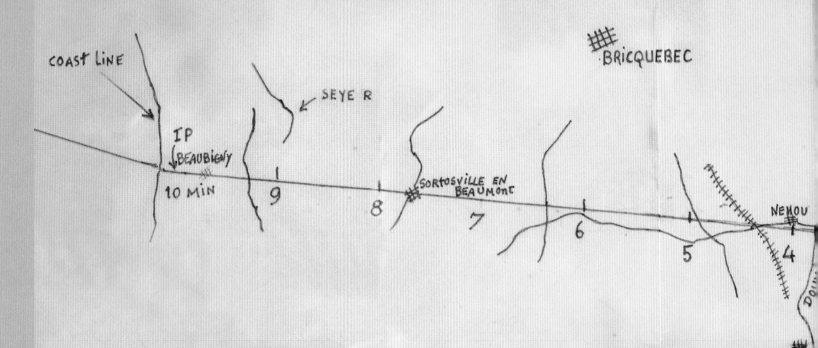

EXPLANATORY NOTES

1) Line of flight is graduated in unit minutes, one (1) to ten (10)

2) Check points consist of primary roads, rivers, railroads and towns.

3) Directional flight IP to DZ – 96 degrees true north or 105 degrees magnetic north.

4) Distance IP to DZ – 21.5 miles.

COAST LINE

BRICQUEBEC

SEYE R

IP
BEAUBIGNY

10 MIN   9   8   SORTOSVILLE EN BEAUMONT   7   6   5   4   NEHOU

Bq 505 Prcht. Inf
APO 169 USA
3 June 1944

JUMPMASTERS SKETCH – OVERLAY (to accompany flight plan)
Showing IP to DZ check points.

Map. FRANCE 1:100,000 Sheets 5E & 6E

ERMAN
Cadg

OFFICIAL

NORTON
S-3

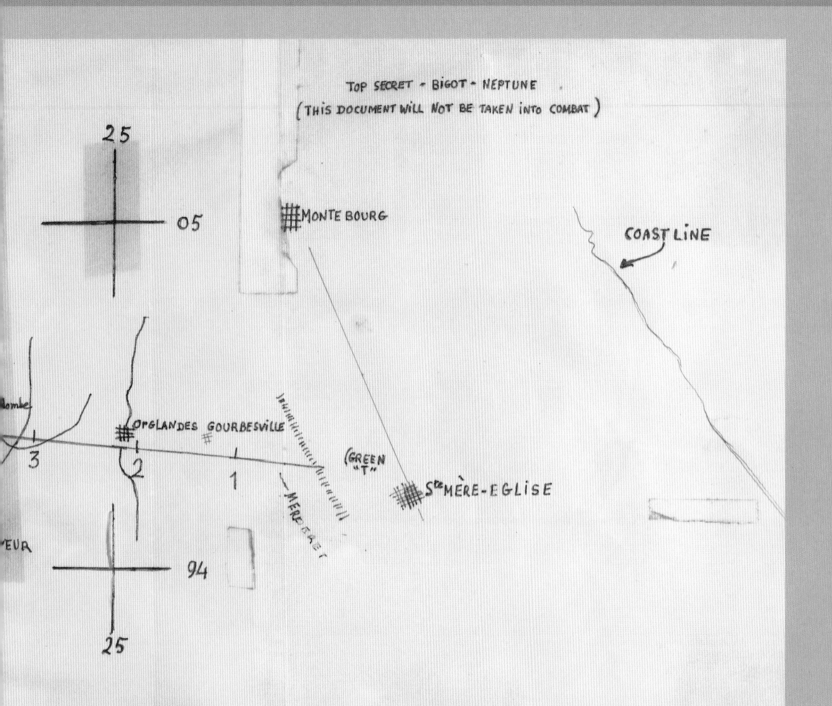

BELOW & OVERLEAF *A diary from June 1944 kept by Staff Sergeant Murray Goldman of the 3rd Medical Battalion, 505th Parachute Infantry Regiment of 82nd Airborne Division.*

June 5 – Left Cottesmore about eleven – flew all over England than over channel came into France at 0200 – nice and quiet + lots of smoke commented that this was easy. Suddenly tracer + flack – red and green. Plane started violent evasive action. Green light and went – Plane was on its side and low, about 150. terrific tracer coming up into chutes. Slipped away for all I was worth. one man screaming i

Landed easy and stayed flat – reason – grazing fire – terribly scared. crawled into hole and took off equipment. Lots of firing – c47's still coming – men still jumping into hell. One plane burning, but men bail out met two jumpers + joined met 8 more – met 20 more – feel good now – all kinds of weapons. Now we seek trouble – tore down telephone wires. No germans.

June 6 next morning

Joined a mixed group of
502-506-508-505 men
and came to farmhouse
produced map and frenchman
showed St Mere Eglise to
us. Occasional sniper
fire but inaccurate
Reached St mere Eglise about
noon and found that Co H.
had town taken. Moved
into a big building and
set up hospital.
Gliders had taken a hell
of a beating - crashed all
-over countryside Wounded
pouring in now

companies set up town
defence and prepare to
hold town at all costs as
ordered - already we are
surrounded and fighting
Town being shelled and
mortared. Eighty-eight
artillery tearing hell out
of us - Wounded pouring
in now - Hospital hit
repeatedly. Germans
want that town. Getting
dark now - this night will
be pure hell cause we
are all alone + cut off. The
boys are fighting like
cornered lions. Even
advancing. German

wounded in hospital.

night

Violent Enemy artillery and infiltterating attacks – some Germans enter town. They dont leave it again – they are dead – tanks knocked out justoutside of town by GI's with grenades. Our guys are strictly mean now. They are fighting mad. Morning and we still hold town. But what a price. Hospital choked with wounded. Wounded from all over,

countryside coming in now. what a god damned mess. and still the bastard beach force does not relieve us. Hospital being shelled & hit repeatedly. Kitchen blown in. Back yard full of shell holes – no windows glass & plaster and bloody rags and wounded and dying men all over the place. Hanful of aid men dog tired. Sleep. what is that?

June 7. Next Morning

Repeat performance. Artillery
And Snipers + attacks, got
wounded again. No more.
room any place in hospital
but still they come.
The afternoon the 4th
Div. 8th day comes in.
Hooray. So this no good
bastard command attacks
with our own heavy
gun attaching anything
unattached infantry
in our rear. Some Big
Yankee guy wants us all

June 11. Push ahead - Lessville
June 12. Push ahead - Granville
June 13 - close to Montberg + Valognes
June 14 - change sectors. drive for St Sauen
June 15. drive
June 16 - Enter St Sauen - "Got it"
June 17 - Still "Hot." plenty
June 18 - Occasional Shelling
June 19 - move for more hot stuff -
June 20 - Interesting bivouac
area - 15 germans + 2 M.G's +
plenty of stuff Murphy gets
busted in legs. capture 12
of reds.
June 21. Woods - bastard
artillery. chopping us down plenty
clothes full of blood - moral
is very low.

UTAH BEACH

BAD WEATHER HAD ALREADY CAUSED THE POSTPONEMENT OF THE INVASION BY ONE DAY, AND D-DAY ITSELF WAS LAUNCHED IN WHAT EISENHOWER'S CHIEF METEOROLOGIST HOPED WOULD BE A BRIEF BUT USABLE WINDOW IN THE WEATHER.

Conditions were very unpleasant in landing craft as they wallowed in the swell, and visibility was so poor that the bombers sent to provide last-minute softening-up of the defences at Utah and Omaha were largely ineffective. The landings were to take place after low water on a rising tide, and local conditions meant that they would begin at 6.30 am in the US sector and 7.30 am in the British. Fast German patrol boats alerted at about 3.30 am, attacked the invasion flotilla (the only serious casualty was the Norwegian destroyer *Svenner*) and at 5.35 am, only 15 minutes before Allied warships began their own bombardment, German coastal batteries began to open fire.

ABOVE *US 4th Infantry Division.*

LEFT *American infantrymen crossing the sea wall and the dunes behind it: the gradient here is far gentler than at Omaha.*

BELOW *US Army-issue Bible carried into battle on Utah Beach in the breast pocket of Staff Sergeant Louie Havard. During D-Day an enemy bullet struck Havard's rifle, ricocheted off it and struck the Bible, which saved his life. Louie Havard survived the Second World War.*

ABOVE *American troops in foxholes on Utah while beach clearance goes on in the background.*

ABOVE *US Army soldiers disembark from a landing craft during the D-Day landings of 6 June. Sherman tanks and White half-tracks can be seen drawn up on the beach.*

THEODORE ROOSEVELT Jr

was son of the president of the same name, and a brigadier general. He served in the First World War and helped create the American Legion after it. He distinguished himself as assistant division commander of 4th Infantry Division on D-Day, but died of a heart attack on 12 July, the day he was due to take command of his own division. Awarded the Congressional Medal of Honor, America's highest gallantry award, he lies buried at St-Laurent, beside his brother Quentin, killed in 1918.

BELOW *Eisenhower's exhortation to the troops of the Allied Expeditionary Force who were about to embark on the D-Day invasion and liberation of Europe.*

BELOW *The watch worn on D-Day by Staff Sergeant Glen E. Gibson of the 70th Tank Battalion. Gibson was the sole survivor from the crews of four amphibious tanks which were destroyed when their landing craft hit a mine off Utah Beach. His watch was stopped by the explosion at 5.46 am.*

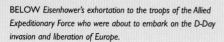

**SUPREME HEADQUARTERS
ALLIED EXPEDITIONARY FORCE**

Soldiers, Sailors and Airmen of the Allied Expeditionary Force!

You are about to embark upon the Great Crusade, toward which we have striven these many months. The eyes of the world are upon you. The hopes and prayers of liberty-loving people everywhere march with you. In company with our brave Allies and brothers-in-arms on other Fronts, you will bring about the destruction of the German war machine, the elimination of Nazi tyranny over the oppressed peoples of Europe, and security for ourselves in a free world.

Your task will not be an easy one. Your enemy is well trained, well equipped and battle-hardened. He will fight savagely.

But this is the year 1944 ! Much has happened since the Nazi triumphs of 1940-41. The United Nations have inflicted upon the Germans great defeats, in open battle, man-to-man. Our air offensive has seriously reduced their strength in the air and their capacity to wage war on the ground. Our Home Fronts have given us an overwhelming superiority in weapons and munitions of war, and placed at our disposal great reserves of trained fighting men. The tide has turned ! The free men of the world are marching together to Victory !

I have full confidence in your courage, devotion to duty and skill in battle. We will accept nothing less than full Victory !

Good Luck ! And let us all beseech the blessing of Almighty God upon this great and noble undertaking.

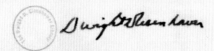

Although the overriding importance of the deep-water port of Cherbourg always made it desirable for a landing to take place at the base of the Cotentin, it was only when the original Cossac plan was modified early in 1944 to involve a five-division assault that planners were able to add Utah Beach to their schedule. Even then it was not ideal, for it was separated by rivers from the other beaches, and the low ground behind it had been flooded, restricting the routes inland. Major General Raymond Barton's 4th Division of VII Corps was to land there on a two-battalion front, with 36 Duplex Drive (DD) swimming tanks supporting the first wave.

There was good luck and bad. A mixture of a strong coastal current and the obscuration of navigation landmarks by the smoke of the naval bombardment meant that the whole invasion force landed about 2,000 yards further south than had been planned, and the tanks arrived late. But the area where the troops came ashore, around La Grande Dune, was actually much less heavily defended than the planned attack sector, and casualties on the run-in and the landing itself were mercifully light. There might have been confusion as junior commanders realized that they were in the wrong place, but the assistant division commander, the arthritic but dogged Brigadier General Theodore Roosevelt (son of the president of the same name), had pressed to be allowed to go ashore with the first wave. Under fire most of the day, he repeatedly led groups over the sea wall and pointed them inland. His bravery earned him the Congressional Medal of Honor, and helped ensure that within three hours of the first landing the beach was secure and cleared, with engineers and naval demolition parties dealing with beach obstacles, making gaps in the sea wall and clearing minefields. By nightfall infantry had pushed as far inland as the main Cherbourg–Bayeux road at Les Forges.

6 – 8 JUNE 1944
UTAH BEACH

PLANNED H-HOUR: 06.30

ALLIES

ASSAULTING DIVISION: US 4th Infantry

DIVISION COMMANDER:
Major General Raymond O. Barton

INFANTRY ASSAULT UNITS: 1st and 2nd
Battalions of the 8th Infantry Regiment

MEN LANDED: 23,250

CASUALTIES (DEAD, WOUNDED &
MISSING): c.200

AXIS

DEFENDING DIVISIONS: Elements
of 709th Infantry and 352nd Infantry

709TH INFANTRY DIVISION
COMMANDER:
Lieutenant General Karl-Wilhelm
von Schlieben

352ND INFANTRY DIVISION
COMMANDER:
Lieutenant General Dietrich Kraiss

- ▪ German strongpoint
- ─ Frontline 12.00 hrs 6 June
- ─ Frontline 7 June
- ➤ US advance movements
- ▨ Sandy shoreline
- ▨ Rocks
- ▨ Flooded area

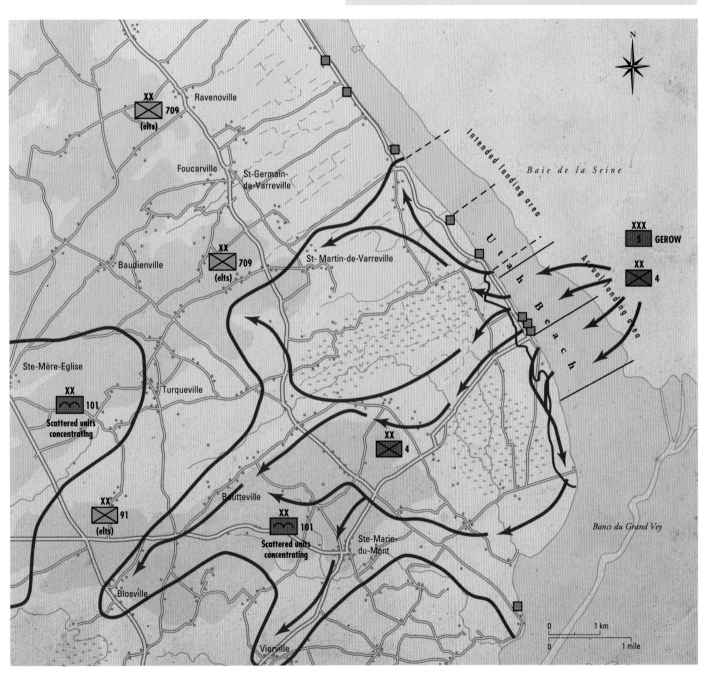

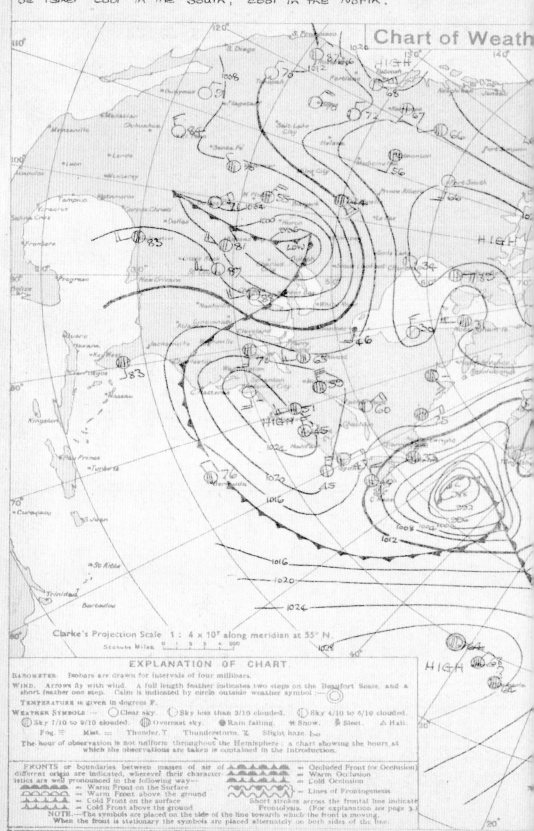

RIGHT *Meteorological Office weather map for Monday 5 June 1944, showing the deep depression centred off the north-east coast of the British Isles and resultant high winds in the English Channel which forced Eisenhower to postpone the invasion by 24 hours.*

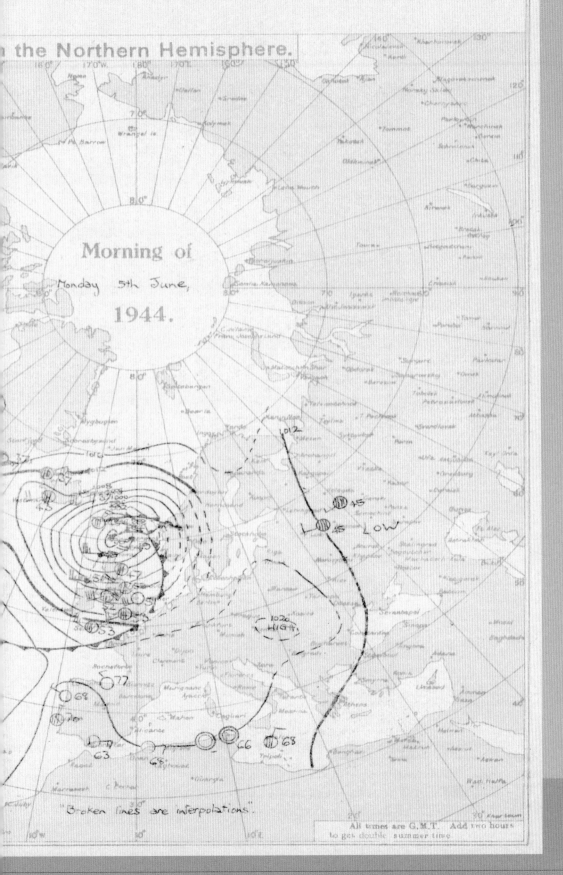

FURTHER OUTLOOK

...in spreading into W. Ireland, and W. Scotland later tomorrow afternoon moving east.

Gale warning in operation in districts 13A, 13B. time of issue 0800 4.6.44. and in districts 11, 15, and 16 at 13.55. 4.6.44.

...the Northern Hemisphere.

Morning of
Monday 5th June,
1944.

"Broken lines are interpolations".

All times are G.M.T. Add two hours to get double summer time

POINTE DU HOC

THE POINTE DU HOC (HOE IN THE US OFFICIAL HISTORY – THE WORD STEMS
FROM OLD FRENCH FOR A VESSEL'S JIB) WAS AS IMPORTANT TO THE AMERICANS
AS PEGASUS BRIDGE AND MERVILLE WERE TO THE BRITISH.

The clifftop site, rising 177 feet from the shore, was believed to house six 155mm guns in concrete emplacements: they could either fire onto Utah Beach or at the force assaulting Omaha. These defences had been damaged by bombing, but aerial and naval bombardment could not guarantee to destroy them. Their location meant that neither parachutists nor glider troops could be used, and the mission was given to Lieutenant Colonel James E. Rudder's 2nd Ranger Battalion, which would storm from the sea.

Colonel Rudder's first wave of three companies would land at the foot of the cliffs, scale them, and then be reinforced by another two companies, while his sixth company continued to Omaha, whence it would join the rest of the battalion by land. Most of the Rangers would be in landing craft, but four amphibious DUKWs, fitted with turntable ladders supplied by the London Fire Brigade, mounted twin Lewis machine guns. To climb the cliffs, ropes attached to grapnels were to be fired by special projectors.

BELOW *The battleship USS* Texas *pounding the Pointe du Hoc with her 14-inch guns on D-Day. She formed part of the Western Task Force under Rear Admiral D. P. Kirk, USN.*

OPPOSITE *A-20s of the US Ninth Air Force attacking the Pointe du Hoc (bottom right) on D-Day.*

JAMES EARL RUDDER

was a college teacher and football coach with a reserve commission when he was called to active duty in 1941. He took command of 2nd Ranger Battalion in 1942, leading it in its assault on the Pointe du Hoc. Rudder was a full colonel in 1945, and subsequently combined careers as university president, civic leader and reserve officer, rising to major general. President Johnson awarded him the Distinguished Service Medal, the highest peacetime service award, in 1967.

ABOVE *US 2nd Rangers Battalion.*

ABOVE US Rangers hauling ammunition up the cliff face at the Pointe du Hoc after its capture.

BELOW *The Air and Naval Bombardment Plan for Omaha and Utah sectors showing the positions of German batteries.*

AMERICAN NEPTUNE AREA
BATTERY BOMBARDMENT PLAN

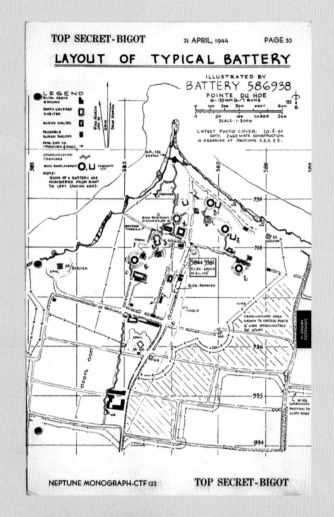

TOP SECRET-BIGOT   21 APRIL, 1944   PAGE 53

LAYOUT OF TYPICAL BATTERY

ILLUSTRATED BY
BATTERY 586938
POINTE DU HOE
6-155MM (6.1") GUNS

NEPTUNE MONOGRAPH-CTF 122   TOP SECRET-BIGOT

Rudder's men transferred to their landing craft and DUKWs 12 miles out, lost two craft in heavy seas, and lost two more when they ran in parallel to the coast after making the wrong landfall. Although the garrison was ready for them, the Rangers began their ascent at once, undaunted by the fact that waterlogged ropes prevented the grapnels from rising far enough. A last-minute attack by B-26 bombers rattled the defenders, and the destroyers USS *Satterlee* and HMS *Talybont* fired as the Rangers climbed. There were no guns in the casemates — they had been moved inland to escape the bombing, but Rudder's men found and destroyed them. The Rangers were then counter-attacked and forced back into the original German defences, but they held until relieved on 8 June. They lost 135 of the 225 men landed: the follow-up companies did not receive the success signal and went on to Omaha.

LEFT *An Allied secret briefing map showing the German defensive positions on the Pointe du Hoc in April 1944.*

BELOW *Allied bombing and naval gunfire had done terrible damage to German defences before the Rangers landed.*

OPPOSITE *This aerial reconnaissance photograph of Pointe du Hoc (the point itself is at the top) gives a good view of the damage done by bombing before D-Day. The map overlay is a detail from the map on the left.*

PLANNED H-HOUR: 06.30

ALLIES

ASSAULTING UNITS: D, E and F Companies of 2nd Ranger Battalion

COMMANDER: Lieutenant Colonel James E. Rudder

MEN LANDED: 225

CASUALTIES: 135 (by 8 June 1944)

AXIS

DEFENDING UNIT: Elements of 716th Coastal Defence Division

NUMBER: 200

716TH COASTAL DEFENCE DIVISION COMMANDER: Lieutenant General Wilhelm Richter

OMAHA BEACH

OMAHA WAS THE RESPONSIBILITY OF THE US V CORPS. MAJOR GENERAL CLARENCE R. HUEBNER'S 1ST DIVISION WOULD LAND WITH TWO REGIMENTS ABREAST, THE 116TH INFANTRY (FROM THE 29TH DIVISION) ON THE RIGHT AND THE 16TH INFANTRY ON THE LEFT. ONCE THE BEACH WAS SECURED, THESE REGIMENTS WOULD BE SUPPORTED BY TWO OTHER REGIMENTS, AND THE ATTACKERS WOULD THEN SEIZE THE BAYEUX ROAD TO THE SOUTH AND PERHAPS REACH ISIGNY TO THE WEST.

The beach's gentle-sloping sand led to coarse shingle, and immediately behind rose high sandy bluffs. There were only five exits through them, and these valleys ("draws" to their attackers) were protected by concrete bunkers. Nowhere else were assaulting troops confronted with such serious obstacles. The area was defended by the over-extended 716th Division (responsible for the coastline from the Orne to the west of Omaha), but at Omaha it had been reinforced by the higher-quality 352nd Division, undetected by Allied intelligence. While the British had placed emphasis on getting specialist armoured vehicles ashore at the very beginning to deal with obstacles, the American approach was less technological, and beach-clearing was to be done by unarmoured engineer teams. Lastly, the long run-in through heavy seas

ABOVE *The Purple Heart, for all US personnel wounded or killed in combat. Around 3,000 were awarded to the D-Day casualties on Omaha.*

LEFT *Seconds to the landing. US infantrymen in a landing craft approaching Omaha Beach. Smoke on the shoreline comes from naval gunfire supporting the landing.*

NORMAN "DUTCH" COTA

was an ebullient New Englander. Assistant division commander of the 29th Division, he was the first general ashore on Omaha Beach. Showing characteristic vigour in getting men off the beach, he shouted to one group of soldiers that, as Rangers, they should be leading the way. Promoted to command the 28th Division, he led it through Paris in the liberation parade, and in heavy fighting in the Hürtgen Forest. His division was badly mauled in the German Ardennes offensive.

'WE HIT THE EYE OF THE STORM. THE BATTALION WAS DECIMATED. HELL, AFTER THAT WE DIDN'T HAVE ENOUGH TO WHIP A CAT WITH.

SGT JOHN R. SLAUGHTER, D CO., 116TH INFANTRY REGIMENT, 29TH DIVISION

ABOVE *The photographer Robert Capa landed at Omaha, but most of the film he shot was ruined by an over-enthusiastic developer. This photograph shows infantrymen moving through the surf and the beach defences.*

ABOVE US troops wade through thigh-high water, the pull of underwater current and ongoing German gunfire as they disembark from USS Samuel Chase onto the sector of Omaha Beach that they called Fox Green.

6–8 JUNE 1944

OMAHA BEACH

PLANNED H-HOUR: 06.30

ALLIES

ASSAULTING DIVISION: US 1st Infantry

US 1ST DIVISION COMMANDER:
Major General Clarence R. Huebner

INFANTRY ASSAULT UNITS: 2nd and 3rd Battalions of
the 16th Infantry Regiment, and 1st and 2nd Battalions of
the 116th Infantry Regiment attached from US 29th
Infantry Division

MEN LANDED: 34,250

CASUALTIES (DEAD, WOUNDED & MISSING): c.3,000

AXIS

DEFENDING DIVISIONS:
Elements of 352nd Infantry and 716th Coastal
Defence

352ND INFANTRY DIVISION COMMANDER:
Lieutenant General Dietrich Kraiss

716TH COASTAL DEFENCE DIVISION
COMMANDER:
Lieutenant General Wilhelm Richter

MAP KEY

- German strongpoint
- U.S. positions by 12.00 hrs 6 June
- Frontline 24.00 hrs 6 June
- Frontline 7 June
- Frontline 8 June
- ⊢XXX Army boundary lines
- ⊢ XX Divisional boundary lines
- U.S. advance movements
- Sandy shoreline
- Rocks
- Flooded area

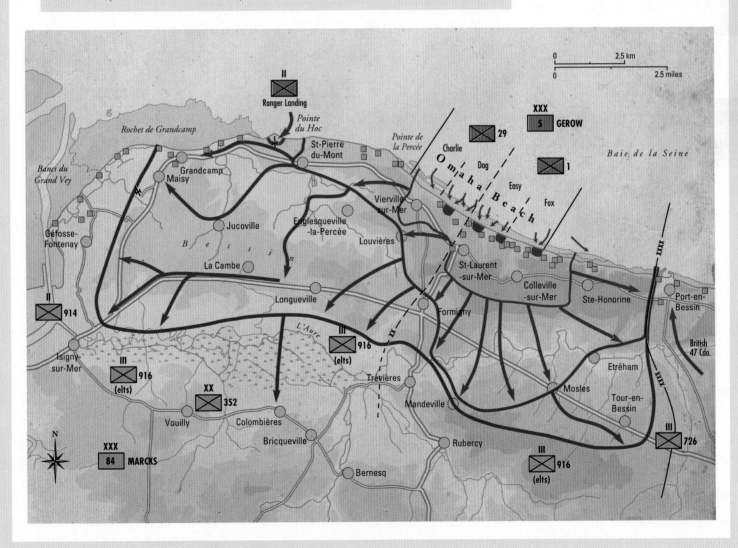

caused losses before the attackers reached the shore, and the coastal current meant that most landing craft beached eastwards of their intended landfall.

At 5.40 am the first DD tanks were launched 6,000 yards out, but most foundered at once, and of the 32 only five reached the shore, doing so after the assaulting infantry. The artillery expected to fire on the way in did little better: all but one of the 105mm guns of 11th Field Artillery Battalion were lost, as were six of 7th Field Artillery Battalion's pieces. Although naval bombardment had temporarily neutralized the defences, they came to life as the landing-craft neared the shoreline, and the nine companies of the first assaulting wave were disgorged –

overloaded, soaking and often sea-sick – onto the surf of a bullet-swept beach. Undamaged obstacles gave them a degree of cover but posed a terrible risk to incoming DUKWs and landing craft.

The failure of the first wave meant that the specialist engineer teams were unable to work as planned, despite suffering 40 per cent casualties that day. After the first dreadful hour the 116th Infantry had a toehold just west of Les Moulins, and, as much by luck as by judgement, it was there that the regimental command group under Colonel Charles D. W. Canham and the assistant division commander, Brigadier General Norman D. Cota, landed. The view from the sea was depressing: one officer reported that the beach was clogged with infantry while landing

craft milled about like "a stampeded herd of cattle". Lieutenant General Omar N. Bradley, the US First Army commander, aboard USS *Augusta*, even briefly considered redirecting the remaining units to Utah Beach.

By this time there was progress on the beach as destroyers came dangerously close inshore to engage defences at point-blank range, and determined groups of men fought their way off the beach. Sometimes they were formal leaders, and sometimes they were not: decorations honoured the achievements of Brigadier General Cota at one extreme and several gallant NCOs and private soldiers at the other. By the day's end the Americans held a narrow strip of land between St-Laurent and Colleville, but they lacked most of the resources needed for the planned advance inland. Omaha Beach had cost V Corps around 3,000 casualties, more than were suffered on the other beaches in total.

OPPOSITE *A medic tends a wounded man on Omaha. Note the drip held by his assistant: promptly administered, intravenous saline replacements were invaluable in reducing deaths from shock.*

LEFT *The body of a US soldier lies on Omaha Beach beside a couple of hastily abandoned rifles and one of the ineffective arrangements of defensive wooden poles widely known as "Rommel's Asparagus".*

BELOW *This aerial view of Omaha Beach shows the 6 June landing on the Normandy coast of two American infantry regiments, 18th and 115th, along with their landing craft and various vehicles.*

BELOW With the beach secured, landing ships put cargo ashore in the days after the operation, and the nearby sea bustles with shipping. Barrage balloons are flown overhead for protection from air attack and a halftrack convoy forms on the beach.

TOP-SECRET
BIGOT

REGISTER NO. 839

NEPTUNE
Monograph

PREPARED BY
COMMANDER TASK FORCE 122
APRIL 1944

TOP-SECRET
BIGOT

Left Page

NEPTUNE
Monograph

FOREWORD

The material from which the Monograph has been compiled comes from various agencies, as well as studies by Commander Task Force ONE TWO TWO. The main sources of information have been: Allied Naval Commander, Expeditionary Force; Theatre Intelligence Service of Supreme Headquarters Allied Expeditionary Force; the British Admiralty; The Hydrographer of the Royal Navy; 21st Army Group; Royal Air Force; Office of Naval Intelligence; Commander U. S. Naval Forces, Europe; Commander Amphibious Training Command, U. S. Atlantic Fleet; 1st U. S. Army; U. S. Army Engineers and the 9th Air Force.

Certain subjects, such as enemy light and heavy defenses, are omitted, as these are covered by annexes issued by the Allied Naval Commander, Expeditionary Force.

Some of the material contained in the Monograph is subject to revision as new information is received. Such late information will be promulgated by the Allied Naval Commander, Expeditionary Force or the Naval Commander, Western Task Force.

If any information promulgated by the Allied Naval Commander, Expeditionary Force or higher authority conflicts with that disseminated by Commander Task Force ONE TWO TWO (Naval Commander, Western Task Force) the former will govern.

This monograph is informative in character and none of the material in it is to be considered as a directive.

A G Kirk

Right Page

"OMAHA" BEACH
(COLLEVILLE - ST LAURENT - VIERVILLE)

LIMITS

	WEST	TO	EAST
Coordinates:	"T" 637927		"T" 696893
Latitude:	49° 23' 17" N.		49° 21' 36" N.
Longitude:	0° 55' 08" W.		0° 50' 10" W.

i.   GENERAL DESCRIPTION:

"OMAHA" BEACH, 7,500 yards long, is composed of firm sand with shingle occuring from the back of the beach for a distance of about 25 yards. Several sand bars exist inside the tidal area. The beach is flanked by hard shale. At the western end, this rock formation extends 1,300 yards along the beach, and at a point 500 yards from the western end, the rocks extend 120 to 150 yards to seaward.

Except for its western end, the beach is backed by a low wavecut embankment, faced for part of its length by a masonry wall, behind which is a level, sandy grass covered shelf averaging 100 yards in width. Back of the shelf is an 80-foot grass covered bluff broken by four natural valley exits, through which run roads. The western quarter of the beach is backed by a steep 80-foot cliff. A level cultivated plateau lies inland of this entire section of the coast.

The valleys are blocked by anti-tank obstacles, mines and wire, and the entire beach is defended by strong points and batteries. A line of obstacles exists along the beach at a distance of 50 to 130 yards to seaward from the back of the beach.

A detailed description follows: Refer to Folios A and B.

ii.   LENGTH: 7,500 Yds. (Coastline).
7,446 Yds. (Between coordinates).

iii.   WIDTH: Varies with the height of the tide. See SHORELINE SKETCH (Folios A and B) including TIDAL DATA and GRADIENTS on back thereof.

iv.   LANDMARKS:

(a) 647910 - VIERVILLE Steeple (100 feet high).
(b) 638926 - Tower (30 ft. high).
(c) 690895 - Valley.
(d) 678900 - Valley.
(e) 665907 - Valley.
(f) 648918 - Valley.

v.   APPROACH: Clear to seaward from low water mark. (See MAP CHART F-1015 for best data available on soundings.)

MARKINGS:

(a) POINTE DE LA PERCEE is border-

ed by a bank which, with depths of less than 5-fathoms, extends about 3/4 of a mile NE and about one mile ENE of the point. When the wind is against the tidal stream, a tide race, known as RAZ DE LA PERCEE, is formed over this bank. Under all wind conditions, turbulent currents are to be expected in this area, except during slack water.

(b) On both flanks of the beach there are underwater rocks composed of hard shale. At the western end, a strip of shale and shingle runs for 1,300 yards along the beach near the high tide mark. At a point 500 yards from the western end, a spur from this shale extends seaward 120 to 150 yards from the back of the beach.

(c) A rocky outcrop near the high water mark will be found in the vicinity of 651917.

vi.   GRADIENTS: In general flat up to Mean Level (13 ft.), then increasingly steep. (See GRADIENT DATA on back of Folios A and B.)

vii.   SAND BARS: A series of low sand bars exists along the entire length of the beach. The depressions between the bars drain off as the tide recedes. The sand bars are subject to slight shifting due to storms. Best information on bars is shown on SHORE-LINE SKETCH (Folios A and B).

viii.   CURRENTS: See SHORELINE SKETCH (Folios A and B) (Front and back.)

ix.   TIDAL RANGE:

Springs: 23 feet.
Neaps :   19 feet.
Mean Level: 13 feet, above Datum, which is approximate level of low low water.

x.   CONSISTENCY: Hard, well compacted sand from low water line to within 25 yards from back of beach. Beyond the sand to the back of the beach, there is shingle, averaging 6 inches in diameter. This area has an average slope of 1 in 8. In front of LES MOULINS, the shingle forms a bank 5 feet high average. The seawall west of LES MOULINS has sand and shingle piled up to a height of 2 to 3 feet. The eastern end of VIERVILLE seawall has a shingle and rock bank 4.5 feet high average. Rocks and debris occur in the western 1300 yards at the foot of the cliff. There is an outcrop at 651917 and small rock patches at 655914, 662910, and 674903.

xi.   OBSTACLES:

(a) OFFSHORE –
(1) NATURAL: See par. v, AP-PROACH and SHORELINE SKETCH (Folios A and B).
(2) ARTIFICIAL: None.
(b) WITHIN NORMAL TIDAL AREA:
(1) NATURAL: See Par. x, CONSISTENCY.
(2) ARTIFICIAL: As of 4-9-44 1000 obstacles have been laid on the beach, forming a continuous single-row barrier 648918 to 688897, the line varying from the 11' to the 18' contour above LLW. Obstacles are of the steel hedgehog type. Further installation is anticipated. For mines, wire etc., see ANCXF, ANNEX "A" – ASSAULT BEACH DEFENSE MAPS SCALE 1/12,500.

(c) BACK OF NORMAL TIDAL AREA:
(1) NATURAL:
(a) 696894 to 673902: Grassy bank, 4-6 ft. high, sloping approx. 1 in 4.
(b) 673902 to 662909: Wave-cut embankment, 4 to 8 ft. high.

(c) 659911 to 655913: Wave-cut embankment, 4 to 8 feet high.
(d) 649917 to 647919: Six-foot embankment.
(e) 647919 to 637927: Vertical cliffs up to 100 feet high with debris slope and shingle at base.
(2) ARTIFICIAL:
(a) 673902 to 662909: Beach is backed by a wave-cut embankment 4 to 8 feet high with intermittent rough stone wall.
(b) 662909 to 659911: Masonry wall, 4 to 8 feet high, with 15 jetties 55 ft. long and spaced 55 ft. apart, projecting seaward at a 60° angle. The surf has broken a part of the wall for a distance of 150 ft., from 65959106 to 65929109.
(c) 659911 to 655913: Wave-cut embankment, 4 to 8 ft. high, with intermittent rough stone wall.
(d) 655913 to 649917: Masonry and stone seawall, 8 to 12 ft. high, sloping approximately 45°. Nine jetties project seaward at western end of wall. These jetties are old and weathered and only pilings and a few connecting pieces remain.
(e) 649917 to 647919: A 6-foot embankment from which 6 jetties project seaward and on top of which are houses and stone fences.
(f) For obstacles of a defensive nature, see ANCXF, ANNEX "A" – ASSAULT BEACH DEFENSE MAPS, SCALE 1/12,500.

xii.   EXITS:

(a) COASTAL – (On shelf between bluff and beach).
(1) 696894 to 691895: Four-foot sandy trail along coast, turning inland at 691895.
(2) 687896: Road off beach branching immediately. One fork leads inland to COLLEVILLE, the other proceeds westward as an 8-foot sandy road turning inland at 679900, continuing in this direction to 677900.
(3) 677900 to 671904: 8-foot sandy road mentioned above parallels beach 75 yards inland.
(4) 679900 to 678900: 4-foot trail continues along coast where 8-foot sandy road mentioned in (2) above turns inland.
(5) 671904 to 665907: 10-foot tarmac road parallels the beach.
(6) 665907 to 648917: Road mentioned in (5) above broadens into a 12-foot tarmac road paralleling the coast.

WARNING

This road is being washed out at 659911 by action of the sea.
(b) INLAND:
(1) 696893: 10-foot unsurfaced road leads up slope to strong point atop bluff and inland to village of CABOURG. At the back of the beach, this road forks to the west, and an 8-foot trail leads inland into CABOURG and COLLEVILLE.
(2) 687896: 10-foot tarmac road to COLLEVILLE.
(3) 676900: 10-foot unsurfaced road leading to ST. LAURENT.
(4) 665907: 10-foot tarmac road leaves coast at LES MOULINS inland for ST. LAURENT.
(5) 648917: 15-foot tarmac road leaves VIERVILLE inland.

xiii.   OBSTACLES TO MOVEMENT INLAND:

(a) NATURAL –
(1) BLUFF: A bluff backs the entire beach area with the exception of the easternmost end. The bluff area thus presents a continuous obstacle to tracked and wheeled vehicles, restricting their movements inland to the four exits mentioned in par. xii (b) (2), (3), (4) and (5). At the eastern end of the beach area, the slopes are believed negotiable by all

tracked vehicles and possibly lighter wheeled vehicles.
(2) FIELD BOUNDARIES: Fields on the plateau behind the bluff are bounded by hedges, rows of bushes, trees and occasionally by stone walls. Most of the fields themselves are clear of trees, but there are a few orchards and small groves.
(b) ARTIFICIAL: For road blocks, anti-tank ditches, minefields, obstacles, demolitions, etc., see ANCXF, ANNEX "A" – ASSAULT BEACH DEFENSE MAPS, SCALE 1/12,500.

xiv.   DEFENSES:

(a) LIGHT DEFENSES: Beach is heavily defended by light artillery units, heavy and light machine guns, mines, wire, pillboxes, demolitions etc.. Almost continuous construction activity has been noted since October 1943. For details, see ANCXF, ANNEX "A" – ASSAULT BEACH DEFENSE MAPS, SCALE 1/12,500.
(b) HEAVY DEFENSES: The beach is defended by heavy coastal batteries, located to the east and west of the beach area. For details, see:
(1) ANCXF, ANNEX "C" – TEXT AND DIAGRAM OF NEPTUNE BATTERIES.
(2) ANCXF, ANNEX "D" – TEXT AND TRACES OF COAST DEFENSES.

BEACH NEAR VIERVILLE-SUR-MER LOOKING EAST SHOWING RETARDS IN FOREGROUND
(Small buildings on beach have been removed)

BEACH NEAR ST. LAURENT-SUR-MER LOOKING WEST SHOWING SHINGLE AT BACK OF BEACH
(Buildings in background have been removed)

Section VI - ENEMY DEFENSES and INSTALLATIONS

A. INTRODUCTION

Coast and Beach defense along the enemy held channel coast consists of a number of well emplaced coastal and field batteries sited to cover both sea approaches and beach areas, and a line of concreted infantry strongpoints along the coast to provide interlocking fire over beaches and exits. Batteries are generally located well inland behind beach areas, and on coastal headlands. Strongpoints are spaced along the coast, thickly in areas where landing might be made, and more widely scattered along rocky or steeply sloping coastline.

Since the beginning of the year construction activity has increased to a marked degree in the defensive belt. Batteries are being casemated with great rapidity; in some instances prefabricated concrete blocks have been used. Existing strongpoints are being strengthened and new field defences are being built at from 1,000 to 10,000 yards inland of the coast line.

NOTE: Strongpoints are permanent positions with heavy concrete construction for defense and are usually buried for further protection. Field defenses are less permanent positions comprising movable guns protected normally by wire, occasionally by mine fields, but without permanent armor. Field defenses are set up as a rule for strategic defense of highways, dumps or other military features. They are usually reserve positions.

Large quantities of steel underwater obstacles are being brought to the coast and placed in position on the beaches, and natural terrain obstacles are being supplemented by anti-tank ditches and walls to hold invading troops within the area of fire of beach strongpoints. This activity is occurring along the entire coast and is probably a result of Field Marshal Rommel's inspection of the west wall during December and January.

In the American Neptune area this activity has resulted in the following changes: Existing batteries are being casemated, new casemated positions and new open field battery emplacements are being prepared. This activity is particularly noticeable in the North East corner of the Cotentin Peninsula. New pillboxes and shelters are being built in coastal Strongpoints; no inland Strongpoints have been begun as yet. Steel beach obstacles have been laid in parts of the area, and new anti-tank ditches and barbed wire installations are in evidence.

B. BEACH DEFENSES
STRONG POINTS, PILL BOXES, OBSTACLES, WIRE

The line of strongpoints behind the beaches provide defensive fire for the Neptune landing areas. There is no present defense in depth. Recent prepared defenses in addition to strongpoints include underwater obstacles, sea walls behind the beaches, anti-tank ditches and walls blocking valley exits (OMAHA), inundated areas blocking exits over low land (UTAH), and a liberal use of mines and wire. Most of the houses left standing on the coast have been fortified.

A typical strong point consists of a group of pillboxes, open weapon pits, and underground shelters, usually protected by wire, mines and anti-tank ditches. Flame thrower installations have been reported. On OMAHA the strong points are situated on the low land immediately behind the beach, on the beach and on the cliffs and bluffs just inland. On UTAH the strong points are located along the sea wall behind the beach. Pillboxes and shelters are usually of reinforced concrete, with a minimum thickness of 3'. Shelters are usually completely buried and pillboxes nearly so. A network of trenches connects these structures. Anti-tank emplacements or casemates and light field gun emplacements are frequently found in coastal strong points. Strong points are also found around heavy batteries and radar installations.

There are three common types of underwater obstacles (see sketch). There is a single line of "hedgehog" obstacles on OMAHA beach between the 11' and the 18' contour above LLW, and two lines on the northern half of UTAH between the 11' and 18' contour, which extend off the beach to the north. Installation is still in progress on both beaches.

TYPICAL STRONG POINT

ILLUSTRATED BY POSITION 668903 AT LES MOULINS, BEACH "OMAHA".

BURIED SHELTER

MACHINE GUN PITS

PILL BOX

OBLIQUE VIEW OF PILL-BOX

LEGEND

- PILLBOX (NM) (OBLIQUE)
- MACHINE GUN
- WIRE
- COMMUNICATION TRENCH
- OPEN EMP
- BURIED SHELTERS
- PROB. BURIED STORES

OBLIQUE VIEW OF STRONG POINT

THIS SECTION OF STRONG POINT STILL UNDER CONST

TOP OF CLIFF

TOP OF CLIFF

PILL BOX UNDER CONST

SEE OBLIQUE VIEW OF PILL-BOX ABOVE

SANDY SHELF BEHIND BEACH

GRID NORTH

HIGH HIGH WATER MARK

PLAN VIEW OF STRONG POINT   SCALE 1:3000

BELOW D-Day situation report messages sent by the U.S. Information Team on Omaha Beach, commanded by Colonel B. B. Talley, to Major General Leonard T. Gerow ("LTG"), U.S. V Corps commander, who was on a ship offshore. All 21 officers and men were decorated for gallantry on D-Day, one of the largest single-unit awards in U.S. Army history.

THESE SPACES FOR MESSAGE CENTER ONLY

TIME FILED	MSG CEN No.	HOW SENT

MESSAGE

(CLASSIFICATION)   (SUBMIT TO MESSAGE CENTER IN DUPLICATE)

NO **10**   DATE

TO **LTG**

From one thousand yds off Dog Red Beach I see several companies one six Inf on Easy Red and fox red Beaches X enemy artillery and Machine gun fire still effective X Love charlie Tares shifting ~~from~~ Dog X about thirty CTs standing by to land

OFFICIAL DESIGNATION OF SENDER   TIME SIGNED

SIGNATURE AND GRADE OF WRITER

GPO   16—20158

THESE SPACES FOR MESSAGE CENTER ONLY

TIME FILED	MSG CEN No.	HOW SENT

MESSAGE

(CLASSIFICATION)   (SUBMIT TO MESSAGE CENTER IN DUPLICATE)

NO   DATE

TO **10 contd**

~~Rifle and~~ Obstacles seem thicker than in photos X Bty Able seven FA in Dukws just arrived X Love charlie item eight five hit and smoking after unloading X have seen Two ~~these~~ Love charlie Tares ~~Hit~~ Burn Count Ten Tanks on Fox X landing resuming on Dog

OFFICIAL DESIGNATION OF SENDER   TIME SIGNED

SIGNATURE AND GRADE OF WRITER

GPO   16—20158

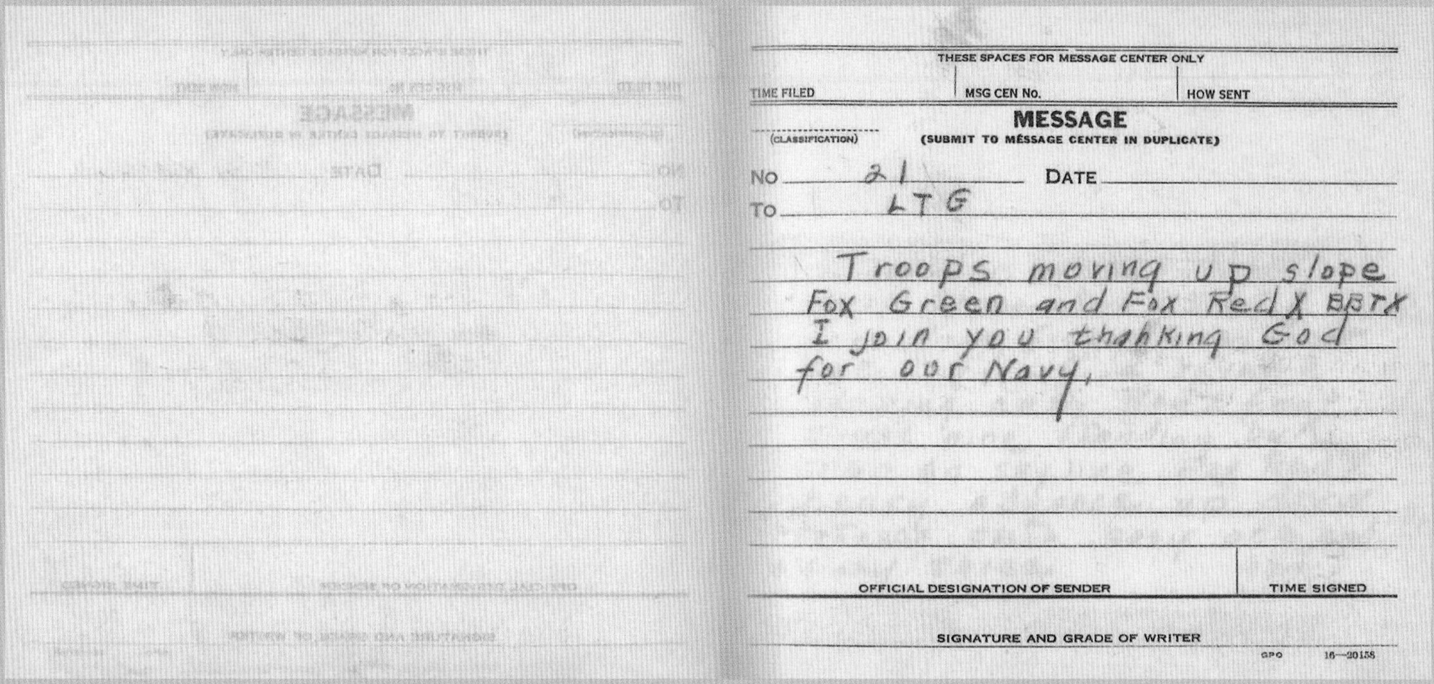

THESE SPACES FOR MESSAGE CENTER ONLY

| TIME FILED | MSG CEN No. | HOW SENT |

MESSAGE

(CLASSIFICATION) (SUBMIT TO MESSAGE CENTER IN DUPLICATE)

No ___ 21 ___ DATE ___

To ___ LTG ___

Troops moving up slope
Fox Green and Fox Red X BBTX
I join you thanking God
for our Navy.

| OFFICIAL DESIGNATION OF SENDER | TIME SIGNED |

SIGNATURE AND GRADE OF WRITER

GPO 16—20158

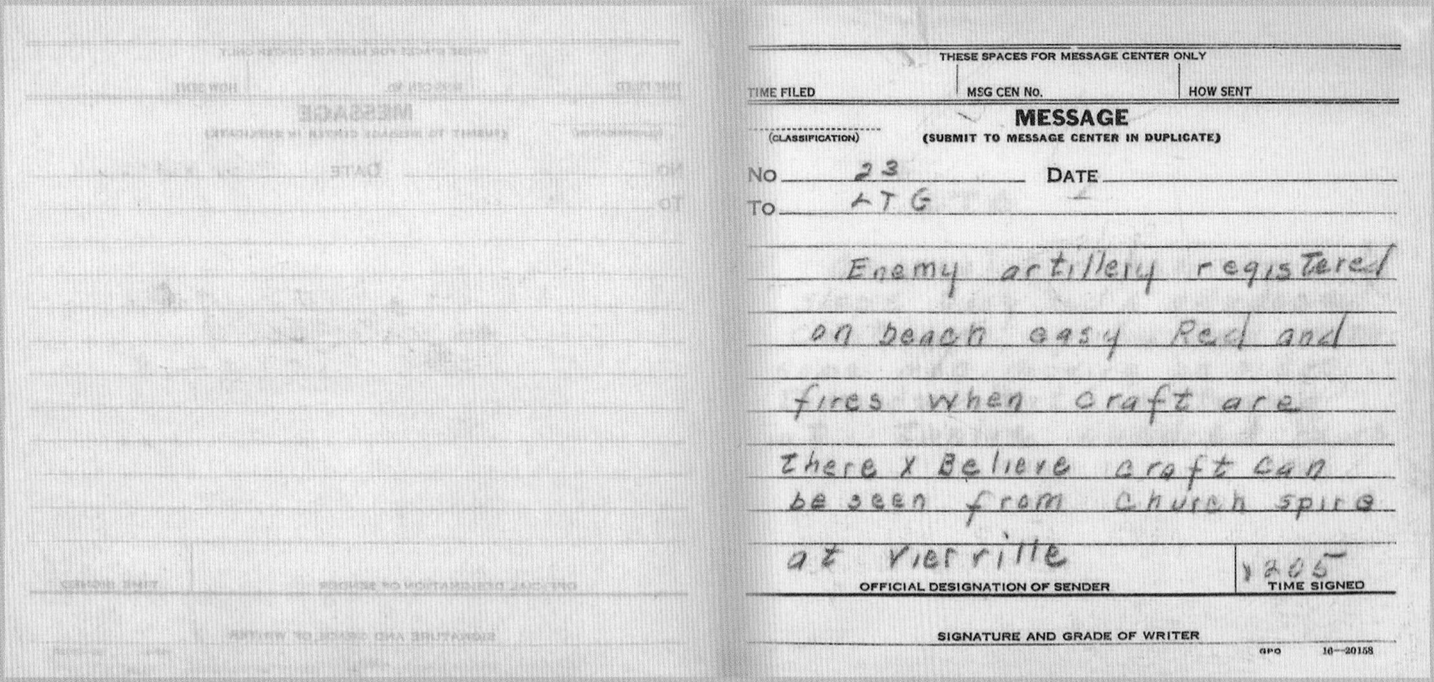

THESE SPACES FOR MESSAGE CENTER ONLY

| TIME FILED | MSG CEN No. | HOW SENT |

MESSAGE

(CLASSIFICATION) (SUBMIT TO MESSAGE CENTER IN DUPLICATE)

No ___ 23 ___ DATE ___

To ___ LTG ___

Enemy artillery registered
on beach easy Red and
fires when craft are
there X Believe craft can
be seen from church spire
at Vierville

| OFFICIAL DESIGNATION OF SENDER | 205 TIME SIGNED |

SIGNATURE AND GRADE OF WRITER

GPO 16—20158

TUESDAY 6 JUNE 1944

GOLD BEACH

GOLD, THE WESTERNMOST OF THE BRITISH/CANADIAN BEACHES, WAS TO BE ASSAULTED BY
MAJOR GENERAL D. A. H. GRAHAM'S 50TH DIVISION OF XXX CORPS, WHICH WAS TO
ADVANCE TO TAKE BAYEUX, AND HOOK RIGHT TO CAPTURE ARROMANCHES (WHERE THE
BRITISH MULBERRY HARBOUR WAS TO BE BUILT) AND THEN LINK UP WITH THE AMERICANS.

50th Division had begun the war as a Territorial formation recruited from the north-east (its distinctive divisional flash bore TT, for Tyne-Tees), and it had fought in France in 1940 and subsequently in the Western Desert. Its regional composition had been much diluted and, sadly, dwindling numbers of British soldiers available for service in the infantry were eventually to result in its disbandment: but not before it added further lustre to its laurels on D-Day.

FAR LEFT *British 50TH Infantry Division.*

LEFT *British 8TH Armoured Brigade.*

BELOW *Infantry of a follow-up wave coming ashore from a landing craft near Ver-sur-Mer on Gold Beach.*

OPPOSITE *Troops inspect a knocked-out German anti-tank gun on Gold Beach.*

'IT WAS A SOBERING SIGHT AS THE HAMPSHIRES LEFT THEIR SMALLER INFANTRY LANDING CRAFT. ... MEN WERE DROPPING WHILE STILL IN SHALLOW WATER, TO BE DRAGGED FORWARD BY THEIR MATES AND LEFT ON THE SAND, WHILE THEIR COMRADES RAN ON IN A PURPOSEFUL STEADY JOG TROT, WHICH BETRAYED NO SIGN OF PANIC.

TROOPER JOE MINOGUE, THE WESTMINSTER DRAGOONS

50th Division was to land with two brigades forward, 231st on the right and 69th on the left, with 56th Brigade following up on the right and 151st on the left. The division had 8th Armoured Brigade under command, and this provided one regiment of DD tanks with each assaulting brigade, the Nottinghamshire Yeomanry on the right and the 4th/7th Dragoon Guards on the left. Once the beach was secure, 47th Royal Marine Commando would land and make for Port-en-Bessin on the inter-Allied boundary. In contrast to American policy, specialist armoured vehicles, of the Westminster Dragoons and 6th Assault Regiment Royal Engineers, were to land just ahead of the infantry to deal with beach obstacles, mines and the sea wall. On Gold Beach alone there were almost 2,500 obstacles of one sort or another, embodying almost 900 tons of steel, concrete or wood.

Strong defences at Le Hamel briefly held up 231st Brigade – 1st Hampshire lost its commanding officer and second-in-command – but by 8.30 the whole brigade was ashore and making progress. On the left, 69th Brigade also ran into resistance just behind the beach, but the garrisons of a battery on Mont Fleury and the village of Ver-sur-Mer had been so cowed by naval and air bombardment that they offered little opposition. With the assaulting brigades ashore, naval beachmasters began to organize the beaches so that follow-up units could land smoothly: 151st Brigade arrived at about 11.00, with 69th Brigade not far behind. By the day's end almost 25,000 men had gone ashore.

Progress inland was encouraging. The commandos dug in overlooking Port-en-Bessin, and Arromanches was cleared by nightfall. During the advance of 69th Brigade, Company Sergeant Major Stan Hollis of the Green Howards earned the Victoria Cross, the only one awarded as a result of D-Day, for valour that began on Mont Fleury and ended in the village of Crepon. By nightfall 151st Brigade had reached the Bayeux-Caen road. Bayeux itself was hopelessly exposed, and fell the following day.

STAN HOLLIS

was a company sergeant major in 6th Green Howards, a Yorkshire Territorial battalion, on D-Day. He personally cleared German bunkers on Mont Fleury, and later attacked a field gun in the village of Crepon. Hollis was awarded the Victoria Cross, Britain's highest award for military bravery: it was the only one given for D-Day. The citation referred to his "utmost gallantry". After the war Hollis ran a pub, and told his wife to sell his VC when he died because it was, in effect, his pension.

TOP *The Victoria Cross, the highest award for gallantry awarded to British and Canadian servicemen.*

ABOVE *British 231st Infantry Brigade.*

LEFT *British Sherman tanks move through the town of Bayeux, captured on 7 June. The first major French town to be liberated, Bayeux fell without much resistance. It was spared the terrible damage visited on Caen and St-Lô.*

6 JUNE 1944 UP TO 12.00 HOURS

GOLD BEACH

PLANNED H-HOUR: 07.25

ALLIES

ASSAULTING DIVISION: British 50th Division

DIVISION COMMANDER: Major General D.A.H. Graham

INFANTRY ASSAULT UNITS:
1st Battalion Hampshire Regiment, 1st Battalion Dorset Regiment, 5th Battalion East Yorkshire Regiment, 6th Battalion The Green Howards

FIRST-WAVE DD TANKS: Nottinghamshire Yeomanry, 4th/7th Royal Dragoon Guards

MEN LANDED: 24,970

CASUALTIES (DEAD, WOUNDED & MISSING): c.400

AXIS

DEFENDING DIVISIONS:
Elements of 716th Coastal Defence and 352nd Infantry

716TH COASTAL DEFENCE DIVISION COMMANDER:
Lieutenant General Wilhelm Richter

352ND INFANTRY DIVISION COMMANDER:
Lieutenant General Dietrich Kraiss

MAP KEY

■   Area of strongest German resistance

●   German resistance points

♛   German battery

♜   Mines

—   Frontline at 12.00 hours

ABBREVIATIONS

Hants   Hampshire

Cdo   Commando

GH   Green Howards

EY   East Yorkshire

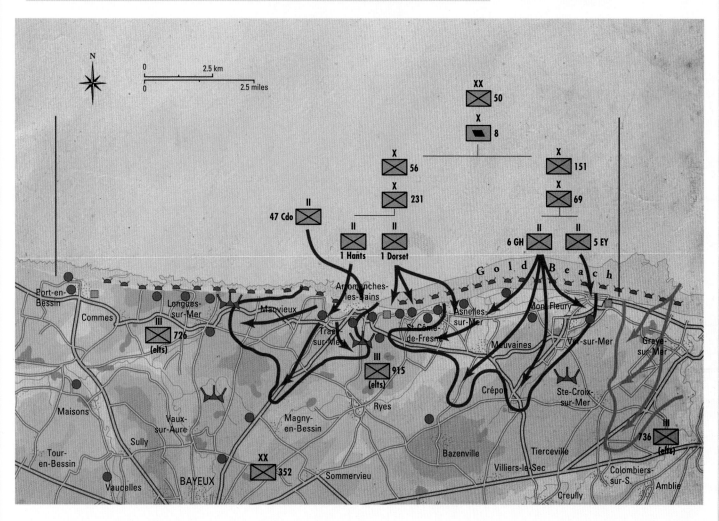

BELOW *Cromwell tanks of 4th County of London Yeomanry, then part of 7th Armoured Division, moving ashore from Gold Beach on 7 June.*

JUNO BEACH

CANADA MADE A DISTINCTIVE CONTRIBUTION TO THE ALLIED EFFORT IN BOTH WORLD WARS, AND IT WAS FITTING THAT MAJOR GENERAL R. F. L. KELLER'S 3RD CANADIAN DIVISION, PART OF I CORPS, SHOULD LAND ON JUNO BEACH.

Canadian 3rd Infantry Division

The Canadian armed forces reflected, not without tensions, Canada's cultural divide: though most units serving overseas bore English titles and contained a majority of English-speaking men, Le Régiment de Maisonneuve and Les Fusiliers Mont-Royal, for example, were to play their part alongside the Black Watch of Canada and the South Saskatchewan Regiment in Normandy. Two Canadian destroyers, HMCS *Sioux* and *Algonquin,* were among the warships bombarding Juno, and they reflected the Canadian navy's costly service escorting Atlantic convoys.

ABOVE *Men of 48 (Royal Marine) Commando going ashore on Nan, the easternmost sector of Juno Beach.*

BELOW *Canadian infantrymen of Le Régiment de la Chaudière, the follow-up battalion of 8th Canadian Brigade, landing near Bernières on the morning of D-Day.*

HOBART'S "FUNNIES"

Major General Sir Percy Hobart, brother-in-law of General Montgomery, was recalled from retirement in 1941, at the instigation of Winston Churchill, to take command of the 79th Armoured Division and mastermind the development of specially adapted armour to support a seaborne invasion. The "funnies", as they were known, were invaluable on Sword, Gold and Juno for facilitating rapid exit of the first waves of infantry and support vehicles off the beaches.

ABOVE A standard M4 Sherman tank with a revolving drum fitted to a frontally extended frame, known as a "flail tank" or "crab". The chains attached to the drum exploded mines and cleared belts of barbed wire, leaving a safe path for following troops.

BELOW A Duplex Drive (DD) Sherman tank with a collapsible canvas screen, which, when raised, gave it sufficient buoyancy to float. It had two propellers and a top speed in the water of over 4 knots. Amphibious armour was used for the first time on D-Day and gave the first-wave infantry invaluable fire support, which came as a complete surprise to the German defenders.

The attack was complicated by the fact that the coast was protected by offshore rocks, exposed at low tide, except at the mouth of the River Seulles and the small port of Courseulles, where the Germans had thickened their defences. The town was the objective of 7th Canadian Brigade, the division's right assault brigade, while 8th Canadian Brigade was to land further east, at Bernières and St-Aubin-sur-Mer. Each assaulting brigade comprised three infantry battalions and an armoured regiment. As on British beaches, specialist armour, in this case from the 22nd Dragoons and 5th and 6th Assault Regiments Royal Engineers, was to deal with the beach defences. 9th Canadian Brigade would follow 8th onto the beaches. The defenders of Juno came from thinly-spread 716th Division, which had about three companies – no more than 400 men – in the path of an attack which would put 2,400 men and 76 tanks ashore in its first wave.

The Canadians landed slightly later than planned, which helped them get over the offshore rocks but meant that they arrived among beach defences. The landing craft had to jockey their way in and out among obstacles and 70 out of 306 were lost or damaged. Courseulles was stubbornly defended, and did not fall until well on in the afternoon, after Royal Marine Centaur tanks and Royal Engineer assault tanks supported the Royal Winnipeg Rifles and the Regina Rifles. Further east, the Queens Own Rifles suffered severely crossing the beach at Bernières, but soon stormed the village, and the New Brunswickers of the North Shore Regiment had a similar experience in St-Aubin. On the Canadian left, 48 (Royal Marine) Commando landing at about 9.00 am, lost landing craft to the now-submerged beach obstacles, and was galled by machine gun fire from St-Aubin, but swung left to capture Lagrune-sur-Mer, on the boundary with the British 3rd Division. Although the Canadians ended the day in contact with 50th Division on their right, and just short of the Bayeux-Caen road to their front, there remained a gap between them and Sword Beach on their left.

BELOW *Anti-tank obstacles in the streets of St-Aubin-sur-Mer. The soldier taking cover from snipers is probably a member of the North Shore (New Brunswick) Regiment.*

BELOW *Sherman tanks of 3rd Canadian Armoured Brigade using an artificial trackway built by engineers to move up the beach: a sharp contrast to Dieppe.*

JUNO BEACH

PLANNED H-HOUR: 07.45

ALLIES

ASSAULTING DIVISION: Canadian 3rd Division

DIVISION COMMANDER: Major General R.F.L. Keller

INFANTRY ASSAULT UNITS:
The Royal Winnipeg Rifles, the Regina Rifle Regiment, the Queen's Own Rifles of Canada, the North Shore (New Brunswick) Regiment

FIRST-WAVE DD TANKS: 6th Canadian Armoured Regiment, 10th Canadian Armoured Regiment

MEN LANDED: 21,500

CASUALTIES (DEAD, WOUNDED & MISSING): c.1,000

AXIS

DEFENDING DIVISION: Elements of 716th Coastal Defence Division

DIVISION COMMANDER: Lieutenant General Wilhelm Richter

MAP KEY

▪ Area of strongest German resistance

● German resistance points

♔ German battery

♕ Mines

▬ Frontline at 12.00 hours

ABBREVIATIONS

RWR Royal Winnepeg

RR Regina Rifles

QOR Queens Own Rifles

NSR North Shore Regiment

RM Cdo Royal Marine Commando

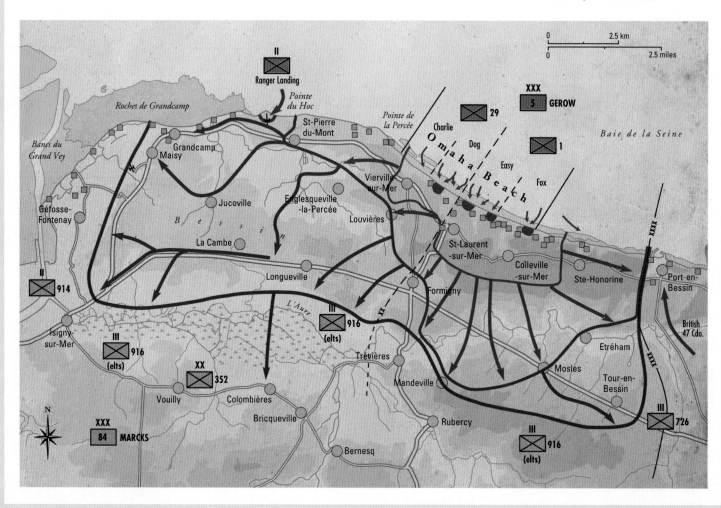

BELOW & OVERLEAF *Letter from Canadian Lance Sergeant Edwin Owen Worden to his wife, written on the boat while waiting to cross the Channel on 5 June. Worden served with the 1st Battalion, Regina Rifle Regiment. He survived D-Day but died in Holland during the Allied advance in April 1945.*

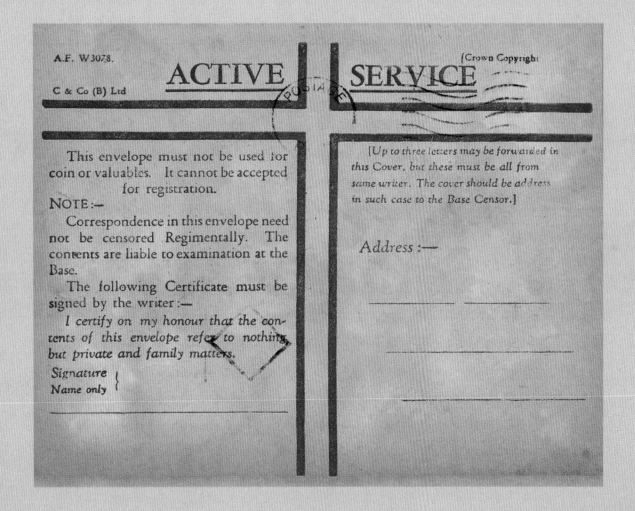

L27027
Rfn E.O. Worden.
1st B tln Regina Rifl
Can army England. Mon 5. 44.

To my darling wife:
How are you to- night? fine
I hope. Lee darling I find
it very hard to write
this to you. I only wish
I could have seen you. but
I can say this. I am fine.
and feel a 100 per cent. ~~for~~
I know I have someone
waiting for me, who is
very brave and knows how
to smile.
We are going in to-
morrow morning. as I write
this we are ~~out~~ on the

2.
water. so the big day has
come. I often ~~had~~ wondered
how I would feel but
~~to~~ I don't feel any
difference, as I ever did
before. thanks to you. I
know ~~and th~~ I can
truthful say if it was
not for you I would
feel different. but it is
the love and trust I have
for you. and that will
help me over ~~many~~ a
~~rough~~ spot.
I am glad in away
that it has come. for it

CANADIAN LEGION
WAR SERVICES Inc.

CANADIAN Y.M.C.A.
OVERSEAS

ON ACTIVE SERVICE

CANADIAN
KNIGHTS OF COLUMBUS
WAR SERVICES

THE SALVATION ARMY
CANADIAN
WAR SERVICES

3

means you and I can be
togeather sooner. something
I have allways prayed
for. and I know you have
to. So promise darling
you will not worrey. for
I'll be allright. and home
befor you know it.
Just you and mum look
after each other. and time
will pass swiftly.
Now before I close I want
to say again. that I love
you very much and you mean
the world to me.

So now darling I'll say
good-night and God bless
you till we meet again
soon
          Yours forever.
              Love.
                Ted.

P.S. Tell mum that I am
thinking of her too. and
not to worrey but look
after you.
I am encloseing a message
they gave us. good-night
I'll write as soon as I
get a chance.

CFA 170(4213)   PLEASE WRITE ON BOTH SIDES

SWORD BEACH

SWORD, THE EASTERNMOST INVASION BEACH, WAS THE OBJECTIVE OF MAJOR GENERAL
T. G. RENNIE'S 3RD DIVISION. THIS DIVISION HAD FOUGHT (UNDER MONTGOMERY'S
COMMAND) IN 1940, BUT HAD NOT BEEN ENGAGED SINCE.

Its task was important and complex. Inland was the city of Caen, capital of Normandy and an important communication hub. Montgomery believed that its early capture was crucial because it would give him room for manoeuvre on the British flank. 3rd Division's orders specified that by nightfall it was to have "captured or effectively masked" the city. Next, the division had to facilitate a link with 6th Airborne Division via Pegasus Bridge, though the commandos of 1st Special Service Brigade, landing on the eastern edge of Sword Beach and taking Ouistreham, were going to make the junction. Finally, it was known that the only German armour close enough to launch a counter-attack, 21st Panzer Division, was in the area, so it was likely that 3rd Division would encounter German armour.

The presence of offshore rocks and the proximity of the mouth of the Orne and the town of Ouistreham meant that 3rd Division landed on the front of a single brigade, which made its deployment sequential rather than simultaneous. The leading brigade, 8th, used two of its battalions, 1st South Lancashire and 2nd East Yorkshire, to secure the coastal strip,

RIGHT *The commandos appear calm aboard the landing craft on their approach to Sword Beach.*

OPPOSITE *Commandos of Brigadier Lord Lovat's 1st Special Service Brigade, destined to relieve the paratroops at Pegasus Bridge, landing at La Brèche in the Queen Red sector.*

LORD LOVAT

or Shimi to his friends, came from a Highland family with a stormy past – an ancestor was the last peer beheaded for treason. He joined the Commandos in 1940, and led 4 Commando on the Dieppe raid, capturing a coastal battery. On D-Day he was accompanied ashore on Sword Beach by his piper, Bill Millin, and carried a hunting rifle. He was later severely wounded, and after the war acted as Churchill's emissary to Stalin before becoming a noted cattle breeder.

British 3rd Infantry
Division.

'I STARTED THE PIPES UP AND MARCHED UP AND DOWN. THIS SERGEANT CAME RUNNING OVER, "GET DOWN YOU MAD BASTARD. YOU'RE ATTRACTING ATTENTION ON US." ANYWAY I CONTINUED MARCHING UP AND DOWN UNTIL WE MOVED OFF THE BEACH.'

PIPER BILL MILLIN, 1ST SPECIAL SERVICE BRIGADE

ABOVE *Royal Marine Commandos advancing inland from Sword Beach.*

ABOVE *Infantry advance with a Duplex Drive Sherman of 13ʰ/18ʰ Hussars just outside Ouistreham.*

PHILIPPE KIEFFER

was born in Haiti to a family originating in Alsace. A reserve officer aboard the old battleship Courbet *in 1940, he immediately joined the Free French forces. Impressed by British commandos, he raised the first French commando unit. He led 177 of his men ashore on Sword Beach, and took the casino in Ouistreham and the lock gates on the canal: his commandos suffered heavy casualties and he was twice wounded. After the war he sat in the National Assembly.*

and then pushed its third battalion, 1ˢᵗ Suffolk, assisted by tanks of the 13ᵗʰ/18ᵗʰ Hussars, inland to attack a German battery near Colleville and a strongpoint codenamed Hillman just south of the same village. This took longer than had been expected, largely because Hillman, which had not been bombed or shelled, was too serious an obstacle for the Suffolks to take, save by a formal attack with proper armoured support. As long as Hillman remained in German hands, it acted like a cork in the bottle.

The next brigade to land, 185ᵗʰ, had been ordered to capture Caen, with the infantry of 2ⁿᵈ King's Shropshire Light Infantry riding on tanks of the Staffordshire Yeomanry to spearhead the advance. However, the narrowness of the front and congestion on and behind the beach caused delay, and although the leading elements of the brigade eventually reached the northern edge of Lebisey Wood, just three miles short of Caen, they were unable to get further. When 9ᵗʰ Brigade arrived, after further delay, Major General Rennie ordered it to defend the Orne bridges against attack from the west. His concern was understandable, for he had already heard that 21ˢᵗ Panzer Division had begun its counter-attack.

21ˢᵗ Panzer had been re-raised to replace the original division, lost in North Africa. Its commander lacked relevant experience: on the dawn of the invasion it was inconveniently close to the Orne and the Caen Canal, and it took time for a decision to attack west of the water obstacles. Colonel von Oppeln-Bronikowski's battle group was launched northwards, but was sharply engaged by tanks and anti-tank

guns, well posted on the Perières ridge, west of Hillman, and though it just reached the coast between the 3ʳᵈ British Division and the 3ʳᵈ Canadian Division, it achieved little. Although 3ʳᵈ Division had shrugged off the only major D-Day counter-attack, it had failed to take Caen. With the benefit of hindsight it seems that the plan was too ambitious given the proximity of German armour and the need to squeeze all attacking brigades, one by one, across the same beach.

PLANNED H-HOUR: 07.25

ALLIES

ASSAULTING DIVISION: British 3ʳᵈ Division

DIVISION COMMANDER: Major General T. G. Rennie

INFANTRY ASSAULT UNITS: 1ˢᵗ South Lancashire Regiment, 2ⁿᵈ East Yorkshire Regiment

FIRST-WAVE DD TANKS: 13ᵗʰ/18ᵗʰ Hussars

MEN LANDED: 28,845

CASUALTIES (DEAD, WOUNDED & MISSING): c.630

AXIS

DEFENDING DIVISION: Elements of 716ᵗʰ Coastal Defence Division

DIVISION COMMANDER: Lieutenant General Wilhelm Richter

06 JUNE 1944 UP TO 12.00 HOURS

SWORD BEACH

MAP KEY

- ▢ Area of strongest German resistance
- ● German resistance points
- ⩜ German battery
- ⩊ Mines
- ▬ Frontline at 12.00 hours

ABBREVIATIONS

SS	Special Service
RM Cdo	Royal Marine Commando
SL	South Lancashire
EY	East Yorkshire

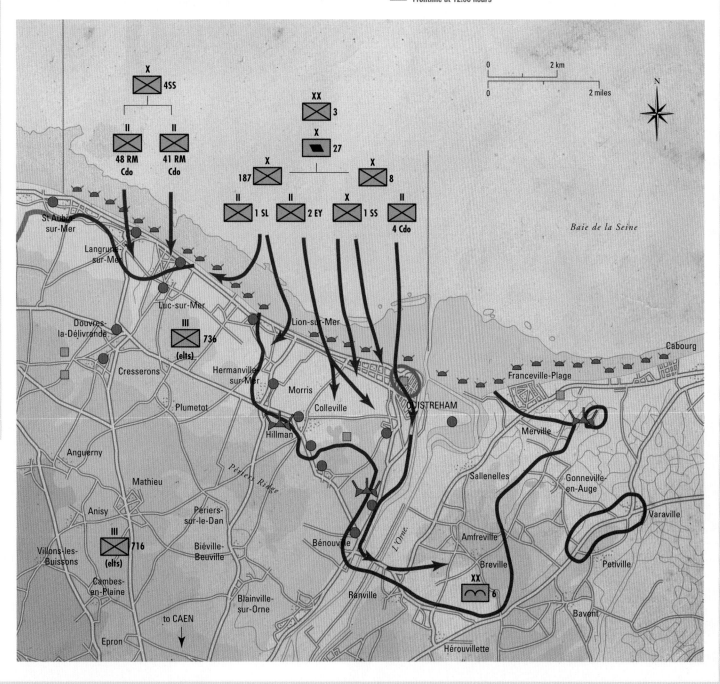

SAPPER CYRIL HAWKINS

SAPPER JIMMY LEASK

SAPPER FRED SADLER

LEFT *The scene on Queen White sector of Sword Beach at about 8.30 a.m. on D-Day. Sappers of 84th Field Company Royal Engineers are in the foreground. In the background are men of 1st Battalion, the Suffolk Regiment and Lord Lovat's commandos.*

ABOVE *A Royal Artillery forward observation group from 3rd Division use portable wireless sets during the advance inland from Sword Beach.*

BELOW *Troops pass through La Brèche, having landed at Sword Beach.*

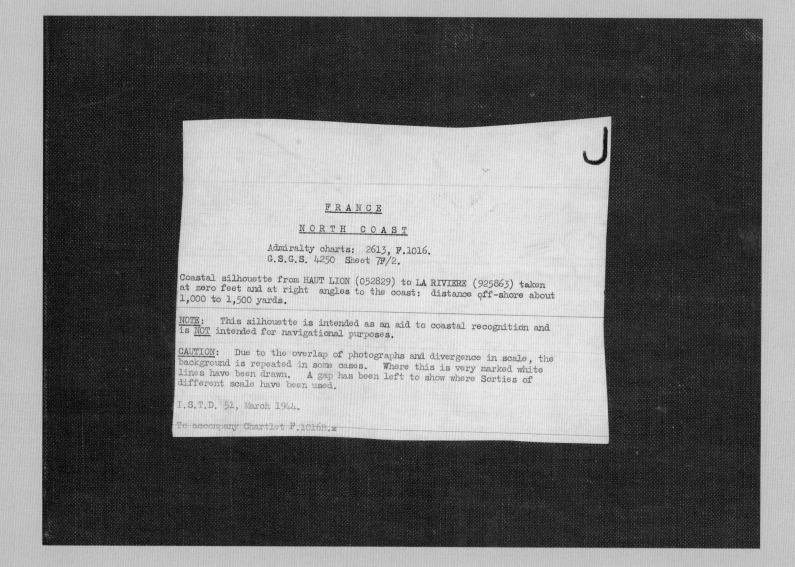

FRANCE

NORTH COAST

Admiralty charts: 2613, F.1016.
G.S.G.S. 4250 Sheet 7F/2.

Coastal silhouette from HAUT LION (052829) to LA RIVIERE (925863) taken at zero feet and at right angles to the coast: distance off-shore about 1,000 to 1,500 yards.

NOTE: This silhouette is intended as an aid to coastal recognition and is NOT intended for navigational purposes.

CAUTION: Due to the overlap of photographs and divergence in scale, the background is repeated in some cases. Where this is very marked white lines have been drawn. A gap has been left to show where Sorties of different scale have been used.

I.S.T.D. 51, March 1944.

To accompany Chartlet F.1016B.x

LANGRUNE-SUR-MER

BELOW Letter from General Montgomery to his friend Major General Frank Simpson, director of military operations at the War Office, summarizing the overall situation on D+2. Montgomery wrote the letter from his tactical headquarters on the day he landed in Normandy.

SECRET

1.

Tac 21 Army Group

8 - 6 - 44

Seen by CIGS 10 June & Angas.
... 11 June

My dear Simbo

You may like the following news of our battle.

1. There is no doubt that the Germans were surprised, and we got on shore before they had recovered. The speed, power, and violence of the assault carried all before it.

2. Generally, the beach obstacles presented no difficulty; where they were troublesome it was because of the rough weather — and on some beaches it was pretty rough.

3. DD Tanks.
(a) Used successfully on UTAH beaches.
(b) Failed to reach the shore on OMAHA beaches and all sank — too rough.
(c) Were not launched on 50 DIV front as it was too rough; were landed "dry" behind the leading flights; casualties to AVRE sappers high as a result, and to leading infantry.
(d) landed "dry" on Canadian front.
(e) Used successfully on 3 DIV front.
generally it can be said that the DD tanks

2.

proved their value, and casualties were high when they could not be used.

4. As a guess prisoners about 6000 so far. They consist of Germans, Russians, Poles, Japanese, and two Turks.

5. British casualties about 1000 per assault Division.
American casualties not known.
High proportion of officer casualties, due to sniping behind our front.
Two Inf. Bde. Comds wounded:
    Cunningham   9 Bde
    Senior   151 Bde
Good many Inf. C.O.'s killed, including HERDON, o.c. 2 Warwicks.
No general officers are casualties.

6. The Germans are fighting well; Russians, Poles, Japanese, and Turks, run away; and if unable to do so, surrender.

7. Our initial attack was on a wide front, and there were gaps between landings. The impetus of the assault carried us some way inland and

3

many defended localities were by-passed; these proved very troublesome later. In one case a complete German Bn, with artillery, was found inside 50 DIV area; it gave some trouble but was eventually collected in (about 500 men). There is still one holding out — the radar station west of DOUVRES; it is very strong and is held by stout-hearted Germans.

8. Sniping in back areas has been very troublesome, as a result of para 7. The roads have been far from safe and we have lost several good officers. I have been all right myself, though I have toured the area all day. There have been women snipers, presumably wives of German soldiers; the Canadians shot 4 women snipers.

9. The Germans are doing everything they can to hold on to CAEN. I have decided not to have a lot of casualties by battering up against the place; so

4

I have ordered second Army to keep up a good pressure at CAEN, and to make its main effort towards VILLERS BOCAGE and EVRECY and thence S.E. towards FALAISE.

10. First US Army had a very sticky party at OMAHA, and its progress at UTAH has not been rapid. I have therefore ordered it to join up its two lodgement areas and to secure CARENTAN and ISIGNY. It will then thrust towards LA HAYE DU PUITS and cut off the Cherbourg peninsula.

11. The two armies have now joined hands east of BAYEUX.

No time for more.

Yrs. ever

B. L. Montgomery.

P.T.O.

VILLERS-BOCAGE

DESPITE BLOODY OMAHA AND THE BRITISH FAILURE TO TAKE CAEN, D-DAY WAS A
TRIUMPH: BY ITS CLOSE OVER 130,000 ALLIED SOLDIERS HAD BEEN LANDED.

Over the next few days the Allies consolidated their position. First contact between British and Americans was made on 7 June, and on the 9th American troops from Utah and Omaha met. The Allies now had a continuous beachhead, although it took more fighting to secure the Carentan area and make the link between the two US corps really secure.

Having failed to take Caen early, Montgomery ordered XXX Corps to attack through Villers-Bocage and Noyers, cross the River Odon, and then push south and south-east of

ABOVE *British 7th Armoured Division.*

RIGHT *German tanks, heavily camouflaged and well spaced out to minimize the risk of air attack, moving up near Villers-Bocage.*

OPPOSITE *German tanks moving up the battle area were repeatedly harried from the air. This photograph of Lancaster heavy bombers in action shows what the original caption calls a "really good concentration of bomb bursts" on German armour at Villers-Bocage.*

7TH ARMOURED DIVISION

originated as the Mobile Division, formed in Egypt in 1938, and fought throughout the desert campaign, moving on to Italy before being recalled for the invasion of Europe. The division, with its extensive experience in the Mediterranean, and a measure of war-weariness, initially found the new conditions of Normandy trying, and its commander, Major General G. W. E. J. Erskine (left) was replaced. However, the division rose above the summer's misfortunes, and it took the surrender of Hamburg and participated in the 1945 Berlin victory parade. Its jerboa badge and nickname "Desert Rats" have been inherited by the modern 7th Armoured Brigade.

'[THE TIGER] IMMEDIATELY KNOCKED OUT COLONEL ARTHUR'S TANK, AND THAT OF THE REGIMENTAL SECOND IN COMMAND, MAJOR CARR, WHOM HE SERIOUSLY WOUNDED, FOLLOWED BY THE REGIMENTAL SERGEANT MAJOR'S TANK. CAPTAIN DYAS IN THE FOURTH TANK, REVERSED AND BACKED INTO THE FRONT GARDEN OF A NEARBY HOUSE.

MAJOR W. H. J. SALE, 4TH COUNTY OF LONDON YEOMANRY

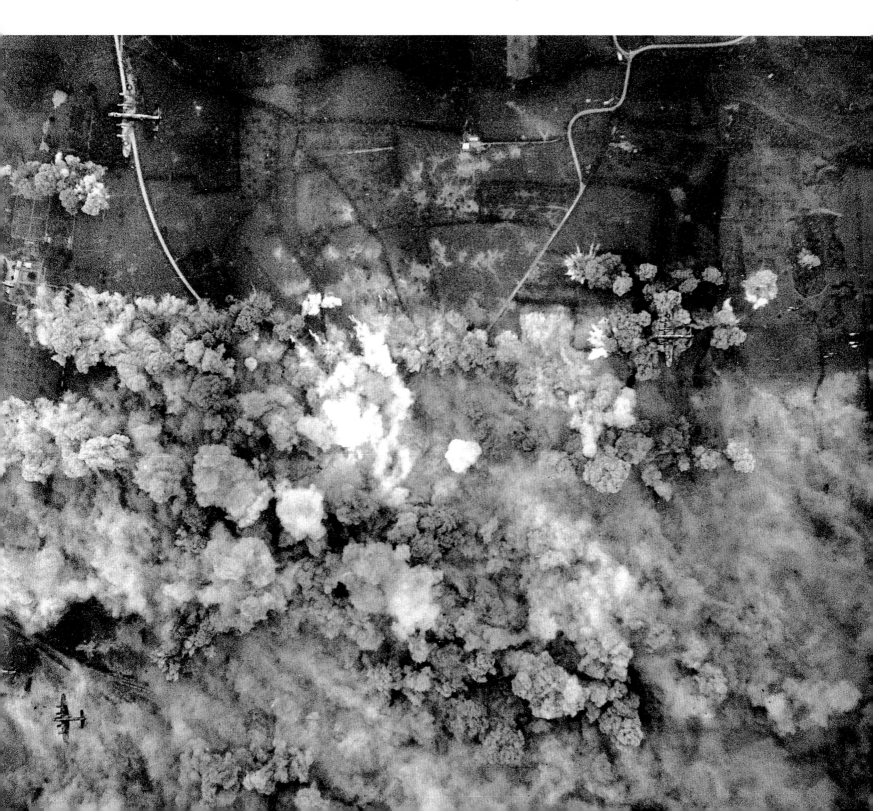

MICHAEL WITTMANN

was one of the war's most outstanding tank commanders. Between March 1943 and January 1944 his Tiger of 1st SS Panzer Division destroyed over 100 Soviet tanks and assault guns. Transferred to Normandy in command of an SS heavy tank company, he distinguished himself at Villers-Bocage, adding swords and oak leaves to his Knight's Cross. On 8 August, during Operation Totalize, his tank was knocked out by a Sherman of the 1st Northamptonshire Yeomanry with no survivors.

Tilly-sur-Seulles, outflanking Caen. Major General G. W. E. J. Erskine's 7th Armoured Division was to lead, with 22nd Armoured Brigade at its head. On 10 June the advance began, but the bocage of little fields bounded by thick hedges was easier to defend than attack. Infantry from 56th Infantry Brigade, borrowed from 50th Division, came up that night, and the advance was resumed with infantry on hand to help with close-quarter fighting, but progress was again poor.

On 12 June 7th Armoured tried again, this time with its own infantry of 131st Brigade to help. It had crossed the River Aure and swung south so that at nightfall on the 11th its leading elements were only two miles from Caumont and five from Villers-Bocage, which was taken without

difficulty on the 12th. But as the leading elements of 4th County of London Yeomanry with infantry of the Rifle Brigade moved out along the Caen road, they were assailed by a tank company commanded by SS Captain Michael Wittmann; he knocked out 12 tanks, 13 troop carriers and two anti-tank guns. Although his own tank was destroyed, he and his crew escaped. As the counter-attack gained momentum, Major General Erskine decided, with his corps commander's approval, to pull back to Tracy-Bocage, and then fell back on Livery. The action, termed "disappointing" by the British official history, was eventually to contribute to both divisional and corps commanders losing their jobs.

ABOVE *A knocked-out Cromwell tank of 4th County of London Yeomanry in the main street of Villers-Bocage.*

RIGHT *The Tiger tank with its 88mm gun. Although slower than the Sherman, and less mechanically reliable, its thick armour and fearsome fire power made it a formidable defensive weapon in Normandy. The Allies reckoned that on average it cost them three tanks to knock out one Tiger.*

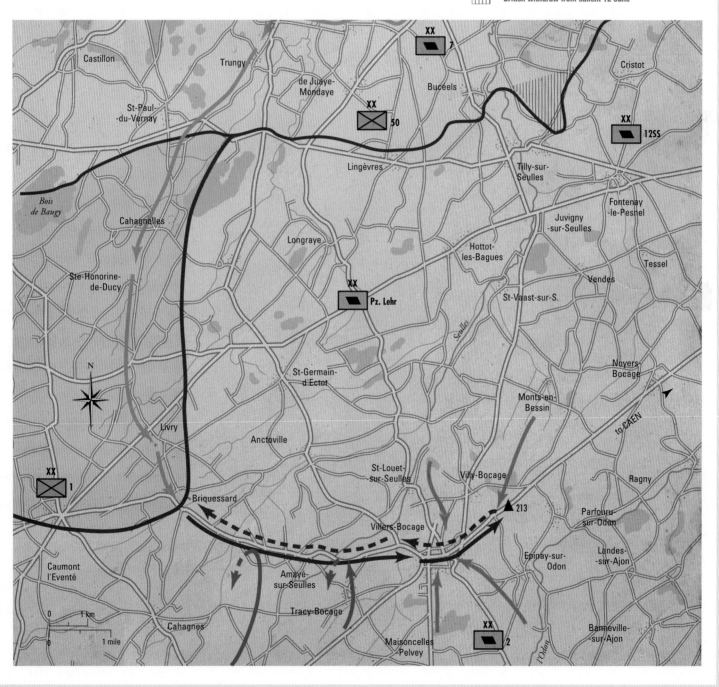

11–13 JUNE 1944

VILLERS-BOCAGE

MAP KEY

— Frontline 24.00 hrs. 11 June

— Frontline 24.00 hrs. 24 June

↙ Advance of 7th Armoured Division 12 June to 24.00 hrs.

↖ Advance of 7th Armoured Division 13 June

↙ German counter-attacks 13 June

◂-- Retreat of 7th Armoured Division 13 June

↙ German counter-attacks 14 June

◂-- Retreat of 7th Armoured Division 14 June

▦ British withdraw from salient 12 June

Castillon

Trungy

de Juaye-Mondaye

Buceels

Cristot

St-Paul--du-Vernay

XX 7

XX 50

XX 12SS

Lingèvres

Tilly-sur-Seulles

Bois de Baugy

Fontenay-le-Pesnel

Cahagnolles

Juvigny-sur-Seulles

Longraye

Hottot-les-Bagues

Tessel

Ste-Honorine-de-Ducy

XX Pz. Lehr

Vendes

St-Vaast-sur-S.

Seulles

St-Germain-d'Ectot

Noyers-Bocage

N

Monts-en-Bessin

to CAEN

Livry

Anctoville

St-Louet--sur-Seulles

Villy-Bocage

Ragny

XX 1

Briquessard

▲ 213

Parfouru-sur-Odon

Villers-Bocage

Landes--sur-Ajon

Caumont l'Eventé

Amayé-sur-Seulles

Epinay-sur-Odon

0   1 km

Tracy-Bocage

0   1 mile

Cahagnes

XX 2

Banneville-sur-Ajon

Maisoncelles--Pelvey

l'Odon

BELOW *Royal Engineers fill the wreck of a German Tiger IE tank with landmines in order to destroy it.*

LES ARMEES
ALLIEES
DEBARQUENT

Le général Eisenhower s'adresse aux peuples des Pays Occupés

PEUPLES DE L'EUROPE OCCIDENTALE:

Les troupes des Forces Expéditionnaires Alliées ont débarqué sur les côtes de France.

Ce débarquement fait partie du plan concerté par les Nations Unies, conjointement avec nos grands alliés Russes, pour la libération de l'Europe.

C'est à vous tous que j'adresse ce message. Même si le premier assaut n'a pas eu lieu sur votre territoire, l'heure de votre libération approche.

Tous les patriotes, hommes ou femmes, jeunes ou vieux, ont un rôle à jouer dans notre marche vers la victoire finale. Aux membres des mouvements de Résistance dirigés de l'intérieur ou de l'extérieur, je dis : " Suivez les instructions que vous avez reçues ! " Aux patriotes qui ne sont point membres de groupes de Résistance organisés, je dis : " Continuez votre résistance auxiliaire, mais n'exposez pas vos vies inutilement ; attendez l'heure où je vous donnerai le signal de vous dresser et de frapper l'ennemi. Le jour viendra où j'aurai besoin de votre force unie." Jusqu'à ce jour, je compte sur vous pour vous plier à la dure obligation d'une discipline impassible.

CITOYENS FRANÇAIS:

Je suis fier de commander une fois de plus les vaillants soldats de France. Luttant côte à côte avec leurs Alliées, ils s'apprêtent à prendre leur pleine part dans la libération de leur Patrie natale.

Parce que le premier débarquement a eu lieu sur votre territoire, je répète pour vous, avec une insistance encore plus grande, mon message aux peuples des autres pays occupés de l'Europe Occidentale. Suivez les instructions de vos chefs. Un soulèvement prématuré de tous les Français risque de vous empêcher, quand l'heure décisive aura sonné, de mieux servir encore votre pays. Ne vous énervez pas, et restez en alerte !

Comme Commandant Suprême des Forces Expéditionnaires Alliées, j'ai le devoir et la responsabilité de prendre toutes les mesures nécessaires à la conduite de la guerre. Je sais que je puis compter sur vous pour obéir aux ordres que je serai appelé à promulguer.

L'administration civile de la France doit effectivement être assurée, par des Français. Chacun doit demeurer à son poste, à moins qu'il ne reçoive des instructions contraires. Ceux qui ont fait cause commune avec l'ennemi, et qui ont ainsi trahi leur patrie, seront révoqués. Quand la France sera libérée de ses oppresseurs, vous choisirez vous-mêmes vos représentants ainsi que le Gouvernement sous l'autorité duquel vous voudrez vivre.

Au cours de cette campagne qui a pour but l'écrasement définitif de l'ennemi, peut-être aurez-vous à subir encore des pertes et des destructions. Mais, si tragiques que soient ces épreuves, elles font partie du prix qu'exige la victoire. Je vous garantis que je ferai tout en mon pouvoir pour atténuer vos épreuves. Je sais que je puis compter sur votre fermeté, qui n'est pas moins grande aujourd'hui que par le passé. Les héroïques exploits des Français qui ont continué la lutte contre les Nazis et contre leurs satellites de Vichy, en France, en Italie et dans l'Empire français, ont été pour nous tous un modèle et une inspiration.

Ce débarquement ne fait que commencer la campagne d'Europe Occidentale. Nous sommes à la veille de grandes batailles. Je demande à tous les hommes qui aiment la liberté d'être des nôtres. Que rien n'ébranle votre foi — rien non plus n'arrêtera nos coups — ENSEMBLE, NOUS VAINCRONS.

Dwight D. Eisenhower

DWIGHT D. EISENHOWER,
Commandant Suprême des
Forces Expéditionnaires Alliées

Z.F.1.

BELOW & OPPOSITE The *7 June 1944 edition of* Stars and Stripes, *the daily newspaper of the U.S. armed forces in the European Theatre of Operations, with first news of the D-Day landings. This copy was owned by Wilson Wood, who briefed Marauder bomber pilots on their D-Day missions over Utah Beach, described on the front page.*

Many thanks – from the 323rd Bomb Group, which flew over Utah Beach on D-Day! see the Bud Hutton article.

1D. THE STARS AND STRIPES 1D.

Daily Newspaper of U.S. Armed Forces in the European Theater of Operations

Vol. 4 No. 185 — New York, N.Y.—London, England — Wednesday, June 7, 1944

Allies Driving Into France

Opposition Less Than Expected; Troops 10 Mi. In

Allied armies, supported by more than 4,000 ships and 11,000 warplanes, stormed the northern coast of France in the dark hours of yesterday morning to open the decisive battle for the liberation of Europe, and by nightfall had smashed their way ten miles inland to Caen, between the vital ports of Cherbourg and Le Havre. Enemy radio stations said heavy street fighting was in progress.

By reaching Caen, the invasion forces may have cut the railway running from Paris to Cherbourg, main route for the supply of Hitler's troops on the peninsula.

German opposition in all quarters—sea, air and land—was less than expected, according to information reaching supreme headquarters and losses appeared to be astonishingly light.

American naval losses were only two destroyers and one LST (landing ship, tank) craft, while American air losses were kept to one per cent, President Roosevelt revealed in Washington on the basis of a noon dispatch from General Eisenhower. The President said operations were "up to schedule."

Losses of troop-carrying aircraft were extremely small, although more than 1,000 of such planes were used, headquarters disclosed. The airborne troops themselves were "well established," Prime Minister Churchill had announced earlier.

And as for the forces which landed on the beaches, Adm. Sir Bertram Ramsay, Allied naval commander-in-chief, reported that "naval ships landed all their cargoes 100 per cent." He added that there was "slight loss in ships, but so slight that it did not affect putting armies ashore. We have got all the first wave of men through the defended beach zone and set for the land battle."

Along a front described by the Germans as 80 miles long—from the mouth of the Seine River at Le Havre to the tip of the Cherbourg peninsula—American, British and Canadian troops landed on French soil from the choppy waters of the English Channel and from the storm-studded skies.

From 600 naval guns, ranging from four to 16 inches, and from massive fleets of supporting planes, ton upon ton of high explosives thundered into the concrete and steel of the West Wall which Hitler erected to guard his conquered countries.

The actual landings took place in daylight after an aerial assault on the coastal defenses which lasted from before midnight to dawn, a communique disclosed late last night. The airborne troops, however, had landed behind enemy positions during darkness.

Between 6.30 and 7.30 two naval task forces—one commanded by Rear Adm. Sir Philip Vian, aboard HMS Scylla, and the other by Rear Adm. Alan Goodrich Kirk, aboard the U.S.S. Augusta—launched their assault forces at enemy beaches.

It was on the cruiser Augusta that President Roosevelt and Prime Minister Churchill signed the Atlantic Charter in August, 1941.

The mightiest air and sea armadas ever assembled paved the way for the successful landings. American warships participating included battleships, cruisers and destroyers, as well as hundreds of smaller craft and troopships.

Thirty-one thousand Allied airmen, not counting airborne troops, made a continuous road through the night in the skies over France. Between midnight and 8 AM more than 10,000 tons of high explosives were hurled upon the Normandy invasion area by Allied aircraft, which flew 7,500 sorties.

Against this aerial might the Luftwaffe was able to mount only 50 sorties, despite an order of the day from Goering that "invasion must be beaten off even if the Luftwaffe perishes." Allied fighters swept 75 miles inland without opposition.

After an initial communique made the momentous announcement of the landings, Prime Minister Churchill gave the first word that the assault had been successful. To a cheering House of Commons he announced shortly after noon that landings were proceeding according to plan, that sea obstacles planted by the Nazis had been less serious than had been feared, that the fire of shore batteries had been largely quelled, and that airborne landings had been effected successfully behind the enemy lines.

Later, after visiting Gen. Eisenhower's headquarters with King George VI, Churchill said that "many dangers and difficulties which appeared at this time last night to be extremely formidable are behind us. The passage of the sea has been made with far less loss than we apprehended."

A spokesman at Supreme Headquarters Allied Expeditionary Forces (SHAEF) declared last night that the "first four or five hurdles" in establishing Allied forces on the Continent had been overcome, and that the positions of the Allied troops definitely gave "no cause for pessimism." No specific information was given on the landing points or the progress made.

It was left to the Germans to give most of the details, and all day long came a steady stream of reports from German agencies of new airborne and sea landings, most of them between Le Havre and Cherbourg and some airborne landings southwest of Boulogne.

Enemy radio stations late last night painted a picture of growing Allied successes, with new beachheads established and a general spreading-out from positions on coastal stretches already occupied.

German Overseas News Agency said fierce fighting was in progress along the whole 19-mile stretch of road between Carantan and Valognes on the Cherbourg peninsula. Paratroops established themselves on both sides of the road and later were reinforced by glider troops, the agency added.

Vichy radio said Allied reinforcements were pouring into the beachheads and "it must be admitted the Allied landing area has been considerably extended."

The French radio station at Brazza-

(Continued on page 4)

Greatest Umbrella for Landing

Armadas of Allied Planes Hammer Nazi Targets

Unleashing the full fury of Anglo-American air power, Allied aircraft yesterday bombed and strafed mile after mile of French beaches, seizing undisputed mastery of the air and heaping record-breaking tons of explosives on Nazi coastal installations in providing the greatest umbrella in history for the invasion forces.

Between midnight and 8 AM yesterday alone, 10,000 tons of steel went cascading down on German targets on the coast of Normandy. In the same period more than 31,000 Allied airmen, not including airborne troops, dominated the sky over France.

It was estimated that in a final recapitulation the number of sorties flown yesterday would soar to more than 20,000.

In spite of the staggering number of sorties flown by the Americans only 1 per cent of the aircraft operating were lost, President Roosevelt announced in Washington at noon.

Luftwaffe Stays Down

So sparse was Luftwaffe opposition that most airmen did not encounter a single German fighter. Few of the 1,750 fighter planes which it is estimated the Nazis can muster to oppose the invasion put in an appearance.

High-ranking officers of Supreme Headquarters emphasized, however, that there was no reason to believe the Luftwaffe had been defeated.

"Fighting of the greatest severity is in store before the Luftwaffe is wiped out," according to one air officer.

American heavies, flying three missions for the second time in four days, roared out at 6 AM, at noon and again in the mid-afternoon at a cost of only four bombers.

In the first assault a record force of more than 1,300 Fortresses and Liberators struck more than 100 German targets on the French coast. Later in the day a medium force of B24s and B17s flew behind the West Wall to pound a defended German position. Most of the bombers in the second raid returned with their loads because the presence of Allied troops made it inadvisable to bomb through overcast. Another Nazi strongpoint was battered on the third mission.

Not one enemy fighter was encountered.

Bombing, strafing and patroling fighter aircraft of the Ninth Air Force were in the air continuously yesterday from 4.30 AM, covering the movement of the Allied Expeditionary Force over sea and on to the beaches, and probing ahead of the landing parties for tactical objectives beyond the operations zone.

Starting yesterday morning with air-

(Continued on page 3)

'This Was the Invasion'

Flying S & S Writer Files First Eyewitness Story

By Bud Hutton
Stars and Stripes Staff Writer

Six thousand feet below, troops surged over the beaches of France and against Hitler's Atlantic Wall, and as the first black dots moved over the white sand a gunner said over the interphone: "Jesus Christ! At last."

On the dirty dark green of the Channel waters, battleships, cruisers, destroyers and more man-carrying craft than you could count rolled steadily toward the green fields and the white towns the Nazis had taken from France. Through a smoke screen the wraith-like shapes of warships loomed a moment, chameleoned into blobs of flame as another broadside roared off to find some Wehrmacht strongpoint beyond the coast.

This was the invasion.

North and south, all across the Channel and deep into the reaches beyond the concrete-bound coasts of the Continent, some 7,000 American and Allied warplanes flew in the greatest aerial armada in history. They drove the Luftwaffe from the skies with guns, and with bombs the German gunners and infantry from their camouflaged strongpoints beneath. Marauders and Havocs, Fortresses and Liberators, Mustangs, Thunderbolts, Lightnings and all the myriad craft of the RAF filled the sky until there was no room for more.

From a Marauder medium bomber of

(Continued on page 4)

Teheran Set Landing Time With Stalin's OK, Says FDR

WASHINGTON, June 6—President Roosevelt disclosed today that the approximate invasion time was set at the Teheran conference last December and that Marshal Stalin was completely satisfied with it. The precise date, however, was determined only within the last few days.

Citing losses far lower than expected, Mr. Roosevelt told his press conference that politicians who had been demanding a second front for months would see now why the Allies had waited—the extra time had enabled Gen. Eisenhower to have many more divisions and landing craft.

Eisenhower's Order of Day

The following order of the day was issued yesterday by Gen. Eisenhower to each individual of the Allied Expeditionary Force:—

"Soldiers, sailors and airmen of the Allied Expeditionary Force!

"You are about to embark upon the great crusade, toward which we have striven these many months. The eyes of the world are upon you. The hopes and prayers of liberty-loving people everywhere march with you.

"In company with our brave allies and brothers in arms on other fronts, you will bring about the destruction of the German war machine, the elimination of Nazi tyranny over the oppressed peoples of Europe, and security for ourselves in a free world.

"Your task will not be an easy one. Your enemy is well trained, well equipped and battle hardened. He will fight savagely.

"But this is the year 1944! Much has happened since the Nazi triumphs of 1940-41. The United Nations have inflicted upon the Germans great defeats in open battle, man to man. Our air offensive has seriously reduced their strength in the air and their capacity to wage war on the ground.

"Our home fronts have given us an overwhelming superiority in weapons and munitions of war, and placed at our disposal great reserves of trained fighting men. The tide has turned! The free men of the world are marching together to victory!

"I have full confidence in your courage, devotion to duty and skill in battle. We will accept nothing less than full victory!

"Good luck! And let us beseech the blessing of Almighty God upon this great and noble undertaking."

The order was distributed to assault elements after their embarkation. It was read by commanders to all other troops in the Allied Expeditionary Force.

Late Bulletins

FIRST U.S. RAID FROM USSR BASES

U.S. BOMBER BASE, Soviet Union, June 6 (Reuter)—In the first American raid of the war from new shuttle bases on Soviet soil, scores of U.S. heavy bombers showered tons of high explosives and incendiaries on airdrome installations at Galatz, Rumania, today and then returned here.

STALIN LAUDS ALLIES ON ROME

A congratulatory message from Marshal Stalin on "the great victory of the Allied Anglo-American forces" at Rome was made public last night by Prime Minister Churchill. Stalin wrote that the news of Rome capture was "greeted in the Soviet Union with great satisfaction."

INVASION JAMS U.S. PAPERS

WASHINGTON, June 6 (Reuter)—Many newspapers announced tomorrow's editions would not contain advertising because of pressure of space,

Page 4 THE STARS AND STRIPES Wednesday, June 7, 1944

U.S. Hears News Soberly; FDR Pens a Prayer

President Sits Up Late to Follow Action; Lights Blaze in Pentagon

NEW YORK, June 6—Prayers were said in churches and homes throughout America today as the nation grimly and soberly heard the news at last that its sons were embarked on the great invasion.

President Roosevelt, closeted alone in his bedroom, spent the early hours before dawn composing a national prayer for the victory of the Allied liberation forces. Time was reserved on all the radio networks at 10 o'clock tonight (4 AM in the ETO) for the Commander-in-Chief to read his prayer and for listeners all over the land to join in it.

Other prayers were offered during the day in the various states in accordance with D-Day proclamations issued by the governors. In New York, Mayor Fiorello H. LaGuardia arranged a mass prayer meeting at Madison Square Garden.

Times Square Nearly Deserted

It was half-past midnight in New York and the theater crowds had departed from Times Square when the first German announcements came, and the endless belt of lights around the Times building spelled out the news and the radios of the taxicabs along the curbs broadcast cautious bulletins. SHAEF's confirmation did not come until three hours later, when most of the East was asleep.

It was still Monday in Hollywood—the day before D-Day—when the first news reached the movie colony. Bands stopped playing in the night clubs and dance halls while the glib MCs, not so glib for once, announced the opening of the invasion. The gaiety went on—but somehow it was not as gay as it had been. At the Clover Club many prominent film stars bowed their heads while an Army chaplain offered a prayer.

In war plants from coast to coast, men and women on the night shift heard the news over public address systems. In some plants they cheered, in others they listened silently—in all of them they went right on working.

Lights Blaze in Pentagon

There was no sign of anything unusual in Washington before the news broke but soon after 1 AM lights flared up in windows all over the War Department's sprawling Pentagon Building and officials began arriving at other Government offices by taxi and private car.

At the White House, President Roosevelt sat up with a few intimates listening to the radio and receiving direct reports from the War Department. Gen. George C. Marshall, Chief of Staff, had remained at his desk all night but other officials, including Secretary of War Henry L. Stimson, were at home.

Jap Destroyers Sunk in Pacific

U.S. Liberators sank a Japanese destroyer in the Halmahera sea, 300 miles northwest of New Guinea, and probably destroyed another off Manokwari, in the Geelvink Bay area of Dutch New Guinea, on Saturday night, Gen. Douglas MacArthur's communique revealed yesterday.

Meanwhile an American column pushed within two miles of enemy-occupied Mokmer airdrome on Biak Island in Geelvink Bay by outflanking Japanese positions on a ridge north of the field.

Heavy bombers from the Admiralty Islands dumped 79 tons of bombs on Dublon and Eten Islands in Truk atoll and shot down seven of 20 enemy interceptors for the loss of one Allied plane. More than 60 tons were dropped on supply dumps and bivouacs in the Wewak-Hansa areas of British New Guinea.

On the Burma front, Lord Louis Mountbatten's communique reported that Lt. Gen. Joseph W. Stilwell's forces captured a Japanese position at the northern edge of Myitkyina and destroyed enemy defenses to the south and southwest.

Letters to Home Front Kept the Invaders Busy

Movement into marshalling areas had brought about a natural lull in mail from home, but the flow of outgoing mail kept censors and mail clerks chained to their jobs as invasion troops penned letters until boarding the boats.

When they weren't writing letters or playing softball, U.S. troops sprawled in tents jammed with battle equipment, reading or just resting "in the sack."

Two Invaders Cited

Two GIs took a few minutes off in their marshalling area to receive Silver Stars for gallantry in action during the Sicilian campaign. They are T/Sgt. Edward A. Plona, of Newburgh, N.Y., and Sgt. Robert A. Price, of Far Rockaway, N.Y.

German Army Halts All Leave

Basle, Switzerland, June 6 (Reuter)—All military leaves have been stopped in Germany and even convalescent wounded have been recalled, a report from the frontier said today.

Armada Moves Within Firing Range of French Coast

Associated Press Photo

D-Day's invasion coast is barely visible as this aerial picture shows an Allied armada nearing the end of its historical voyage across the Channel early Tuesday morning.

Allied Armies Driving Wedge Into France

(Continued from page 1)

ville said street fighting was in progress in Caen.

German radio also announced that Allied airborne troops, supported by the softening-up firepower of naval units, had landed in the Channel Islands of Jersey and Guernsey, British possessions in the hands of the Germans since 1940.

Between Le Havre and Cherbourg the main landings reported by the enemy were:

Seine Estuary—Strong Allied naval formations convoying troop vessels were attacked, numerous hits being scored on them. Berlin claimed an Allied battleship set on fire, and admitted the loss of one of its own vessels.

Western coast of Seine Bay—Landings made under smoke screens with other airborne landings inland.

Trouville, southwest of Le Havre—Airborne landings, including cargo gliders as well as parachute troops.

Orne Estuary (north of Caen)—Landings from the sea by Allied landing craft which penetrated the estuary. In this area airborne troops, including British units, landed in considerable strength in the Caen area, and last German reports were that they had suffered heavy losses in fighting inside Caen. A whole parachute regiment was wiped out, German Overseas Radio claimed.

Vire Estuary—Landings from the sea similar to those in the Orne Estuary.

Between the two estuaries—Landings reported at Asnel Ouistreham, where 80 vessels appeared off the coast; Asnelles and Arromanches, where 200 vessels landed troops which scaled the cliffs with ladders and later landed tanks.

Berlin also said another landing near the Orne Estuary brought Allied troops a few miles inland between Isigny and Carentan, on the estuary, across the marshy country.

'Cherbourg Battle Grows'—Paris

Despite fierce German resistance, Paris radio—less than 100 miles from the fighting—said that the battle for the Cherbourg peninsula was "widening in depth."

A steady stream of Allied troops continued to pour onto the beaches in the vicinity of the bathing resort at Arromanches at noon, Berlin reported, with light tank formations also ashore.

The invasion force was the greatest ever used in amphibious operations. Commanding it, under the supreme leadership of Gen. Eisenhower, was Gen. Sir Bernard L. Montgomery. There were unconfirmed reports that Hitler himself was rushing to France to take charge of Axis forces.

The weather, which had caused postponement of the invasion for 24 hours, ruffled the Channel and caused "awful anxiety," said a spokesman at SHAEF. But the landings were made, although some of the troops undoubtedly were seasick.

For hours without interruption the vast armada of planes charged with softening up the defenses roared over the coast, while in the water more than 200 minesweepers cleared obstructions before the invasion fleet.

As a result comparatively light opposition was met from enemy naval forces and shore batteries. Coast defense guns were not nearly as effective as they might have been, and despite German claims of heavy damage inflicted by Nazi E-boats, the Allies' naval losses were "very, very small," a SHAEF spokesman said.

The Allied Command said nothing about the great battle being on at last until the Germans found it out for themselves. At 6.35 AM the German Overseas News Agency broadcast a bulletin: "The invasion has begun. German naval forces have engaged enemy landing craft. Paratroops have landed at the mouth of the Seine." Instantly the electrifying news was relayed round the world.

The Allied announcement came at 9.01 AM, when correspondents summoned to the elaborate invasion press room in London's Ministry of Information were given Communique No. 1:

"Under the command of Gen. Eisenhower, Allied naval forces, supported by strong air forces, began landing Allied armies this morning on the northern coast of France."

A few minutes later American and British broadcasting stations sounded the alert for all of Europe, and in the voice of Gen. Eisenhower himself the eager patriots of the other nations were advised to be cautious until the hour for liberation struck in their own lands. He was followed by the exiled rulers and ministers from those countries.

To France the supreme commander directed an even more emphatic appeal. "Follow the instructions of your leaders. A premature uprising of all Frenchmen may prevent you from being of maximum help to your country in the critical hour. Be patient. Prepare."

The two Normandy ports of Le Havre and Cherbourg were the obvious locale for Gen. Eisenhower to spot the first landings. Both are big ports, Le Havre the largest in France, and ports are vital for an amphibious operation on the scale of this offensive. The ports are close together, so that the attacking forces need not be widely split. And each port is on a promontory of the sea rather than a long lateral stretch of coast like the section opposite Dover; this gives the attacking forces a comparatively narrow front to hold while assembling for the advance inland and makes it possible for warships to give supporting fire from both flanks.

The extent of surprise which the Allied troops achieved was not immediately announced by supreme headquarters.

Several times great fleets of Allied vessels had sailed out of British harbors, carrying invasion forces complete even to war correspondents, and had approached within shelling range of the German defenses on Europe's coast only to turn back. German reconnaissance planes had checked closely on the maneuvers, which were carried out at widely separated points.

1st Eyewitness Of 2nd Front

(Continued from page 1)

Col. Wilson R. Wood's Ninth Air Force group, piloted by 1/Lt. Richard E. Robinson, of Pittsfield, Ill., I saw the first Americans go ashore. Just as they went into the low surf, our ship and with it thousands of other bombers and fighters carried out the job toward which Eighth and Ninth Air Force airmen have been aiming since the first Fortress opened its bomb bays above Rouen on Aug. 17, 1942. We poured onto every known German strongpoint in the Cherbourg peninsula area in front of the assault craft the heaviest concentrated bombing any spot in the world ever got.

Fountains of smoke and flame and Nazi-poured concrete leaped up along the ridges behind the beaches.

The airmen had been told that on them would rest the task of making the foot soldier's job less bloody. They accepted that task and in its execution bombed from half the altitude they knew could give them a fighting chance of getting home so that their explosives would not miss. To do that job they had gone through a nightmare of flak before they came to the targets.

For long months, the bombers and the fighters have woven a pattern of craters across the ramparts of the Atlantic Wall. The pattern was cut for invasion. On Monday, I flew in the co-pilot's spot of a Marauder piloted by Maj. Paul Stach, of Rosenberg, Tex., to watch the last attack of the many which had come to be called "the pre-invasion blitz."

The bomber men went back to base. They ate and went to bed. At one o'clock in the morning they were called. Sleepy, worn with the strain of two hauls a day almost every day for two months, they walked through the wet night to the briefing. In a plain, undramatic Texas voice, Wilson Wood told them:

"Thirty-three seconds after your bombs hit the target, hundreds of thousands of American boys just as you are going ashore in France. This is the invasion." He talked some more and ended: "Let's kick the hell out of everything Nazi that's left."

Then they cheered, and went out to work.

The clouds broke over the Channel, and suddenly there were more ships than you could see, with the white wakes of them streaming back to the English coast and the dark green of the Channel flat before them to the coast of Europe.

The flak began to come up, but for once the bomber men weren't watching it, because through the murk above the waters off the coast there burst the angry red of warship broadsides, and inland came the answering crimson a few moments later as the shells hit home.

At half the height they've used for bombing the Marauders swept in.

The heavy flak burst around the formations, and tracer from machine guns streaked up past the wings; that's how low they flew.

We went away from the flak and began the long journey home and talked too much over the interphone, because this had been the day.

London Calm But Tense at D-Day News

No Celebrations, and GIs Take It Like the Rest, Quietly Go to Work

By Arthur W. White
Stars and Stripes Staff Writer

The small number of American troops left in London yesterday saw few outward changes in the life of the Allies' invasion capital. There were no hooters or noisy celebrations, but on practically every street corner long queues, mostly women, stood awaiting the latest editions.

American and Allied soldiers in non-combat jobs quietly read their papers and went to work, their sentiments the same as those of the MP on guard duty at a headquarters building who said fervently, "Christ, I wish I was over there with them."

GI Joes—and London's—reaction was, "We've waited a long time for this, now let's make it good."

There was a new tenseness among the people in the buses and busy thoroughfares, but everyone seemed to be waiting for the next fellow to show how excited he was. Yanks in London who expected to see the population get het up remembered that most of them had fathers or brothers fighting with the invasion troops.

A girl bus conductress said the only difference she had noticed was that passengers were more polite than ever before.

One policeman, on his beat in Piccadilly, compared yesterday with Sept. 3, 1939—the day Britain declared war. "We waited and worried a long time then before we knew for certain whether we had to fight," he said. "We've waited a long time for the invasion. Now it's here I think everybody will be calmer than ever before. It's the waiting and worrying that gets you down."

American MPs patrolled with orders to send soldiers on pass and furlough from camps more than 25 miles out back to their stations.

Most London Red Cross clubs were half-empty, and everywhere the conversation of American and British workers was of the soldiers, now fighting, who have swarmed through the buildings during the last year and more.

Nazis Fear Blow From East Next

German nervousness over an imminent Soviet offensive on the eastern front rose to new proportions yesterday with the Allied landings in France.

"In view of the new military situation," said Col. Ernst von Hammer, German News Agency commentator, "the German high command is paying particular attention to the lower Dniester sector where a strong Soviet offensive army has taken action stations and where Soviet artillery and mortar fire is gaining in intensity. . . .

"Now that the Allied invasion in the west has been launched, it is likely that the Soviet divisions which have been massed here over a matter of weeks will now go over to the offensive in order to force a decision."

The Soviet communique, reporting Red Army troops continued to repulse German infantry and tank attacks for the eighth day north of Jassy, said the enemy lost 41 tanks and 33 planes in 24 hours.

French Say Underground Already Aiding Troops

ALGIERS, June 6 (UP)—Members of the French underground are already in action helping Allied airborne troops, Andre Philip, French Minister of State, said today.

Andre le Troquer, Minister for the Liberated Territories, said the underground would not make its full weight felt, however, until the mass of the German army in France was engaged.

The War Today

France—American, British, Canadian forces, supported by 4,000 ships and 11,000 planes, land on northern coast of France to open battle for liberation of Europe. Advances announced by supreme headquarters and admitted by Germans.

Italy—Fifth and Eighth Armies pursue Germans north of Rome, but find enemy retreating so swiftly they are unable to make contact . . . Roosevelt warns nation against over-optimism after Rome's capture, says "victory still lies some distance ahead."

Pacific—Liberators sink Japanese destroyer 300 miles northwest of New Guinea, probably sink another in Geelvink bay . . . Americans push within two miles of Mokmer airdrome on Biak Island.

Russia—Nazis look for Allied landings in France to signal resumption of Red Army offensive on eastern front . . . Russians repulse tank and infantry attacks north of Jassy for eighth day.

Awesome Sight as Fleet Bombards

By Desmond Tighe
Representing Combined Press

ABOARD A BRITISH DESTROYER OFF BERNIERE-SUR-MER, June 6—Guns are belching flame from more than 600 Allied warships. Thousands of bombers are roaring overhead, fighters are weaving in and out of the clouds as the invasion of Western Europe begins.

Rolling clouds of dense black and grey smoke cover the beaches southeast of Le Havre as the full fury of the Allied invasion force is unleashed on the German defenses. It is the most incredible sight I have ever seen.

We are standing some 8,000 yards off the beaches of Berniere-sur-Mer, and from the bridge of this little destroyer I can see vast numbers of naval craft of all types.

The air is filled with the continuous thunder of broadsides and the crash of bombs. Great spurts of flame come up from the beaches in long snake-like ripples as shells ranging from 16 inches to four inches find their mark. In the last ten minutes alone more than 2,000 tons of high explosive shells have gone down on the beach.

It is now exactly 7.25 AM and through my glasses I can see the first wave of assault troops touching down on the water's edge and fanning up the beach.

Battleships and cruisers are steaming up and down drenching the beaches ahead of the troops with withering broadsides. The guns flash and great coils of yellow cordite smoke curl into the air. Great assault vessels are standing out to sea in their hundreds and invasion craft are being lowered like beetles from the davits and head toward the shore in long lines. They are crammed with troops, tanks, guns and armored fighting vehicles of all types.

Conditions are not ideal. A fairly high sea is running and the sky is overcast and dark clouds scurry across the sky. Bombers are passing over us in their thousands; we cannot see them, as they are well above cloud level, but the air reverberates with the thunder of Fortress engines. We can see the bombs crashing down on the German gun positions and defences just inland of the first assault troops.

Printed in England by The Times Publishing Company, Limited, Printing House Square, London, E.C.4, and Published by the United States Armed Forces—7-6-44.

PLUTO & MULBERRY

THE ALLIES HAD A HUGE LOGISTIC APPETITE: INDEED, FROM 15 TO 19 JUNE THEY LANDED
A DAILY AVERAGE OF ALMOST 35,000 MEN, 25,000 TONS OF STORES, AND 5,894 VEHICLES.

It was evident that the Germans would fight hard to retain Cherbourg, the only major port in the area. When its commander surrendered on 26 June, the docks had already been smashed. But a shortfall in port capacity had long been identified, and in 1941 a War Office port engineering branch was formed under Major (later Brigadier Sir Bruce) White. The Admiralty contributed through the Department of Miscellaneous Weapons Development and the Department of Naval Constructors, and US engineers also became involved. Both Churchill

and Admiral Lord Louis Mountbatten, first director of Combined Operations, acted as the project's "godfathers". Dieppe lent urgency, by suggesting that the Allies would not capture a port intact.

In September 1943 instructions were issued for the construction of two harbours, Mulberry A for the Americans and Mulberry B for the British. They were to be made in Britain, towed across the Channel, and were to handle 12,000 tons of stores a day, about one-third of the total requirement. Concrete caissons (Phoenix) formed the harbour

LEFT *A shore terminal for Tombola, which enabled tankers to pipe fuel ashore. Many of the US troops of the Petroleum Distribution Group had been oil workers in civilian life.*

OPPOSITE ABOVE *One of the gigantic spools, codenamed "Conundrums", which unrolled Pluto, the cross-Channel pipeline.*

OPPSOSTE BELOW *The floating roadway of the British Mulberry at Arromanches, photographed on 14 June, its third day of operation.*

MULBERRIES IN USE:
12 June–
28 November 1944

PERSONNEL LANDED:
231,315

VEHICLES LANDED:
45,181

TONS OF STORES LANDED:
628,000

BELOW *Storm damage sustained by one of the piers at Mulberry A. The American harbour was ruined by the storm, and supply briefly faltered.*

wall. They would be sheltered by breakwaters (Gooseberries) consisting of blockships and floating bombardons (Corncobs) and connected to the shore by floating roadways (Whales). The first blockships, old vessels sailing under their own steam, were sunk on 7 June. One of the stores piers of Mulberry B took loads from coasters into trucks on 14 June, and the first tank landed at Mulberry A, two days later.

On 18 June the weather turned very ugly, and did not improve till the 22nd. Mulberry A was crippled and Mulberry B damaged, but was soon brought back into service. The Americans succeeded in landing stores over open beaches or into small ports, and although the piers and roadway of Mulberry A had disappeared, the Gooseberries still proved invaluable. By the end of October about 25 per cent of stores, 20 per cent of personnel and 15 per cent of vehicles had been landed through Mulberry. The development of the DUKW, essentially an amphibious truck, probably made the floating roadways redundant, but this would not have been obvious in 1943.

As early as November 1939 it had been suggested that petrol could be supplied to the continent by undersea pipe, and Pluto (Pipeline Under the Ocean) was the child of discussions between the Chief of Combined Operations and the Petroleum Warfare Department in 1942. Two pipes ran from Sandown, Isle of Wight, to terminals (one British and one American) near Port-en-Bessin, and another later ran from Dungeness to a terminal near Boulogne. The Normandy Pluto did not become operational till the end of July; until then the Allies received fuel via Tombola, buoyed pipelines connected to tankers moored offshore, which in theory (but seldom in practice) delivered 8,000 tons a day.

ABOVE *Churchill visited Normandy soon after D-Day. This photograph shows his evident satisfaction in an invention he had done so much to support.*

BELOW *Mulberry B at work. An outer line of caissons provided shelter from the waves and enabled some vessels to be unloaded into DUKWs, while vehicles could be landed on the floating pierheads and driven ashore along the piers.*

10, Downing Street,
Whitehall.

PIERS FOR USE ON BEACHES

<u>C.C.O.</u>
or deputy.

They must float up and down with the tide. The anchor problem must be mastered. Let me have the best solution worked out. Don't argue the matter. The difficulties will argue for themselves.

30. 5. 42.

TOP SECRET.

Office of Allied Naval Commander,
Expeditionary Force,
c/o Admiralty,
London, S.W.1.

No. X/0911/6/7/2.   27th May, 1944.

HANDBOOK FOR MULBERRY TUGS
(Short Title : TUG BOOK)
————————————————————

        The enclosed orders are issued for the guidance of
Commanding Officers and Masters of tugs employed on the MULBERRY
project in Operation OVERLORD, and of authorities concerned with
such tugs.

        2.   The orders are to be kept locked up when not in use
and are on no account to be permitted to fall into the hands of
the enemy. On conclusion of the operation they are to be burnt.

        3.   They are to be referred to in signals and correspondence
as TUGBOOK followed by the Article referred to, no mention being
made of Chapter or Section number.

                                        B.H. RAMSAY,

                                        ADMIRAL.

TOP SECRET.

CHAPTER 1 - GENERAL INSTRUCTIONS.

    101.   Operation NEPTUNE is the beginning of the Second Front, and
entails landing U.S. and British armies in NORTHERN FRANCE.

    102.   In order to supply these armies once they are landed it is
necessary to have harbours for ships to unload.   Harbours that are
captured will probably have been rendered unusable by the enemy so it
is intended to build two artificial ones, one in the U.S. sector and
one in the British sector;   these will be called MULBERRIES A and B
respectively.

    103.   The MULBERRIES will consist of:-

    (a)   GOOSEBERRIES, which consist of breakwaters formed
          by blockships (CORNCOBS) who will steam to the
          far shore and will be sunk early in the operation
          to form a breakwater,

    (b)   PHOENIX units, which will be towed across and
          sunk as additional breakwaters,

    (c)   BOMBARDON units, which will be towed across and
          moored to form an outer floating breakwater,

    (d)   WHALE units, which will be towed across to form
          piers for unloading inside the harbour.

    Units.

    104.   PHOENIX. Large concrete caissons 200 ft. long.   There are
six sizes which vary from about 6,000 tons to 2,000 tons.   Maximum
draft 20 ft.

        BOMBARDON. Floating steel structures 200 ft. long and
drawing 19 ft.   Units about 1,000 tons.

        WHALE. A large number of different types of units which
will form the pier roadway and pierheads.   Maximum 2,000 tons.   Up
to six of these pieces may be joined together to form one WHALE tow.

                                                /105 ......

SKETCH NO. CBI/39/163
15-6-43

SKETCH A

140 FT — 460 FT — 2100 FT

7'-0" HW DEPTH — 1-END SPAN — 30 STANDARD SPANS — 2 TELESCOPIC SPANS — 30' 10'-6"

H.W. MARK — SLOPE 1 IN 20 — L.W. MARK — SLOPE 1 IN 200 — ELEVATION AT H.W.

GROUNDING FLOATS 22 — WATER BORNE FLOATS 10 — 10'-6" LW

SLOPE 1 IN 20 — SLOPE 1 IN 200 — 7'-0" DEPTH L.W. — ELEVATION AT L.W.

CONCRETE ABUTMENT UNIT — SPIDER PIER HEAD UNITS

CONCRETE RAMP — 420 — 420 — 560 — SURGE ROPES 560 LG — 560 — 560

PLAN — 6' CONCRETE ANCHORS

PIERS FOR FLAT BEACHES

APPLICATION FOR UNLOADING L.S.T.s (FIRST STAGE)

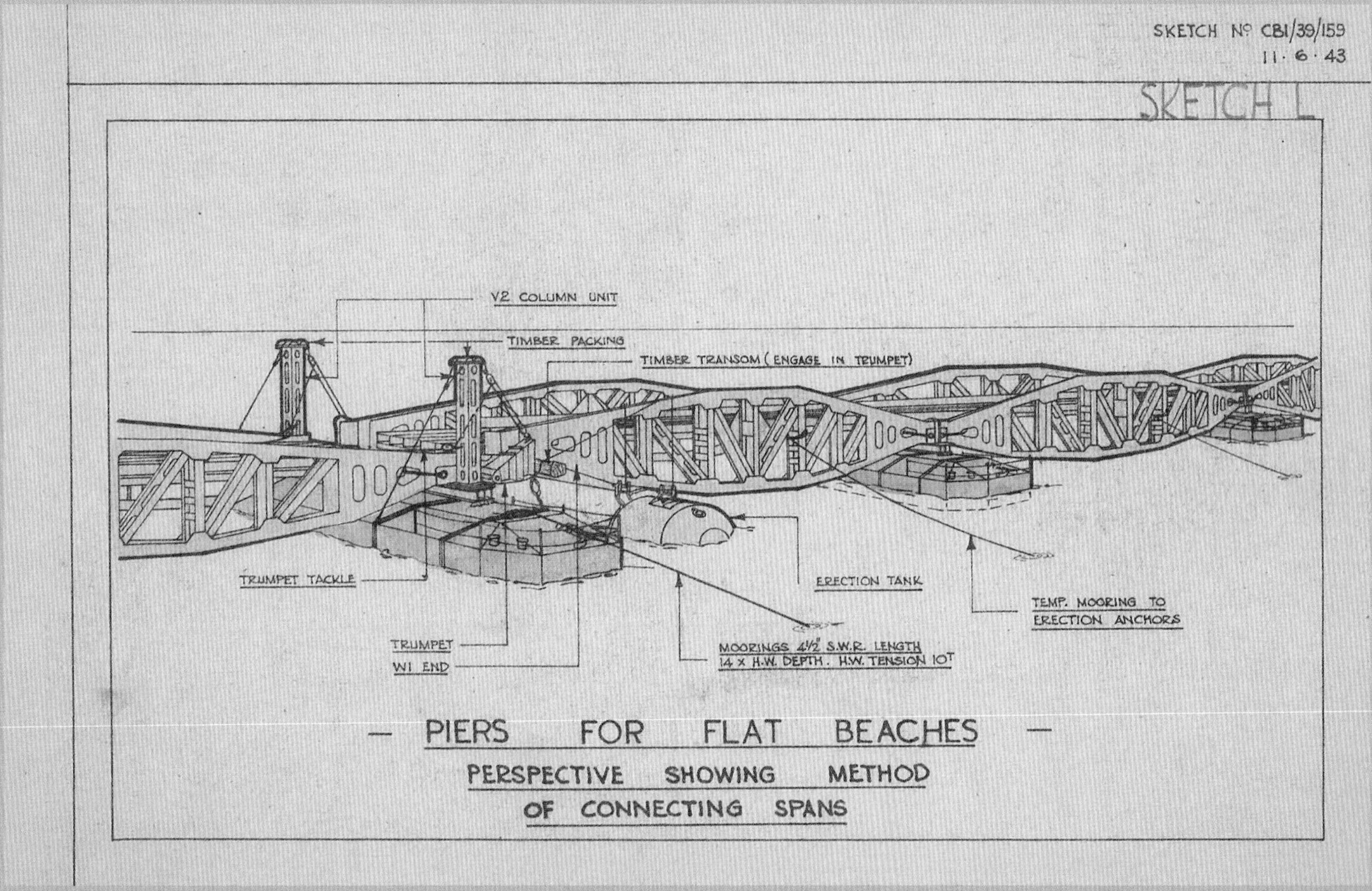

SKETCH Nº CBI/39/159
11·6·43

SKETCH L

V.2 COLUMN UNIT

TIMBER PACKING

TIMBER TRANSOM (ENGAGE IN TRUMPET)

TRUMPET TACKLE

ERECTION TANK

TEMP. MOORING TO
ERECTION ANCHORS

TRUMPET
W! END

MOORINGS 4½ S.W.R. LENGTH
14 × H.W. DEPTH. H.W. TENSION 10ᵀ

— PIERS FOR FLAT BEACHES —
PERSPECTIVE SHOWING METHOD
OF CONNECTING SPANS

OPERATION EPSOM

THE GREAT STORM CAME AT A BAD MOMENT FOR THE ALLIES, FOR BOTH WERE PREPARING
OFFENSIVES: THE AMERICANS INTO THE COTENTIN, HEADING FOR CHERBOURG,
AND FURTHER SOUTH, TOWARDS ST-LÔ, WHILE THE BRITISH WERE GEARING
UP FOR ANOTHER ATTEMPT TO TAKE CAEN.

Despite the damage sustained by the Mulberries, the Gooseberries, which had been inserted off the other invasion beaches, did rather better, though that at Utah was damaged. However, the storm reduced the pace of Allied build-up, and enabled the Germans to shift extra forces into Normandy to buttress their front.

The next British attack was to consist of a minor attack east of the Orne, in which 152nd Brigade of 51st Highland Division was to capture the village of Ste-Honorine-de-la-Chardonnerette, just south of 6th Airborne Division's old dropping zones. The storm delayed the attack until 23 June but it proved successful, and the village was secured by

British 49th Infantry Division.

British 11th Armoured Division.

15th Scottish Infantry Division.

midday. An altogether larger venture was Operation Epsom, on the other side of Caen, which was to involve part of both the bruised XXX Corps and the newly arrived but still incomplete VIII Corps under Lieutenant General Sir Richard O'Connor. There were over 700 guns available to support the attack, and three cruisers and the monitor HMS Roberts were also to assist. The main blow was to fall between Tilly-

sur-Seulles in the west and Carpiquet, not far from Caen, in the east.

On 25 June 49th Division of XXX Corps, fighting its first battle, attacked Juvigny, Vendes and Rauray in an effort to secure the eastern shoulder of the attack sector, and though it made some progress it failed to take the Rauray spur, which caused repeated trouble over the next few days. The following morning, in weather so bad that flying was

OPPOSITE *Royal Scots Fusiliers walk forward into the mist on the first day of Epsom.*

BELOW *Infantrymen, on the lookout for snipers, approach a breached wall in the village of St-Manvieu on the left of 15th (Scottish) Division's attack.*

RICHARD O'CONNOR

was commissioned into the Cameronians in 1909 and was a temporary lieutenant colonel in 1918. He made his reputation commanding the British attack into the Western Desert in December 1941, but was unluckily captured soon afterwards. Escaping captivity after the Italian surrender in 1943, he was a corps commander in Normandy, but never really regained his old touch for armoured warfare. Adjutant general of the army after the war, he resigned on a point of principle in 1947.

out of the question and cross-country going poor, VIII Corps struck out for the Odon but did not quite reach it, though a bridge was seized intact the next day by 15th (Scottish) Division. The Scots were supported by the tanks of 11th Armoured Division and 31st Tank Brigade, in a bitter battle with attacks meeting stern resistance and repeated counter-attacks. By nightfall on the 28th there was a salient five miles deep but only two wide into the German lines, and it had

PAUL HAUSSER

had a conventional army career, retiring as a major general in 1932, but joining the SS two years later. Badly wounded as a divisional commander on the Eastern Front, he commanded 2nd SS Panzer Corps in June 1944, and counter-attacked Operation Epsom. However, his plan fell into Allied hands and the attack failed. He

took command of 7th Army on 29 June. Hausser escaped from the Falaise Pocket and, an SS colonel general, commanded an army group until dismissed in 1945.

attracted most of the German armoured reserves. A series of counter-attacks, which peaked on 1 July, were beaten off, and the battle ended with the British secure across the Odon south-west of Caen, but still without sufficient leverage to wrest that city from the Germans. In one sense Epsom had failed, and had cost 15th Division alone 2,500 casualties. But it had blunted the cutting edge of German armour so badly that there was no longer any chance of it mounting a comprehensive counter-attack on the Allied bridgehead.

TOP *The advance goes on, with a Churchill tank of 31st Tank Brigade moving up in support.*

ABOVE *Firefight in a hedgeline: men of 6th Royal Scots Fusiliers, with a Bren light machine gun in the centre of the picture.*

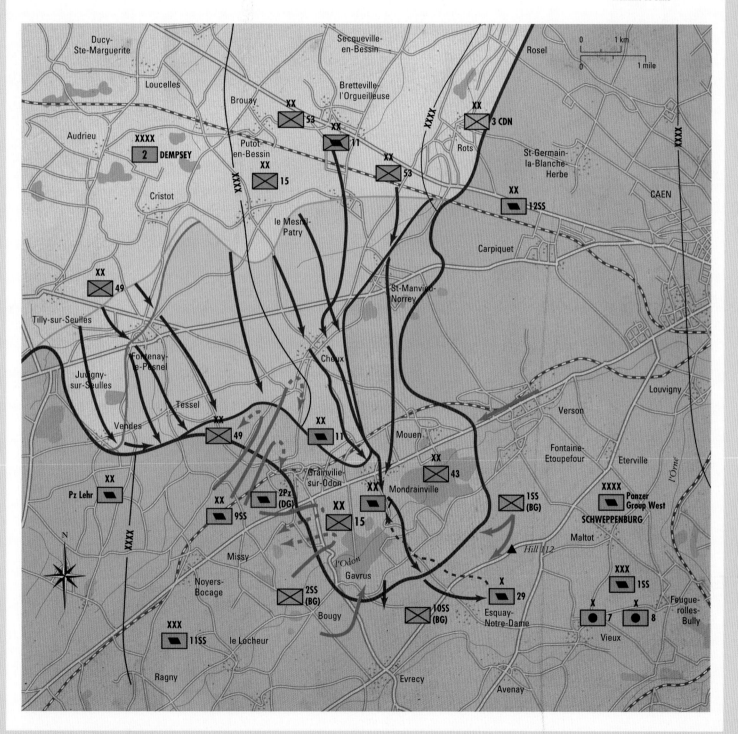

24–30 JUNE 1944

OPERATION EPSOM

Ducy-Ste-Marguerite

Secqueville-en-Bessin

Rosel

0   1 km

0   1 mile

Loucelles

Brouay

Bretteville-l'Orgueilleuse

XX 53

3 CDN

Audrieu

XXXX 2 DEMPSEY

Putot-en-Bessin

XX 11

Rots

St-Germain-la-Blanche-Herbe

XX 15

XX 53

CAEN

Cristot

XXXX

le Mesnil-Patry

XX 12SS

Carpiquet

XX 49

St-Manvieu-Norrey

Tilly-sur-Seulles

Fontenay-le-Pesnel

Cheux

Juvigny-sur-Seulles

Tessel

Mouen

Verson

Louvigny

Vendes

XX 49

XX 11

XX 43

Fontaine-Etoupefour

Eterville

Pz Lehr XX

Grainville-sur-Odon

Mondrainville

XX 7

1SS (BG)

XXXX Panzer Group West

SCHWEPPENBURG

XX 9SS

2Pz (DG)

XX 15

Maltot

Hill 112

Missy

l'Odon

Gavrus

XXX 1SS

Noyers-Bocage

2SS (BG)

X 29

Feugue-rolles-Bully

Bougy

10SS (BG)

Esquay-Notre-Dame

X 7

X 8

XXX 11SS

le Locheur

Vieux

Ragny

Evrecy

Avenay

N

BOCAGE FIGHTING & CHERBOURG

THE TERRAIN OF NORMANDY PRESENTED SHARP CONTRASTS. THE AREA AROUND CAEN AND FALAISE WAS OPEN, WITH BIG FIELDS WHOSE WHEAT STOOD ALMOST SHOULDER-HIGH.

Further west the ground grew more enclosed. The Bessin, around Bayeux, was noted for lush pastures and apple orchards: apples and cream still define cooking à la Normande. John Ruskin declared in 1848 that the Cotentin resembled Worcestershire but was even more beautiful. To its south, around St-Lô, came Norman bocage in its most extreme form, a chequerboard of little fields, stout hedges on high banks, and sunken lanes which reminded visitors of Devon or Dorset.

The advance on Cherbourg through the Cotentin was comparatively straightforward, and Lieutenant General "Lighting Joe" Collins of the US VII Corps defined it, just after the great storm, as "the major effort of the American army". The attack began in earnest on 22 June, with 9th and 79th Divisions moving against the city after heavy air attack, while 4th Division sealed it off from the east. The Germans fought well, their commander, Lieutenant General Karl-Wilhelm von Schlieben, enjoined

US 79th Infantry Division.

US 9th Infantry Division.

LEFT *An American infantryman dashes across a street whose German sign proclaims it the Cherbourg West Diversion.*

ABOVE *Although billed as a combat shot of the advance on Cherbourg, the photograph's careful composition suggests a measure of posing.*

JOE COLLINS

was commissioned into the infantry in 1917, and was commanding a division in Hawaii when war broke out in 1941. His tough style gained him the nickname "Lightning Joe", and he was selected to command VII Corps in the invasion of Europe. In 1944 he came to notice as conqueror of Cherbourg, and was photographed with his defeated opponent Lieutenant General Karl-Wilhelm von Schlieben, commander of 709th Infantry Division and the Cherbourg garrison (pictured overleaf).

ABOVE *The M2 .50 calibre Browning machine gun was used extensively by the Allied forces.*

RIGHT *Coder-decoder machine used by US troops in the field to send and receive coded messages.*

by Hitler to "defend the last bunker and leave to the enemy not a harbour but a field of ruins". Three days later Schlieben told Rommel that the city's fall was inevitable and "further sacrifices cannot alter anything," but was again ordered to "fight to the last cartridge ...". The powerful Fort du Roule fell that day, and Schlieben himself was captured on the 26th, though he refused to surrender his command, and sporadic fighting flickered on a little longer.

Although Hitler ordered Rundstedt to consider a large armoured counter-attack, the opening of Operation Epsom drew German reserves to the east, and Hitler concluded that, for the moment, he would have to fight "a war of attrition" to confine the Allies to their beachhead. This was significantly smaller than planners had hoped, leading to problems in getting the right balance of combat and support troops into the lodgement area, and reducing the programme of airfield construction, notably on the open country around Caen.

Bradley's First US Army began its thrust south at the beginning of July. Reports that the fall of Cherbourg had led to a sharp diminution in German fighting power soon proved incorrect as the advance ran into determined defenders strongly posted in difficult country. US casualties were heavy: 325th Glider Infantry Regiment of 82nd Airborne, with an establishment of 135 officers and 2,838 men, had 55 officers and 1,245 men on 2 July but 41 officers and 956 men four days later: its strongest rifle company had 57 men, its weakest just 12. Junior leadership was at a premium: in 359th Infantry one company and two leaderless platoons of another were commanded by Private Barney H. Prosser. It was clear that there would be no easy ride through the bocage.

LEFT *Major General Collins talking to an American captain at Fort du Roule, one of the last German defences to fall before the capture of Cherbourg.*

13–30 JUNE 1944

THE CAPTURE OF CHERBOURG

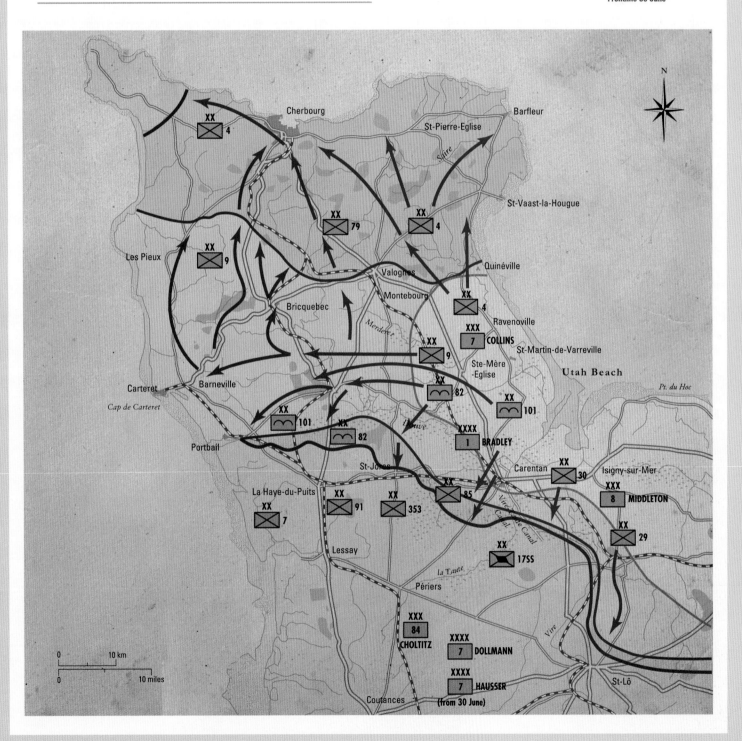

BELOW *Happy warriors? Defenders of Cherbourg march past a statue of Napoleon on their way to prisoner of war cages. The censor has obliterated background detail which would have revealed how badly damaged the docks were.*

BELOW *Soldiers of the US Seventh Corps pass a dead German soldier in the streets of Cherbourg in early July 1944.*

OPERATION CHARNWOOD

AT THE BEGINNING OF JULY, CAEN STILL DENIED MONTGOMERY ROOM FOR
MANOEUVRE ON THE EASTERN FLANK OF THE BATTLEFIELD.

The Canadians captured Carpiquet and its airfield from their old enemies, 12th SS Panzer Division, on 4 July, and on the night of the 7th 450 Lancasters and Halifaxes of RAF Bomber Command, used for the first time in direct support of ground forces, struck Caen itself. The city had already been badly damaged by bombing and by shelling from land and sea – a shell from HMS *Rodney* had felled the fine Gothic spire of the church of St-Pierre – and the preparations for the final Allied assault put the last dreadful touches to its martyrdom. One of the British

British 59th Infantry Division.

LEFT *A Bren-gunner and riflemen in the ruins, amongst blocks of the locally quarried pierre de Caen.*

OPPOSITE *Repeated bombing did terrible damage to the ancient city of Caen. This RAF photograph was taken in the first week of the Normandy campaign.*

'THE TOMMY ATTACKS WITH GREAT MASSES OF INFANTRY AND MANY TANKS. WE FIGHT AS LONG AS POSSIBLE, BUT BY THE TIME THE SURVIVORS TRY TO PULL BACK, WE REALIZE THAT WE ARE SURROUNDED.

PRIVATE ZIMMER, 12TH SS PANZER DIVISION

soldiers who entered the city on 9 July thought it "just a waste of brick and stone, like a field of corn that has been ploughed".

The attack on Caen was carried out by I Corps. While 59th and 3rd Divisions attacked from the north, 3rd Canadian Division struck south-eastwards. The British official history acknowledges that, while the Germans used snipers and mortars to contest the advance through the city, "these gave little trouble compared with the bomb craters, the rubble and the large blocks of locally quarried stone which choked the narrow streets." The attacking corps lost about 3,500 men, and of its opponents, the infantry of 12th SS Panzer Division was reduced to battalion strength and 16th Luftwaffe Field Division had lost three-quarters of its men.

With Caen at last secured, the British mounted a limited operation to widen the bridgehead over the Odon created by Operation Epsom. 43rd Wessex Division, supported by two tank brigades and a Highland infantry brigade and abundant artillery, struck out at Hill 112 in an attack that produced "a battle of shattering intensity even by the standards of Normandy" and cost the British 2,000 casualties. By its end the men from those county regiments, which rarely caught the headlines but always formed the solid weight of the British army, held half the hill, and its long, low crest now bears their memorial.

OPPOSITE *A British sniper in Caen. Despite his camouflaged helmet and firing position, he is running a risk by being so close to the open window.*

BELOW *A section of Royal Engineers moving into Caen to deal with booby traps and unexploded bombs.*

ABOVE A British soldier gives a helping hand to an old lady amid the utter desolation of Caen. One soldier wrote of the inhabitants that "one could hardly look them in the face, knowing who had done this".

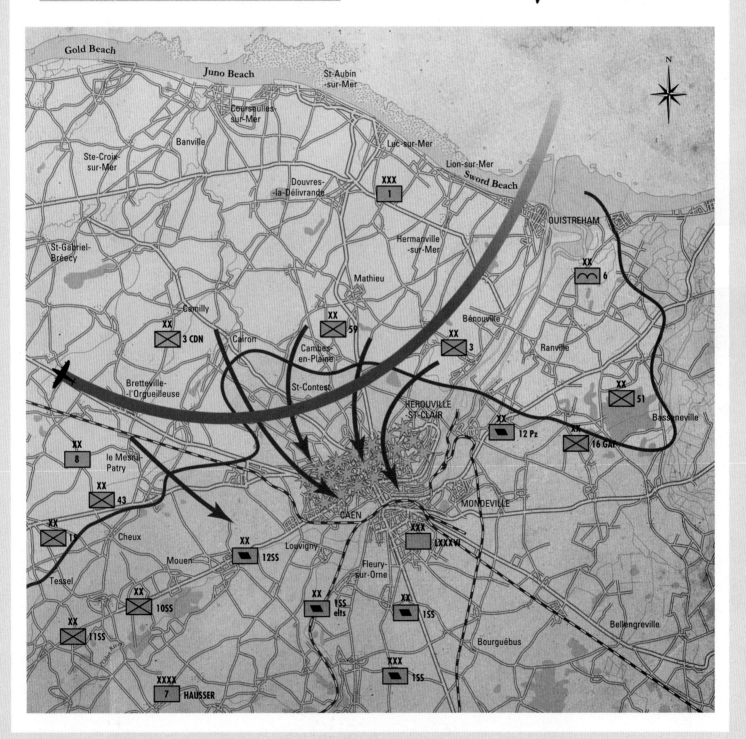

7 – 9 JULY 1944

OPERATION CHARNWOOD

MEDICS

WOUNDS AND DEATH ARE THE CURRENCY OF WAR, AND BOTH SIDES PAID DEARLY
AS THE FIGHTING HARDENED INTO ATTRITION.

By the end of June the British and Canadians had lost 24,698 killed, wounded and missing, and the Americans 37,034, a total of 61,732 Allied casualties. At the end of August these figures were 83,825 and 125,847, 209,672 in total. The dead were often buried near where they fell, with chaplains saying a few words over their graves and carefully recording the sites. The burial grounds we now see, whatever their nationality, are largely "concentration" cemeteries, the bodies beneath their greensward having been moved to new resting places after the tide of war had ebbed away.

Wounded soldiers received aid from comrades or a company medic – all armies had a "First Field Dressing" to staunch the flow of blood – but it was not until they reached their regimental aid post that they

BELOW *US Army medics at work on Omaha Beach. Their patient, who seems to have multiple injuries, probably as the result of a mortar bomb, has been carried to them by stretcher.*

OPPOSITE *An operation in progress in the 79th General Hospital, Bayeux, on 20 June.*

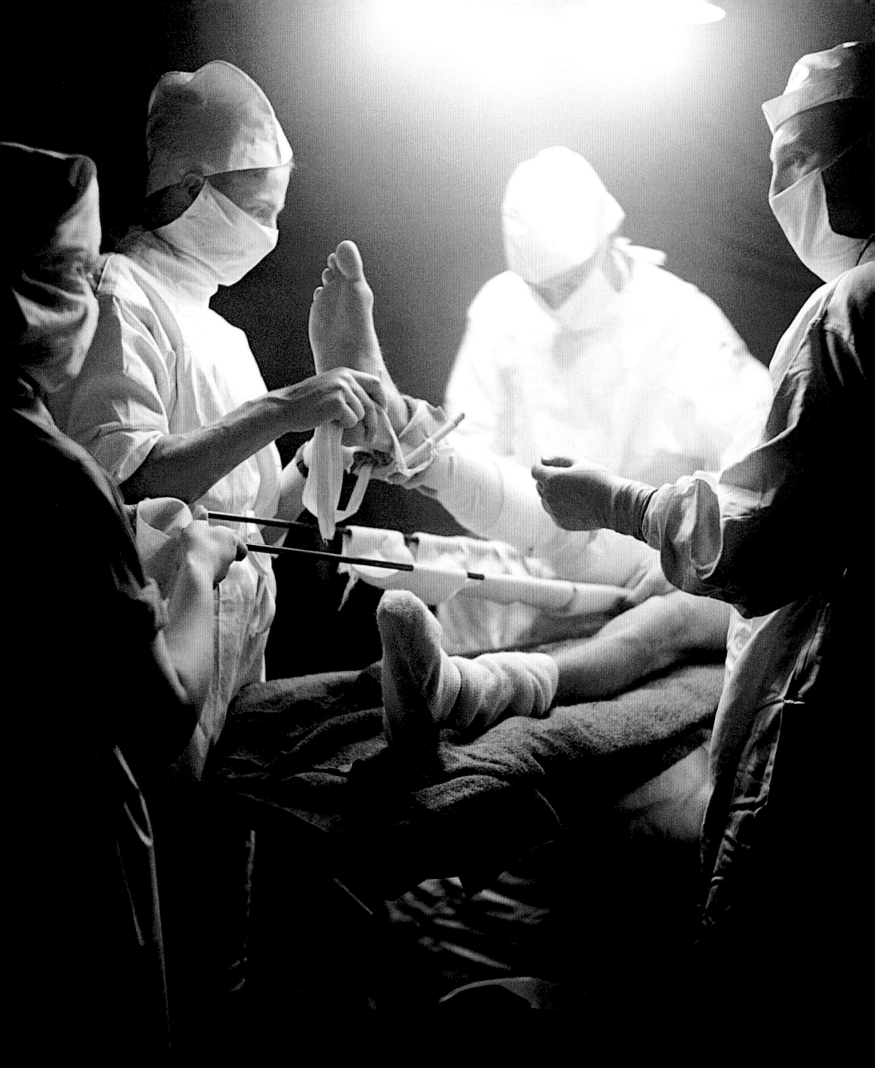

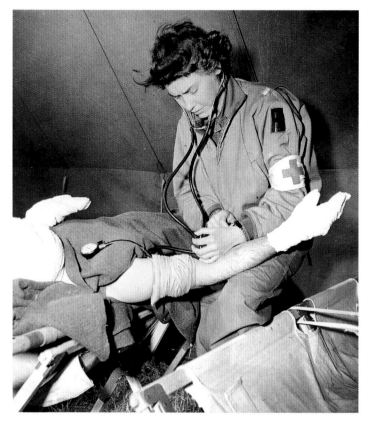

TOP *Air evacuation was widely used in Normandy. Here, a patient is lifted from an ambulance into a C-47 transport aircraft for the flight to England.*

ABOVE *A shell dressing pack carried by medics.*

ABOVE RIGHT *Morphia injection kit carried by officers and medics for pain relief. As soon as the casualty had been injected, the letter "M" was marked on his forehead to prevent overdosing.*

RIGHT *A US Army nurse takes the blood pressure reading of a soldier suffering burns. Allied use of female nurses in Normandy gave a fillip to morale. Montgomery opined: "No man can nurse like a woman, though many think they can."*

could expect qualified medical attention. There, they might be treated and sent back to the line, prepared for evacuation to a dressing station, or made as comfortable as possible to await an inevitable death. Until hospitals could be established in France all casualties would be evacuated to Britain, but an embryo medical organization went in on D-Day. Field dressing stations gave life-saving treatment, and then sent their patients back to casualty clearing stations. General hospitals were speedily established: there were six in the British sector by the end of June. Most men wounded in action or seriously ill were evacuated, but psychiatric casualties, with what was then called "battle fatigue", were treated in France, mainly in divisional recuperation centres. However, psychiatric casualties fell as the grim struggle in the beachhead was replaced by the more open warfare of August, and most centres were closed down.

Casualties sent to Britain at first went by sea, but air evacuation began on 13 June, and by the end of August 57,426 British and Canadian casualties had been evacuated by sea and another 22,646

flown out. Several hospitals were closed in late August so that they could follow the Allied advance across France: of the remaining 29,000 beds in British and Canadian hospitals, only 15,000 were maintained and just 9,700 were occupied.

Normandy produced a casualty pattern which First World War veterans would have recognized, with shells and mortar bombs causing most injuries. However, there had been notable advances since 1918, with the development of antibiotics, new antiseptics, and blood transfusions. In 1943 penicillin was very rare: in Normandy there was sufficient to treat all Allied casualties. Overall, 21 per cent of Allied wounded were operated on in the first "golden hour" after being hit, and another 47 per cent were operated on in the next six. A wounded US soldier, for instance, was half as likely to die in the Second World War as he was in the First.

BELOW *Many soldiers wounded early in the fighting were evacuated on landing craft that had arrived with supplies.*

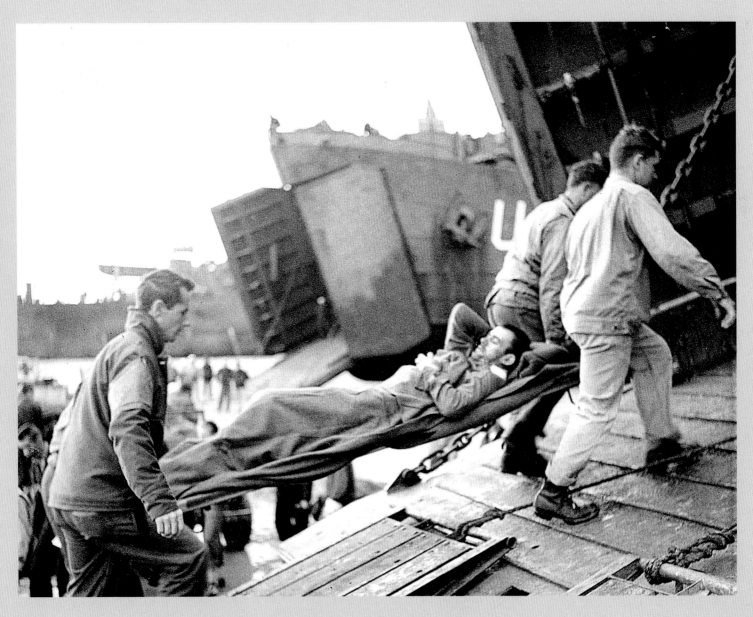

LIFTS WITH BELTS OR WEBBING

1. TWO BELTS. Tie two belts, or webbing, together in a ring. Slip one loop under his arms. Put your head through the other (fig. 9).

Fig.9.

Fig.10.

2. THREE BELTS.

Join three belts together. One loop under his buttocks, the other under his arms. If he can sit, lift him like a haversack. Your hands are free to use a rifle (fig. 10).

3. IF HE CAN'T SIT UP. Lie on your back on top of him. Put your arms through the loops. Roll over. Get up.

NOTES

FIRST AID

FOR

FIGHTING MEN

Your life and those of your comrades may depend upon your having this folder always at hand.

FIRST AID

FOR

FIGHTING MEN

CHARLES KEOGH, F.R.C.S.

This folder is for the Fighting Man, to help him to go on fighting, and to aid his Friend in that cold interval between getting hit and getting help

Printed and Published by
SIFTON, PRAED & CO., LTD.
ST. JAMES'S STREET, S.W.1.

Revised Edition

1. FIRST AID IS COMMON SENSE plus a little specialised knowledge. First Aid saves lives and stops panic.

2. A LIGHTLY WOUNDED MAN, if given First Aid, can go on fighting. Act quickly.

3. A BADLY WOUNDED MAN looks pale and sweaty. Be prepared for this. Treat him like a child. Calm him. Calm the men in your post. This is First Aid.

4. WOUNDS CAN LOOK FRIGHTFUL. Be prepared for this. Remember modern Surgeons can do wonders. Nature does her best to heal all wounds. But give Nature a chance. Stop wounds getting worse. That is your job. That is First Aid.

5. DON'T DISTURB A WOUNDED MAN too much unless you have to. Nature will tell him how to lie in the safest and most comfortable position.

6. LOOK, THINK AND THEN ACT. There may be three men wounded at once. Treat the most urgent first. Keep under cover. If mechanised, turn off petrol. Look out for falling walls. Any fool can be brave and get killed; be brave and don't get killed, and save your friend instead. Look, think, and then act.

7. STOP BLEEDING. A man bleeds to death very quickly. Stop it with your hands. There is no time to wash. Put your fist into the wound. Hold it there. This gives you time. Stuff in a piece of cloth or field dressing. Tie a bandage over it tight. Use another field dressing or strips of cloth for this. Anything will do - but be quick (fig. 1).

FIG. 1

8. IF YOU CAN'T STOP IT that way, slip a piece of string round the leg or arm higher up. A pull-through or sling will do, tie it over his uniform. Tie one knot (fig. 2). Put a pencil or piece of wood on the knot (fig. 3). Tie twice over the stick. Tie a reef knot. Tie any knot if you don't know how (figs. 4 & 5). Twist the stick until the bleeding stops. Keep it in position by tying the ends down This is a Tourniquet.

FIG. 2

FIG. 3

FIG. 4

FIG. 5

9. A TOURNIQUET can save a life and a limb. It can also kill a limb. Loosen a tourniquet every quarter of an hour. Four times an hour. If you don't, the limb will die. So don't put one on unless you have to.

10. IN WAR, a wounded man may be hours or days before he gets to a Surgeon. If ever you put on a tourniquet, put a label on. Write "Tourniquet applied 9 a.m. Tuesday. Loosen four times an hour. Tighten again if bleeding starts." Fix the label where it can be seen.

11. BROKEN BONES. Place the limb in its most natural position and you can't go wrong. Don't let a broken limb flap. Sharp ends of broken bone can cut arteries and nerves to pieces. Tie a broken arm to the chest with any kind of bandage. But tie it firmly (fig. 6). Tie a broken leg to the other leg. Use as many bandages as possible. Foot to foot, knee to knee, thigh to thigh (fig. 7).

FIG. 6

12. SMALL PUNCTURED WOUNDS are often more dangerous than dreadful bloody ones. A spent bullet from the air can go right through a man. Punctured wounds must be seen by a Doctor.

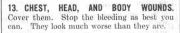
FIG. 7

13. CHEST, HEAD, AND BODY WOUNDS. Cover them. Stop the bleeding as best you can. They look much worse than they are.

14. CARRYING A WOUNDED MAN under fire. Keep under cover. Tie his wrists together. Crawl on hands and knees on top of him. Put your neck under his wrists, and drag him along underneath you. You can go a long way like this, and won't give away the position of your post to the enemy (fig. 8).

FIG. 8

15. WHEN TO GIVE A MAN A DRINK. Give any wounded man a drink of anything you have - but do not give a drink to a man with a wound in the belly, or to a man who cannot swallow. You will kill them if you do. Remember, no drink to those two men. But you can moisten the lips.

16. SHOCK. Shock kills more men than bullets. Shock is a mixture of pain, fear and cold. Do what you can to stop all three. Shock kills brave men.

17. BURNS. Cover burns. You can do no more. Wrap him round in blankets. Keep him warm.

18. PHOSPHORUS BURNS. Hold it under water. Wipe off phosphorus. Keep it wet.

19. GAS. Gas on skin. Wipe it off quickly. Rub in gas ointment. Quick action stops nasty burns. Gas in eyes. Bathe quickly in clean water. Quick action stops blindness. Gas in lungs. Keep him warm. Carry him back. Do not let him walk.

20. KEEP YOUR FEET CLEAN. Keep your underclothes and socks clean. Dirty wounds fester.

21. WHEN A MAN GETS HIT BESIDE YOU. *a.* Calm yourself. *b.* Stop his bleeding. *c.* Keep him warm.

22. THAT IS ALL YOU NEED TO KNOW. Courage in disaster. Courage in the presence of a wounded man. First Aid can save a situation and save a friend.

CHARLES KEOGH, F.R.C.S.,
London Hospital

BATTLE FOR ST-LÔ

THE GERMANS HAD RESTRUCTURED THEIR CHAIN OF COMMAND.

Field Marshal Günther von Kluge replaced Rundstedt (retired for the penultimate time) as Commander in Chief West, and on 17 July also took over Army Group B when Rommel was wounded by strafing RAF aircraft. Panzer Group West (General Heinrich Eberbach) was responsible for the British sector, and 7th Army, commanded by SS General Paul Hausser (who had replaced Colonel General Friedrich Dollmann) was facing the Americans. Hausser had two corps, LXXXIV towards the coast and II Parachute inland. Although many of the latter's

men were parachutists in name only, their robust morale, numerous automatic weapons and plentiful anti-tank Panzerfaust made them ideal for this sort of fighting.

The chief objective of Lieutenant General Omar Bradley's First US Army was the town of St-Lô, as important, in its way, to western Normandy as Caen was to the east, and which, like Caen, had been

BELOW *The perils of the bocage: an American patrol under air-burst artillery fire.*

heavily bombed. It was an important traffic centre, but had, as the US official history admits, accrued psychological value so that its retention or capture "would have a strong effect on the morale of the opposing forces". It lay in the sector attacked by XIX Corps, commanded by Major General Charles H. Corlett. The key to St-Lô was the long Martinville Ridge, crowned by Point 192, east of the city. The central part of the ridge was attacked by 29th Division of XIX Corps, while Point 192 was assailed by 2nd Division of Major General Leonard T. Gerow's V Corps.

Point 192 fell on 11 July after being hit by 45 tons of shells, and its capture enabled the Americans to look along the ridge towards

XIX Corps' objective. After slow progress by 29th Division on 11–12 July, Corlett committed his reserve, the 35th Division, and on 16 July, after a bitter see-saw battle, it took Point 122, the highest point of the ridge in the corps sector. 29th Division entered St-Lô on 18 July, taking with it the flag-draped coffin of Major Thomas D. Howie, commander of 3rd Battalion 116th Infantry, whose last radio message had announced characteristically: "Will do."

ABOVE *An American tank destroyer (a self-propelled anti-tank gun with a limited turret traverse and open top) dealing, at close range, with German positions in St-Lô.*

OMAR BRADLEY

graduated from West Point in 1915 but saw no overseas service in the First World War. In 1941 he jumped from lieutenant colonel to brigadier general, and commanded divisions before taking over II Corps. In Sicily his corps was under Patton's US Seventh Army, but when Bradley commanded US ground troops in Normandy, Patton was under his command. A competent, level-headed general, Bradley tolerated Montgomery better than many. He was later US Army Chief of Staff and chairman of the Joint Chiefs.

U.S 29th Infantry Division.

BELOW *An American soldier looks over the demolished town of St-Lô, destroyed by Allied and Axis bombardment.*

30 JUNE – 24 JULY 1944
BATTLE FOR ST-LÔ

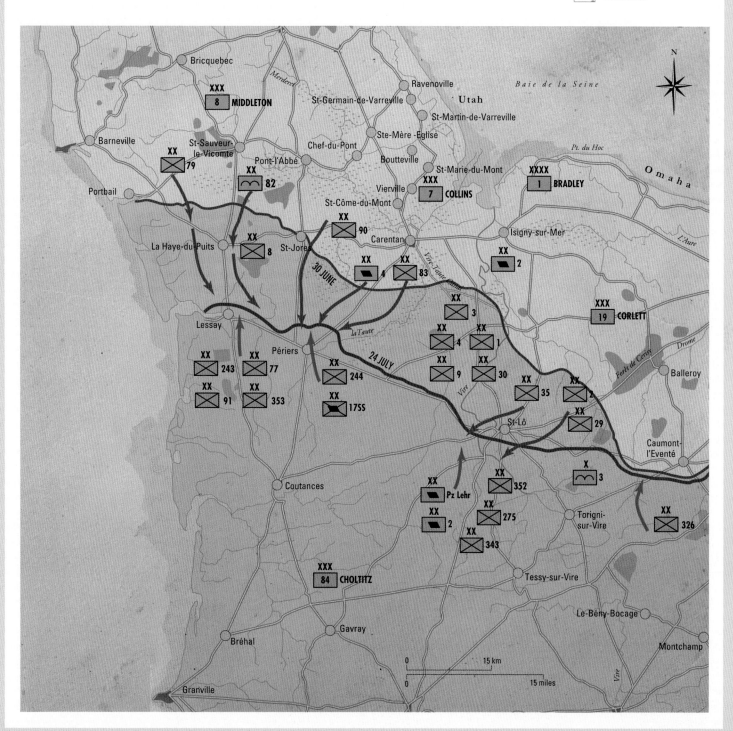

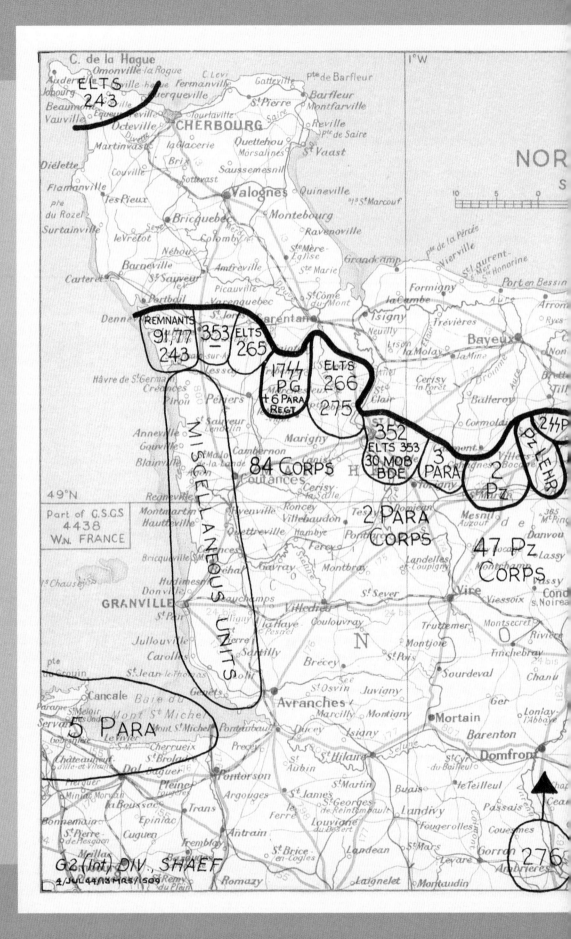

RIGHT & PAGES 174–75 & 176–177 *A series of three SHAEF maps, showing the enemy order of battle during and after the struggle for St-Lô, from 30 June to 28 July.*

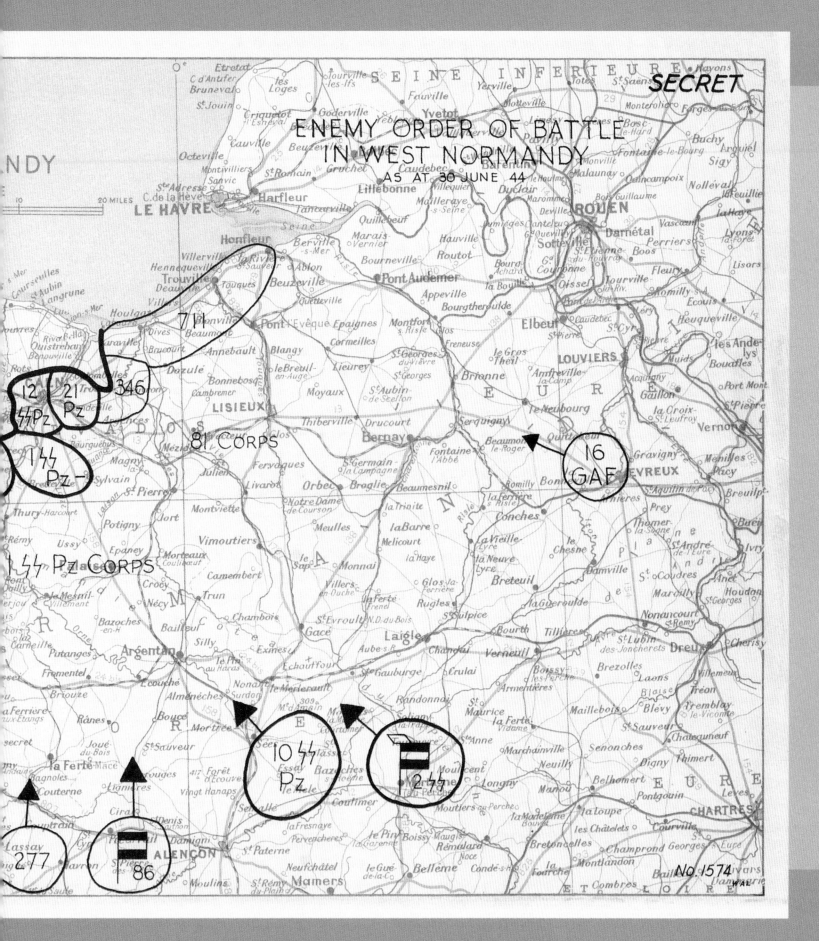

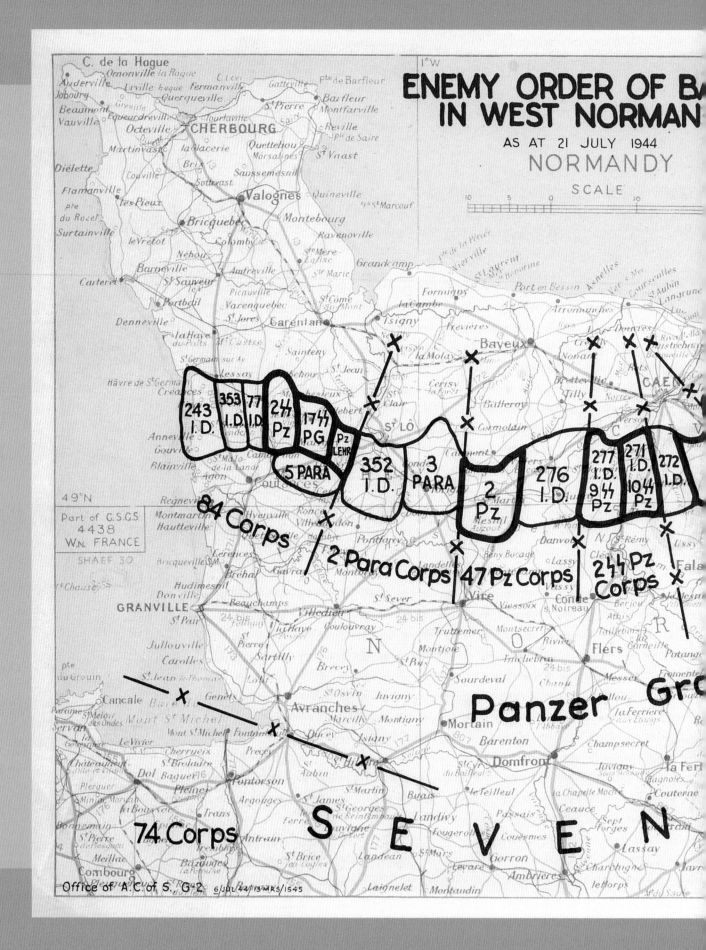

SECRET

7N I.D.

461 I.D.

Pz SGAF

ELTS 12 SS Pz

86 Corps

ELTS 2 SS Pz

Pz Corps

P West

FIFTEENTH

ROUEN

SEVENTH

LOUVIERS

EVREUX

ARMY

WITH	77 I.D	ELTS.	265 & 91 I.D
WITH	174 PG DIV.	ELTS.	6 PARA RGT.
WITH	Pz LEHR DIV	ELTS.	275 I.D
WITH	352 I.D.	ELTS.	266 & 343 I.D.

No. 1636

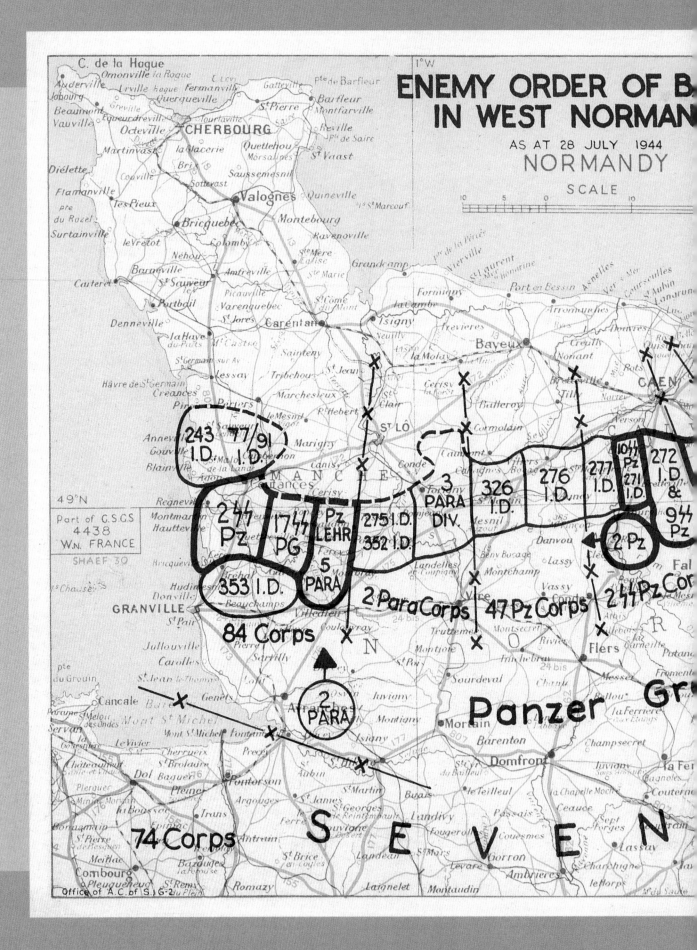

ENEMY ORDER OF B.
IN WEST NORMAN
AS AT 28 JULY 1944
NORMANDY
SCALE

OPERATION GOODWOOD

MONTGOMERY WAS STILL OVERALL GROUND FORCE COMMANDER, ALTHOUGH HIS DAYS AS SUCH WERE NUMBERED.

The Americans would form an army group once they had sufficient troops, leaving Montgomery commanding the Anglo-Canadian 21st Army Group while Bradley stepped up to command the US 12th Army Group. On 10 July Montgomery outlined his plan for the break-out. The Americans were to burst out of the bocage, exploiting down to Brittany and round to Le Mans and Alençon. But before this the British would mount their own offensive, Operation Goodwood. The timings for both operations slipped: it took the Americans longer than expected to secure St-Lô, and bad weather delayed Goodwood.

We cannot be certain whether Goodwood was intended to attract German armour, or was in fact a genuine attempt at a breakout. Major General "Pip" Roberts, of 11th Armoured Division, thought that Falaise was his objective, and Lieutenant General Miles Dempsey, of 2nd Army, believed it was "more than possible that the Huns will break" enabling him to exploit. Even Montgomery told the Chief of the Imperial

ABOVE *British Cromwell tanks assemble in preparation for the opening of Operation "Goodwood" on 18 July 1944. The operation was designed to break through the German line south of Caen, but poor weather and stiff German defences forced a halt by 20 July.*

The Guards Armoured Division.

RIGHT *The British Cromwell tank was armed with one 75mm gun and two 7.9mm Besa machine guns, but was outclassed by the German Panther.*

ABOVE *The impact of strategic bombers, 18 July. Some bombs were fused to explode instantaneously, leaving only small craters which would not impede the advance.*

MILES DEMPSEY

was an infantry officer in the First World War. He did well as a brigadier in 1940, and Montgomery requested him as a corps commander after El Alamein. Thereafter Dempsey moved in Montgomery's wake, commanding 2nd Army from early 1944. He was easy to work with, and Bradley applauded his lack of "jealousy or anger". He made little mark as a commander, probably because he saw himself as Montgomery's loyal lieutenant. Goodwood was essentially his plan, though, and he was optimistic that it would achieve a breakthrough.

OPPOSITE British tanks moving up for Operation Goodwood. Marshalling the three attacking armoured divisions, each with more than 3,000 vehicles, including almost 300 tanks, was no easy task.

ABOVE A shot which captures the heat and confusion of battle shows British infantry preparing to advance near Cagny on the second day of Goodwood.

'THERE WAS A POOR LAD WHO HAD HAD MOST OF THE BOTTOM OF HIS BACK BLOWN AWAY. ... THAT POOR DEVIL SCREAMED FOR ABOUT TWO HOURS; MORPHINE SEEMED TO HAVE NO EFFECT. ... OUR SERGEANT HAD BEEN IN THE WAR FROM THE START, AND EVEN HE WAS WHITE AND SHAKEN.

PRIVATE ROBERT BOLTON, THE QUEEN'S ROYAL REGIMENT

ABOVE A Sherman passes a knocked-out German tank near the village of Cagny.

General Staff that he hoped to "loose a corps of three armoured divisions into the open country about the Caen-Falaise road." Montgomery was subject to increasing pressure to expand the beachhead, and in particular to seize more ground for the construction of airfields. Moreover, he proposed to use heavy bombers to prepare the way for Goodwood, and knew that he would not get them save for an operation of first importance.

The plan was simple enough. Three armoured divisions, the Guards, 7th and 11th, would attack through a narrow corridor between the Orne and the Bois de Bavent, fanning out as soon as there was space, to take the Bourgebus Ridge and exploit beyond it. On the morning of 18 July more than 2,000 RAF and US bombers attacked the little villages forming a framework of defence, and 11th Armoured Division moved off on the heels of the bombing. So narrow was its corridor that it led with a single regiment – 3rd Royal Tanks – and it was not until the advance was well under way that another regiment, 2nd Fife and Forfar Yeomanry, could come up. The first line of defence, furnished by the unlucky 16th Luftwaffe Field Division, was shattered by the bombing, and serious damage had also been done to 21st Panzer Division behind

it. But the defence gradually came to life. Tough-minded officers like Major Hans von Luck, who ordered an anti-aircraft battery commander, at pistol point, to take on advancing tanks, animated the defence, and SS General Sepp Dietrich, commanding 1st SS Panzer Corps, ordered up reinforcements.

The 3rd Royal Tanks were beginning to climb the ridge when they were engaged by 88mm anti-tank guns, and Sherman after Sherman burst into flames. Although the British eventually secured the villages atop the ridge, any chance of a breakthrough had gone. When the battle ended on 20 July, 2nd Army had lost over 400 tanks and 6,000 men. If the tanks could be replaced from stocks in the beachhead, the loss of manpower was more serious, for this was an army scraping the bottom of its recruiting barrel. Montgomery admitted that he was over-optimistic at a press conference on the 18th, and Eisenhower was "as blue as indigo" about poor progress. Much had gone wrong in Goodwood, but one fact was undeniable: it had indeed attracted German armour to the east.

18 - 21 JULY 1944

OPERATION GOODWOOD

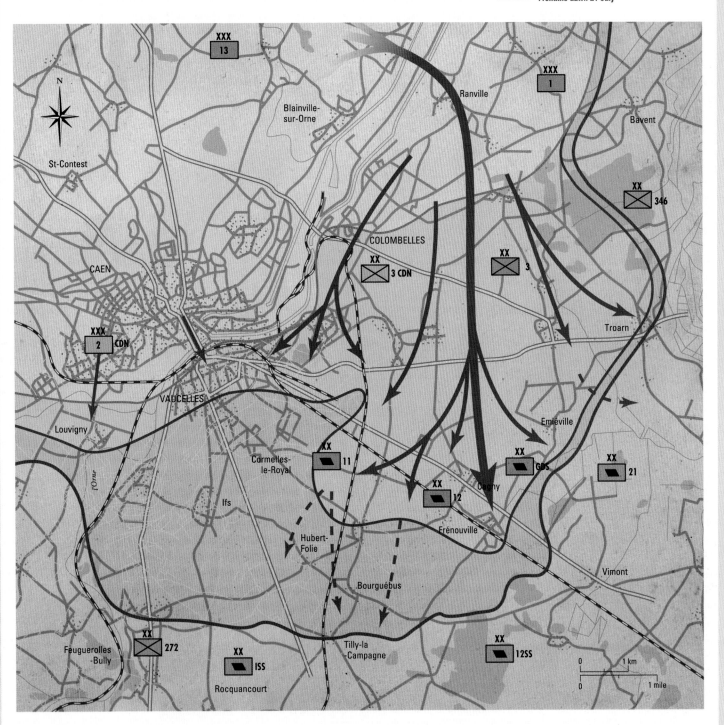

MAP KEY

➡ British and Canadian advance 18 July

⇢ British Armoured Divisions advance 18 July

── Frontline dawn 18 July

── Frontline 24.00 hrs. 18 July

── Frontline dawn 21 July

XXX 13

XXX 1

Ranville

Bavent

Blainville-sur-Orne

XX 346

St-Contest

N

COLOMBELLES

CAEN

XX 3 CDN

XX 3

Troarn

XXX 2 CDN

VAUCELLES

Louvigny

Emiéville

l'Orne

Cormelles-le-Royal

XX 11

XX GDS

XX 21

Ifs

XX 12

Cagny

Hubert-Folie

Frénouville

Vimont

Bourguébus

XX 272

Tilly-la-Campagne

XX 12SS

Feuguerolles-Bully

XX 1SS

Rocquancourt

0   1 km

0   1 mile

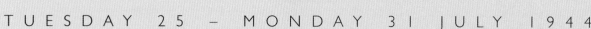

OPERATION COBRA

ON 5 JULY EISENHOWER OBSERVED THAT THREE FACTORS WERE MAKING LIFE HARD FOR THE AMERICANS: GERMAN FIGHTING QUALITY, THE NATURE OF THE COUNTRY, AND THE WEATHER.

By the time they took St-Lô the Americans had learnt a good deal about bocage fighting, and if they were well aware of how unpleasant this was for them, they underestimated the damage that they were doing to the Germans. On 13 July Kluge, who arrived in Normandy full of enthusiasm, warned Hitler's staff that his infantry was worn perilously thin. He needed more tanks "to act as corset stays behind the troops". The situation was now "very serious. ... If a hole breaks open, I have to patch it".

Eisenhower was disappointed by Goodwood, and affirmed that he was "pinning our immediate hopes on Bradley's attack". Montgomery,

meanwhile, ordered Dempsey to "fatten up" his operations in order to ensure that the Germans could not swing to meet the forthcoming attack, Operation Cobra. The original Cobra plan was modest, and envisaged an attack southwards to Coutances and then a jab westwards, to cut off the defenders of the coastal strip, and leave the US First Army consolidating on the line Coutances-Caumont, ready to exploit further. The key breakthrough was to be made by VII Corps, tightly

BELOW *Smoke rising from the "bombing box", just south of the St-Lô–Périers road, as heavy bombers prepare the way for Cobra, 25 July.*

4th Armoured Division.

US Third Army.

GEORGE S. PATTON

came from a well-to-do family with military traditions. Commissioned in 1909, he commanded a tank brigade in France in 1918 with great success. He led an armoured division in 1941 and was an army commander in 1943, but was shelved after slapping two shell-shocked soldiers. Patton commanded Third Army in its dash across France in 1944, but mismanaged the campaign to take Metz. Flamboyant, profane, gifted but flawed, he died after a car crash in 1945.

concentrated just west of St-Lô, and before the attack German positions were to be saturated by heavy bombers. General Collins' infantry would attack after the bombing, and once they had created a gap in the defences his armoured divisions would roll on through.

The bombing was dogged by misfortune. Although the attack was postponed because of bad weather on 24 July some bombers struck anyway, and several Americans were killed or wounded. On the following day the bombers came again, and this time 111 Americans were killed and another 490 wounded. Although the bombing had clearly rattled the defence, the initial infantry attacks still ran into firm

RIGHT *The Allied commanders pose for the camera during a conference in a hayfield in northern France during the rapid Allied advance following Operation "Cobra". General Montgomery, centre, is flanked by (left to right) Lieutenant General Hodges of the US First Army, General Crerar of the Canadian 1st Army, General Bradley, commander of the US 12th Army Group and Lieutenant General Dempsey, commander of the British Second Army.*

BELOW *American infantry and tank destroyers west of St-Lô.*

resistance. However, General Collins believed that the Germans were shaken enough for him to commit his armour, and though the situation on 26 July "did not appear too bright" he did just that. Collins' instincts were correct, and by the end of the day one of his divisional commanders exulted: "This thing has busted wide open." There was indeed a jagged breach in the German defences, and Kluge had too little armour to counter-attack.

Bradley's success lay as much in what followed Cobra as in the battle itself. Recognizing that the Germans could no longer furnish a cohesive defence, he issued orders on 28 July for exploitation of the initial breakthrough. The results were impressive. The Americans reached Avranches on 30 July, and on the following day they seized the little

bridge over the River Sélune at Pontaubault just before the Germans arrived to destroy it. Kluge admitted that "It's a madhouse here", and acknowledged that his whole left flank had collapsed.

On 1 August, with tanks of 4th Armoured Division rattling past Pontaubault towards Brittany, the Americans activated their new command structure, with Bradley stepping up to command 12th Army Group, Lieutenant General Courtney H. Hodges taking over First Army and Lieutenant General George S. Patton assuming command of the newly formed US Third Army. Eisenhower declared that Montgomery would remain ground force commander until SHAEF arrived in France and he assumed personal command. Although there was still much hard fighting to be done, Cobra had changed the pattern of the campaign.

ABOVE LEFT A US Sherman tank with the modification to its hull. These "horns" enabled the tank to rip its way through the hedges-on-banks, so typical of the bocage.

ABOVE A French family carrying what they can on bicycles return to the village of Marigny, recently liberated by the US on 26 July 1944 during Operation "Cobra". Thousands of French people were caught in the crossfire of war and an estimated 60,000 were killed by Allied bombing.

LEFT An American column of jeeps and trucks advancing on Coutances through a badly damaged village following a fierce bombardment.

25 – 31 JULY 1944

OPERATION COBRA & THE BREAKOUT

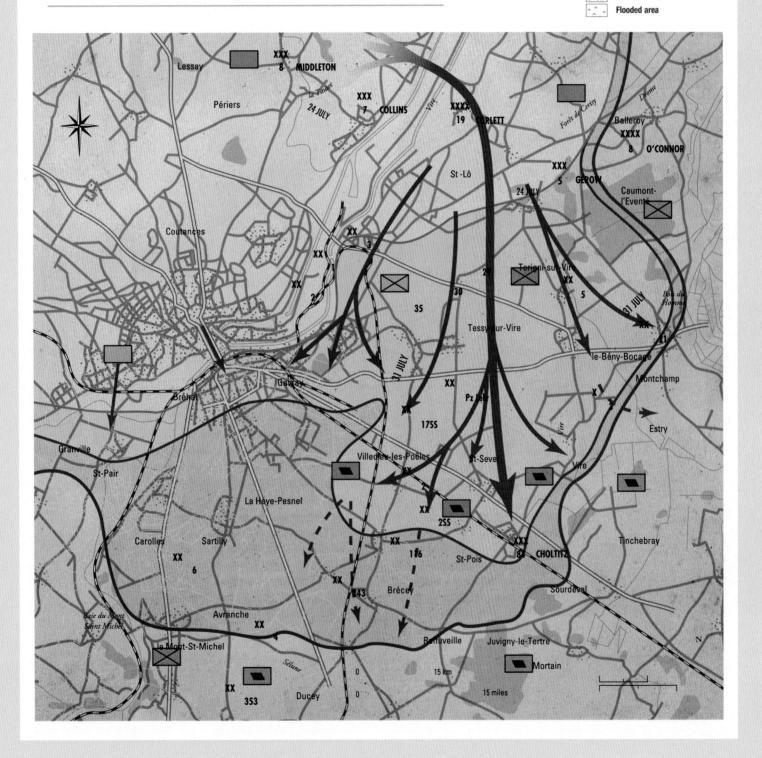

Lessay

XXX
8 MIDDLETON

Périers

la Vallée

XXX
24 JULY

XXX
7 COLLINS

Vire

XXXX
19 CORLETT

Forêt de Cerisy

Drôme

Balleroy

XXXX
8 O'CONNOR

St -Lô

XXX
5 GEROW

24 JULY

Caumont-
l'Eventé

Coutances

XX
1

XX
3

XX
2

35

29

30

Tessy-sur-Vire

Torigni-sur-Vire

XX
5

31 JULY

Bois du
Homme

le-Bény-Bocage

Montchamp

Granville

Bréhal

Gavray

31 JULY

XX

Pz Lehr

Vire

Estry

St-Pair

17SS

Villedieu-les-Poêles

St-Sever

Vire

La Haye-Pesnel

XX

XX
2SS

Carolles

Sartilly

XX
6

XX

116

St-Pois

XXX
84 CHOLTITZ

Tinchebray

Sourdeval

Baie du Mont
Saint Michel

Avranche

XX
4

Brécey

843

Reffuveille

Juvigny-le-Tertre

N

le Mont-St-Michel

Sélune

Mortain

XX
353

Ducey

0

0

15 km

15 miles

RESTRICTED

A POCKET GUIDE

TO

FRANCE

War and Navy Departments
Washington, D.C.

CONTENTS

		Page
I. Why You're Going to France		1
II. The United States Soldier in France		2
1. Meet the People		2
2. Security and Health		5
3. You are a Guest of France		7
4. Mademoiselle		8
III. A Few Pages of French History		9
1. Occupation		9
2. Resistance		11
3. Necessary Surgery		12
4. A Quick Look Back		12
5. Churchgoers		13
6. The Machinery		14
IV. Observation Post		15
1. The Provinces		15
2. The Cafés		16
3. The Farms		17
4. The Regions		21
5. Work		23
6. The Tourist		24
V. In Parting		28
VI. Annex: Various Aids		29
Decimal System		29
Weights and Measures		29
Language Guide		30
Important Signs		*Outside Rear Cover*

30

LANGUAGE GUIDE

You will find all the words and phrases written both in French spelling and in a simplified spelling which you read like English. Don't use the French spelling, the one given in parentheses, unless you have studied French before. Read the simplified spelling as though it were English.

HINTS ON FRENCH PRONUNCIATION

In the simplified English spelling the syllables that are accented, that is, pronounced louder than others, are written in capital letters. In French, unaccented syllables are not skipped over quickly, as they are in English. The accent is generally on the last syllable in the phrase.

Hyphens are used to divide words into syllables in order to make them easier to pronounce. Curved lines (‿) are used to show sounds that are pronounced together without any break; for example, *day-z‿UH* meaning "some eggs," *kawn-B‿YANG* meaning "how much?"

AY	as in *may, say, play* but don't drawl it out as we do in English. Since it is not drawled it sounds almost like the *e* in *let*. Example: *ray-pay-TAY* meaning "repeat."
J	stands for a sound for which we have no single letter in English. It is the sound we have in *measure, leisure, usual, division, casualty, azure*. Example: *bawn-JOOR* meaning "Good day."
EW	is used for a sound like *ee* in *bee* made with the lips rounded as though about to say the *oo* in *boot*. Example: *ek-skew-eny MWA* meaning "Excuse me," or "Pardon."
U or UH	as in *up, cut, rub, gun*. Examples: *nuf* meaning "nine," *juh* meaning "I."
U or UH	as in *up, cut*, etc., but made with the lips rounded. Example: *DUH* meaning "two."
NG, N or M	are used to show that certain vowels are pronounced through the nose, very much in the way we generally say *huh, uh-uh, uh-huh*. Examples: *lahnt-MAHNG* meaning "slowly," *juh kawn-PRAHNG* meaning "I understand," *NAWNG* meaning "no," *PANG* meaning "bread."

31

GREETINGS AND GENERAL PHRASES

English	*Pronunciation and French Spelling*
Hello or Good day	bawn-JOOR (Bonjour)
Good evening	bawn-SWAR (Bonsoir)
How are you?	kaw-MAHN-T‿ah-lay VOO? (Comment allez-vous?)
Sir	muss-YUH (Monsieur)
Madam	ma-DAHM (Madame)
Miss	mad-mwa-ZEL (Mademoiselle)
Please	SEEL voo PLAY (S'il vous plait)
Excuse me	(Pardawn) (Pardon)
You're welcome	eel nee ah pa duh KWA (Il n'y a pas de quoi)
Yes	WEE (oui)
No	NAWNG (non)
Do you understand?	KAWM-pruh-nay VOO? (Comprenez-vous?)
I understand	JUH kawm-PRAHNG (Je comprends)
I don't understand	juh nuh KAWM-prahng PA (Je ne comprends pas)
Speak slowly, please	par-lay LAHNT-mahng, seel voo PLAY (Parlez lentement, s'il vous plait)
Please repeat	RAY-pay-tay, seel voo PLAY (Repetez s'il vous plait)

LOCATION

When you need directions to get somewhere you use the phrase "where is" and then add the words you need.

Where is the restaurant?	oo AY (Ou est) luh RESS-to-RAHNG (le restaurant)
Where is the restaurant?	oo AY luh RESS-to-RAHNG? (Ou est le restaurant?)
the hotel	lo-TEL (l'hotel)
the railroad station	la GAR (la gare)
the toilet	luh la-va-BO (le lavabo)

DIRECTIONS

The answer to your question "Where is such and such?" may be "To the right" or "To the left" or "Straight ahead—" so you need to know these phrases:

To the right	ah DRWAT (a droite)
To the left	ah GOHSH (a gauche)
Straight ahead	too DRWA (tout droit)

OPERATION LÜTTICH

HITLER PERSISTENTLY INTERVENED IN THE CONDUCT OF MILITARY OPERATIONS. SOMETIMES HE WAS RIGHT: HIS DECISION TO STAND FAST IN THE FACE OF THE RUSSIAN COUNTER-ATTACK IN DECEMBER 1941, FOR INSTANCE, WAS WELL JUDGED.

But by August 1944 his grip on reality had been severely eroded, and the unsuccessful assassination attempt of 20 July had increased his paranoia towards the General Staff. The decision to mount Operation Lüttich, the Mortain counter-attack, was his. On the face of things it was not wholly foolish. Exploitation after Cobra had left the Americans with a narrow corridor between Mortain and the coast, and it was not inconceivable that this could be cut, leaving Patton's divisions to the south dangerously short of fuel and supplies. But while Kluge and his staff recognized that a counter-attack could buy time, perhaps enough to fall back to a new defence line, Hitler envisaged something wholly different: a massive counter-stroke which would reverse his fortunes in the west and, as he put it, throw the Allies into the sea.

RIGHT *The Panther tank, with a 75mm gun, was developed by the Germans to counter the threat posed by the Soviet T-34. The Americans and British first encountered it in significant numbers in Normandy.*

ABOVE *A company of Tiger II tanks, part of an SS Panzer division, camouflaged near Mortain on the eve of Operation Lüttich.*

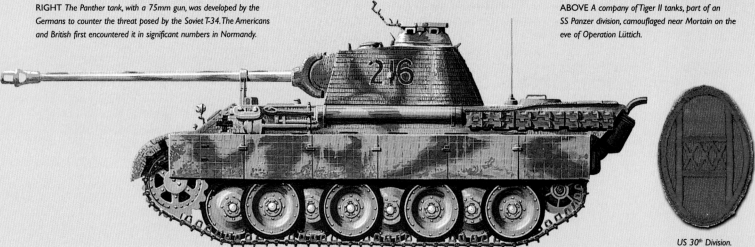

US 30th Division.

'TANKS ARE THE BACKBONE OF OUR DEFENCE, WHEN THEY ARE WITHDRAWN, OUR FRONT WILL GIVE WAY. IF, AS I FORESEE, THIS PLAN DOES NOT SUCCEED, CATASTROPHE IS INEVITABLE.

FIELD MARSHAL GUNTHER VON KLUGE, COMMANDER IN CHIEF WEST

ABOVE *The danger of road moved in daylight. This German convoy has been strafed by USAAF Thunderbolts.*

GUNTHER VON KLUGE

was an army commander from 1939 to 1940, and promoted to field marshal after victory in France. Injured in Russia in 1943, he was re-employed in 1944 as Commander in Chief West, replacing Rundstedt on 3 July. Initially full of enthusiasm, he speedily concluded that his position was hopeless. Ordered to Germany in the wake of the 20 July assassination plot, he took poison on 19 August. His last letter spoke of shame at his failure but of continuing loyalty to Hitler.

BELOW *Soft-skinned vehicles were hideously vulnerable to attack from the air.*

The Mortain counter-attack laboured under many disadvantages: several senior German commanders were markedly lacking in enthusiasm, and most participating units were already under-strength. However, in one respect Hitler's luck held. The weather on 7 August, when the battle began, was poor, grounding Allied fighter-bombers. And if Bradley had brief warning of the attack, produced by Ultra, for some units on the ground the sudden appearance of numerous determined Germans came as a very unpleasant shock. Mortain itself had only just been occupied by the veteran US 30th Division, and although it was driven out of the town, the dominant Hill 317, just to the east, was held by part of an infantry battalion with artillery observers in "one of the outstanding small unit achievements in the course of the campaign." When the weather cleared the observers were able to direct fire onto the main road to the coast, just below them, and USAAF Thunderbolts and RAF Typhoons arrived to lacerate the attackers. Despite there being some early progress, the attack was going nowhere.

Hitler remained convinced that the offensive could have succeeded if it had been heavier, and ordered Eberbach, removed from command of 5th Panzer Army and given a scratch headquarters specifically for the new attack, to try again on 11 August. Eberbach soon recognized that he had too few tanks for the task, and Allied air superiority meant that they could only move while early-morning mist grounded aircraft. And Kluge could see that things were coming unstitched elsewhere: the Canadians were pushing hard down the Caen–Falaise road, and further south the Americans were cutting up from Le Mans towards Alençon. By continuing to strike westwards, the Germans were putting their heads further into the noose, and on 11 August Hitler authorized Eberbach to disengage, although, hopelessly unrealistically, he still hoped to try again later.

07 – 08 AUGUST 1944

OPERATION LÜTTICH

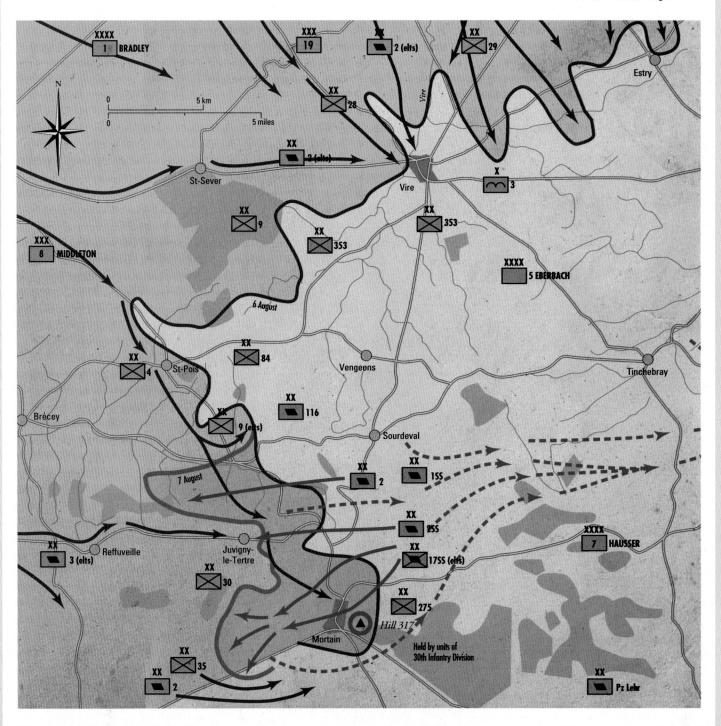

TACTICAL AIR SUPPORT

THE ALLIES ENJOYED AIR SUPERIORITY THROUGHOUT THE CAMPAIGN. THE LUFTWAFFE
HAD BEEN WEAKENED BEFORE D-DAY BY LOSSES IN COMBAT AND THE EFFECTS OF
BOMBING ON THE GERMAN INDUSTRIAL BASE.

Indeed, the erosion of the Luftwaffe's fighter strength was one of the by-products of the strategic bombing campaign. It became harder to train pilots, and by 1944 German air power was in a descending spiral which could have only one result. German soldiers lived with the constant threat of air attack: they joked darkly that the "Normandy look" was an upward stare that gave a man a crick in his neck, and photographs and newsreels reveal constant emphasis on camouflage.

Yet if air power made a crucial contribution to Allied victory, it was not decisive in itself. Armies and air forces were not always comfortable bedfellows. The "bomber barons", like Carl Spaatz and Ira Eaker in the USAAF and Arthur Harris in the RAF, believed that their heavy bombers should be used against strategic targets in Germany, not

BELOW *Marauder medium bombers of the US 9th Air Force
attacking German units moving up to the battlefront by road.*

ELWOOD R. "PETE" QUESADA

had a good range of staff and flying appointments before the war began. He went to North Africa at the head of XII Fighter Command, and was a natural choice for promotion to major general to lead IX Tactical Air Command. He landed near Omaha on D+1, and his airmen opened the first landing strip in France that day. He worked closely with Bradley to orchestrate effective air support in Normandy, and during the German Ardennes offensive.

ABOVE *A rocket-armed RAF Typhoon taking off from a forward airstrip. Aircraft were refuelled and rearmed on these strips, enjoying longer "loiter time" over the battlefield than if they had to return to Britain after each mission.*

tactical targets in Normandy, and the experience of Goodwood and Cobra confirmed them in this view. Even at a lower level, where air power was tactical in function, its effectiveness was limited by personality clashes. Air Marshal Coningham of Second Tactical Air Force cordially detested Montgomery, and Tedder, Eisenhower's deputy, sympathized with him. In contrast, Air Vice Marshal Harry Broadhurst, who supported Dempsey's Second Army, got on well with soldiers. So too did USAAF Major General Elwood R. "Pete" Quesada, whose IX Tactical Air Command supported Bradley. He not only enjoyed an excellent working relationship with Bradley himself, but persuaded him to put aircraft radios into tanks to improve communication between ground and air.

Communication was itself a major difficulty, and one of the reasons why Goodwood made limited progress was that the one forward air controller on the main axis of the advance was in an unarmoured vehicle which was knocked out early on. It was rarely enough to target air attacks on a particular area: pilots had a better chance of success if a forward air controller could give them last-minute directions, perhaps with a smoke shell to mark the target. Next, the limitations of the weapons in use limited the effectiveness of air attacks. Infantry and soft-skinned vehicles could be dealt with by machine-gun or cannon fire, but tanks were harder to destroy, and rockets, like those used by RAF Typhoons, lacked accuracy when used against moving armour. Even when the skies cleared over Mortain, and the flail of Allied air power was applied relentlessly, more tanks were abandoned by their terrified crews than were actually destroyed by rockets. Bad weather often made flying impossible, and "loiter time" over the battlefield was all too short until sufficient aircraft were based on temporary airstrips in France.

HARRY BROADHURST

was commissioned into the RAF in 1926 and quickly established a reputation as a skilled pilot and fine marksman. Heavily involved in the 1940 campaign and the Battle of Britain, he took over the Western Desert Air Force in January 1943 as the RAF's youngest air vice marshal. In 1944–45 he commanded a group in 2nd Tactical Air Force under Sir Arthur Coningham. He enjoyed Montgomery's confidence, and worked well with him during the campaign.

Lastly, the Germans were adept at generating comprehensive ground-based air defence, with 88mm guns reaching up for high-flying aircraft and lighter weapons taking a toll of lower targets. Second Tactical Air Force and UK-based Fighter Command units between them lost 829 aircraft and over 1,000 aircrew killed or missing, and for the campaign as a whole the USAAF lost an average of 34 men and eight aircraft, and the RAF 36 men and nine aircraft, for every thousand sorties. There were times when the efforts of Allied pilots were not appreciated by men slogging it out on the ground, but the skies over Normandy were anything but safe.

BELOW *Canadians pause on their way to Falaise as Allied bombs fall just ahead of them.*

BELOW & OPPOSITE *The logbook of a British Typhoon pilot, Flying Officer Henry "Papa" Ambrose of 175 Squadron (whose motto was "Stop at Nothing"), detailing his ground support sorties from 8 to 31 August 1944.*

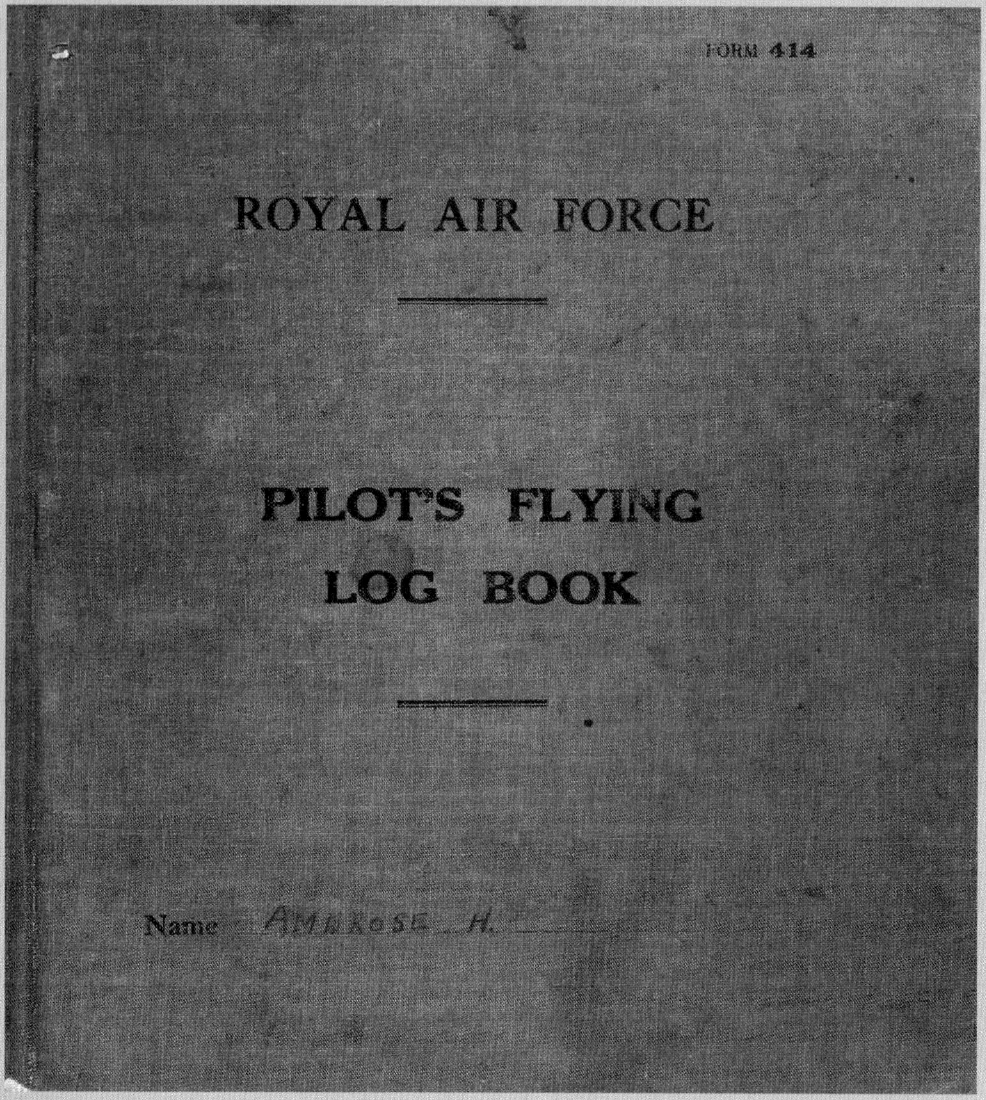

FORM 414

ROYAL AIR FORCE

PILOT'S FLYING
LOG BOOK

Name AMBROSE H.

YEAR		AIRCRAFT		PILOT, OR	2ND PILOT, PUPIL	DUTY
MONTH	DATE	Type	No.	1st Pilot	OR PASSENGER	(INCLUDING RESULTS AND REMARKS)

TYPHOON AIRCRAFT.

CERTIFIED THAT: I have read and understood Pilots Handling Notes.
I understand the hydraulic, oil, petrol and glycol systems.
I have manipulated the undercarriage on a "jacked-up" aircraft including the emergency gear.
I know the engine limitations, petrol and oil consumptions, oil and glycol temperatures, pressures and starting and stopping procedure relevant to a Sabre Engine.
I have had cockpit instruction and have been tested blindfolded.

Signature ....

Engineer Officer: CERTIFIED that I have tested the above named pilot and consider that he is capable of handling the Sabre Engine.
Signature ....

Flight Commander CERTIFIED that the above pilot has had adequate cockpit instruction and has been tested blindfolded by an experienced pilot.
Signature 3.8.43

GRAND TOTAL [Cols. (1) to (10)] .... Hrs. .... Mins.   TOTALS CARRIED FORWARD

CERTIFICATES OF QUALIFICATION AS FIRST PILOT

[K.R. & A.C.I., para. 805, clause 5.]

Name AMBROSE   Rank Sgt/Sgt — P/O — P/O.
                                     F/O F/Lt

(i)   Certified that the above named has qualified as a first pilot (day only)

On (Type)	Date	Unit	Signature and Rank

(ii)   Certified that the above named has qualified as a First Pilot

On (Type)	Date	Unit	Signature and Rank

NIGHT VISION TEST B'MOUTH 19/7/41
AVERAGE:

YEAR 1944		AIRCRAFT		PILOT, OR	2ND PILOT, PUPIL	DUTY	SINGLE-ENGINE AIRCRAFT				MULTI-ENGINE AIRCRAFT						PASS-ENGER	INSTR./CLOUD FLYING [Incl. in cols. (1) to (10)]	
							DAY		NIGHT		DAY			NIGHT					
MONTH	DATE	Type	No.	1st Pilot	OR PASSENGER	(INCLUDING RESULTS AND REMARKS)	DUAL	PILOT	DUAL	PILOT	DUAL	1ST PILOT	2ND PILOT	DUAL	1ST PILOT	2ND PILOT		DUAL	PILOT
							(1)	(2)	(3)	(4)	(5)	(6)	(7)	(8)	(9)	(10)	(11)	(12)	(13)
						TOTALS BROUGHT FORWARD	73·25	566·45	3·35	56·40									
Jan.				175 SQUADRON FRANCE B·5.															
August	8	TYPHOON	Z	SELF		SECTOR RECCO NORMANDY		·35											
	8	"	Z	"		ARMED RECCO		·40			SEVERAL M.T. ATTACKED USED ROCKETS FIRST TIME								
	9	"	W	"		GUNS ATTACKED		·50			N.W. STAVON. IN OPS								
	9	"	W	"		" AND V.C.P. GUNS		1·00			WOODS EAST OF DAETTEVILLE								
	10	"	Y	"		GUN POSITIONS		·40			N. OF MEZIDON.								
	11	"	T	"		GUN POSITIONS S.W. VASSEY		·50			GOOD PRANG								
	11	"	N	"		TROOPS & MORTAR POSITION		·40			FAIR HEAVY FLAK PRANG — SHOT UP BADLY MYSELF.								
	12	"	Z	"		TANKS IN QUARRY S.W. BARBERY		·40			5 TANKS ATTACKED BATTEVILLE SUR LAIZE								
	14	"	Z	"		TRANSPORT EAST FALAISE. R.P.		1·00	Hit in Wing		F/Lt HENMAN BALLO OUT. SELF SHOT UP. F/O ...								
	18	"	U	"		R.P. MET.		1·00			TANKS AND MET AT VIMOUTIERS F/Lt DRIVES FORCE								
	18	"	U	"		R.P. MET		·35			S. OF VIMOUTIERS Y TANKS FRAMES SIX SHOOTERS								
	18	"	Y	"		R.P. MET		1·05			MET AT VIMOUTIERS EXCELLENT RESULTS. HIT BY FLAK								
	19	"	Y	"		R.P. MET		·50			TWO TANKS SIX MET DESTROYED MANY DAMAGED BOIVILLE.								
	24	"	Y	"		SHIPPING ON SEINE		1·00			BARGES DAMAGED								
	25	"	W	"		SHIPPING ON SEINE		·45			MT ATTACKED STAVES SEEN								
	26	"	W	"		RP ON MET.		·50			STUD FOLEY MISSING (27TH) BARGES FLAMING. BELIEVED KILLED								
	28	"	U	"		B5 - St ANDRE		·35											
	31	"	U	"		MET N.E. AMIENS		1·05			GERMAN TRANSPORT FLEEING FROM AMIENS.								
						TYPES					THIS SHOW — PERSONAL SCORE 1 TANK 6 MET 1 HORSE DRAWN TRUCK.								
			SUMMARY AUGUST 1944		TYPHOON ...		{ 14·10												
			UNIT 175 SQUADRON				1·15												
			DATE 31-8-44																
			Sig. M. Ambrose F/O																
	31	"	U			MET N.W. AMIENS		1·15											
					GRAND TOTAL [Cols. (1) to (10)] 714 Hrs. 25 Mins. TOTALS CARRIED FORWARD														
							73·25	580·25	3·35	56·40									

M. ... F/Sgt.
O.C. A. FLIGHT

D.F.C. ... 5/4/44
O.C. 175 SQUADRON

OPERATIONS TOTALIZE & TRACTABLE

IN THE WAKE OF GOODWOOD, LIEUTENANT GENERAL GUY SIMONDS' II CANADIAN CORPS ASSUMED RESPONSIBILITY FOR THE OFFENSIVE TOWARDS FALAISE, AND IN THE PROCESS LANDED TWO HEAVY BLOWS ON THE GERMANS OPERATION TOTALIZE ON 7–10 AUGUST AND TRACTABLE ON 14–16 AUGUST.

Although the rolling countryside crossed by the Caen-Falaise road was well-suited to defence based on the long reach of the 88mm gun, Simonds planned to minimize its effectiveness by attacking with infantry at night, pushing armour through once the defence was breached.

Heavy bombers would support the attacks, and artillery, which had grown in strength and effect as the campaign had developed, would crash out ahead of the advancing troops.

One of the lessons of Goodwood was that unprotected infantry found it hard to co-operate effectively with tanks in open country. Simonds accordingly decided to put much of his infantry into extemporized armoured personnel carriers, from which they would dismount only to attack their objectives. These vehicles were created by removing the guns, seats and ammunition bins from Priest self-propelled guns. Steel

British 51st highland Infantry Division.

Canadian 2nd Armoured Brigade.

LEFT *Canadian troops taking part in the advance towards Falaise in the Caen sector, on 11 August 1944, acquaint themselves with a German Bazooka left behind by the retreating Germans.*

GUY SIMONDS

*was commissioned into the Canadian permanent force between the wars, and was Chief of Staff of
I Canadian Corps before taking command of 1st Canadian Infantry Division in Sicily. He led II Canadian
Corps in Normandy, and after the war became Chief Instructor of the Imperial Defence College,
Commandant of the Canadian National Defence College and finally Chief of the Canadian General Staff.
Simonds was temperamental, but set high standards, and was one of the best Allied corps commanders.*

ABOVE *Canadian infantry in half-tracks advance on Falaise.
The white star on the vehicles was an Allied recognition symbol.*

LEFT *Canadian infantry clearing a village on the way to Falaise.
The second soldier is a sniper.*

sheets were welded across the openings, and as armour plate was in
short supply it was improvised by putting a thin layer of sand between
sheets of mild steel. The new vehicles were known as "holy rollers" or
"unfrocked priests". To help the armoured columns, moving in tight
formation on the axis of the main road, keep their direction in the dark,
there were to be navigational aids like light anti-aircraft guns firing tracer
ammunition in the direction of advance and radio direction beams.

Simonds' corps, comprising 2nd and 3rd Canadian Infantry Divisions,
4th Canadian Armoured Division and 2nd Canadian Armoured Brigade,
was reinforced by the British 51st Highland Division and 33rd Armoured
Brigade, and by 1st Polish Armoured Division. The bombing support for
Tractable began at 11.00 on the night of 7 August, and the attacking
columns moved forward shortly afterwards. There were useful gains
during the night, and after dawn Polish and Canadian tanks moved

KURT "PANZER" MEYER

joined the SS in 1933, and fought in Poland before earning the Knight's Cross in Crete in 1941. In 1944, at the age of 33, he commanded the 12th SS Panzer Division Hitlerjugend in the Caen sector. He was a tough and resolute man. Driving up the Caen-Falaise road at the beginning of Operation Totalize, he found infantry streaming back in panic. He stood in the middle of the road and rallied them, ensuring that their positions around Cintheaux were held. After the war a Canadian tribunal sentenced him to death for the murder of prisoners. The sentence was commuted, and he was released in 1954, dying shortly afterwards.

through the infantry, getting as far as Cintheaux, a total advance of six or seven miles. Subsequent progress, against a hardening defence, was less impressive, and the attack paused on 10 June. Operation Tractable followed a similar pattern, though the first attacks were in daylight, with medium bombers going in at 11.30 on the morning of 14 August and heavies following in the afternoon. The attackers were soon across the little River Laizon, and despite some inaccurate bombing and predictably stiff resistance, the infantry of 2nd Canadian Division had

taken Falaise by midnight on 16 August. Not only did Totalize and Tractable result in the capture of this important objective, but they helped disorganize German plans for an offensive against the Americans. It was small wonder that Hitler admitted that 15 August was the worst day of his life.

BELOW *Canadians pass destroyed vehicles on the Caen-Falaise road.*

7 – 15 AUGUST 1944

OPERATIONS TOTALIZE & TRACTABLE

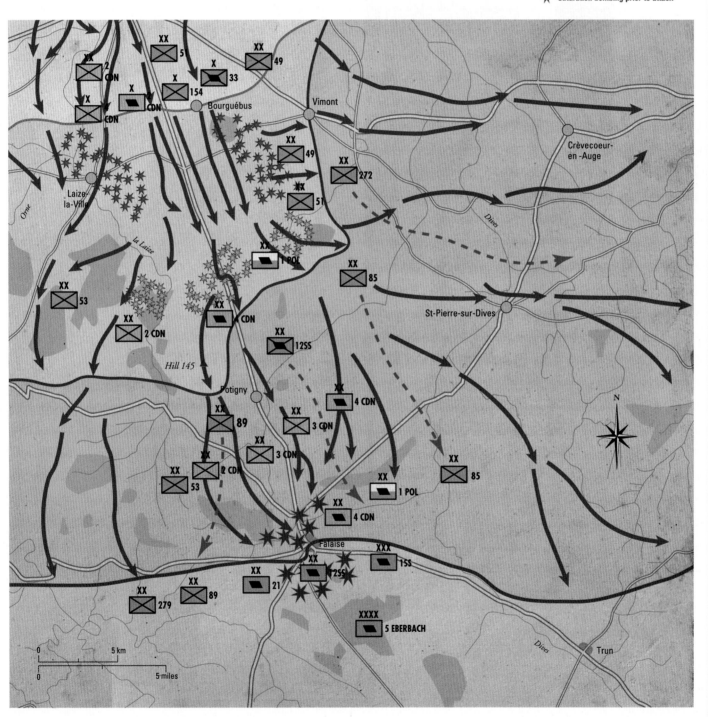

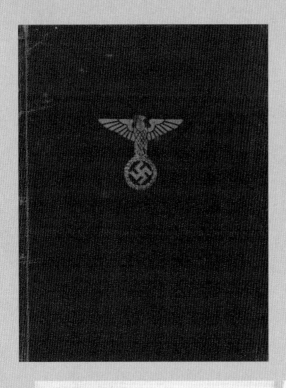

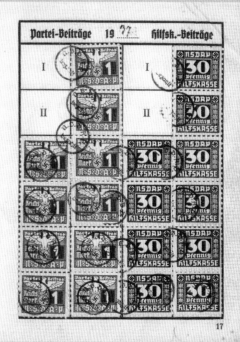

THE FALAISE POCKET

THE BATTLE OF THE FALAISE POCKET WAS IMPROVISED IN RESPONSE TO ALLIED SUCCESSES AND GERMAN FAILURE. BOTH MONTGOMERY AND BRADLEY WERE QUICK TO SPOT THE CHANCE OFFERED THEM.

Bradley told the visiting Henry Morgenthau, US Treasury Secretary, that: "This is an opportunity that comes to a commander not more than once in a century. We are about to destroy an entire German army." The Allies had two major options, a "short hook" to create a pocket near Falaise, or a "long hook" to the Seine to achieve greater encirclement. Both were more difficult and more risky than they appear

in hindsight, for an unplanned envelopment by two national army groups presented extraordinary problems of co-ordination. Moreover, though the German army was indeed beaten, some of its components still displayed their old aggressiveness, and were to show every

BELOW *Allied armour operating in the Falaise sector.*

'FORTY-EIGHT HOURS AFTER THE CLOSING OF THE GAP I WAS CONDUCTED THROUGH IT ON FOOT, TO ENCOUNTER SCENES THAT COULD ONLY BE DESCRIBED BY DANTE. IT WAS LITERALLY POSSIBLE TO WALK FOR HUNDREDS OF YARDS AT A TIME, STEPPING ON NOTHING BUT DEAD AND DECAYING FLESH.

GENERAL DWIGHT D. EISENHOWER

determination of breaking any Allied ring at its weakest point.

A telephone conversation between Bradley and Montgomery on 8 August established the short hook as the preferred option: Bradley's men would jab north towards Argentan, forming the lower jaw of a vice which would meet the British and Canadians jaw crunching down from Caen. Bradley halted his leading corps, Third Army's XV, just south of Argentan on 13 August, arguing that it was "better to have a solid shoulder at Argentan than a broken neck at Falaise". He was across the boundary into 21ˢᵗ Army Group's area, Eberbach's armour was still threatening, and he was uncertain whether there were enough Germans in the Pocket to make the operation worthwhile. Bradley

later complained that Montgomery's caution delayed closing the gap, but it is fair to say that neither commander (nor indeed Eisenhower himself) displayed that killer instinct which would have enabled them to close the gap sooner. Nor ought we to be surprised. These were the armies of mighty democracies nearing the end of a long war, with a chain of command that reflected national and personal tensions.

Early on 16 August Kluge recommended evacuation of the salient, and had begun to withdraw before formal permission reached him later

ABOVE *German transport destroyed by artillery fire. Many combatants found the numerous dead horses in the Pocket particularly depressing.*

DAVID CURRIE

was a Saskatchewan mechanic before joining the Canadian army. Commissioned from the ranks, he was commanding a squadron of the 29th Canadian Armoured Reconnaissance Regiment (South Alberta Regiment) by July 1944. In August he took St-Lambert-sur- Dives, on a German withdrawal route through the Falaise Pocket, and held it in the face of fierce attacks, earning the first Canadian VC of the campaign. He survived the war, and later became sergeant at arms in the Canadian parliament.

that day. It was his last act as a commander, for Field Marshal Walther Model arrived to relieve him on 17 August. As the Germans began to pull back, Bradley, following a phone conversation with Montgomery, ordered Patton to seize Chambois: the jaws of the vice were inching shut. By the evening of 18 August there was still a gap of three miles between the Americans and the Polish armoured division, on the extreme south-east edge of Mongomery's thrust, but on 19 August, Americans and Poles met in Chambois. There was still some very sharp fighting. Major David Currie of the South Alberta Regiment earned the Victoria Cross in St-Lambert-sur-Dives, and the Poles, on what they called "The Mace"

above Chambois, fought desperately to keep Germans in the Pocket and to prevent units outside from boring an escape hole.

When the battle ended on 21 August the killing fields of the Pocket, repeatedly strafed by Allied aircraft, resembled, as Eisenhower put it, something out of Dante's *Inferno,* where it was difficult to walk without treading on human flesh. Although, as subsequent critics pointed out, greater destruction could have been wrought had the Pocket been sealed sooner, it was the culmination of a defeat of shocking proportions. In the previous 10 weeks the defenders of Normandy had lost some 1,300 tanks, at least 50,000 dead, and 200,000 prisoners.

US XV Corps.

Polish Armoured 1st Division.

LEFT *The debris of defeat near Chambois in the Falaise Pocket. Not all the dead in the Pocket were combatants. Chambois alone lost 17 inhabitants.*

BELOW *German prisoners captured in the Falaise Pocket, France on 23 August 1944 on the road between Ecouche and Argentan. British armour can be seen advancing in the background.*

THE FALAISE POCKET

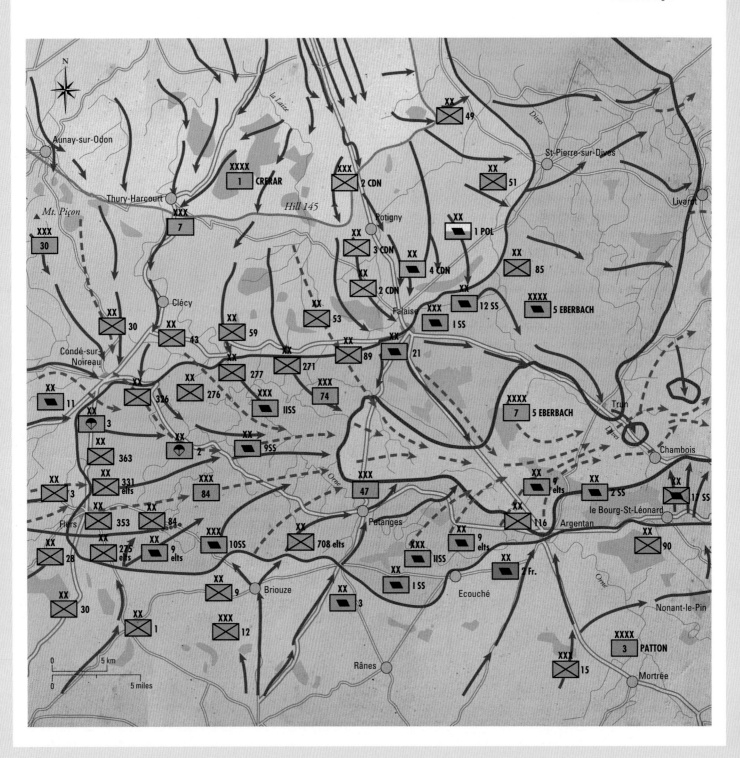

Aunay-sur-Odon

Thury-Harcourt

Mt. Piçon

Hill 145

Potigny

St-Pierre-sur-Dives

Livarot

XXXX 1 CRERAR

XXX 2 CDN

XX 49

XX 51

XX 1 POL

XXX 7

XXX 30

XX 3 CDN

XX 4 CDN

XX 85

XX 2 CDN

XX 12 SS

XXXX 5 EBERBACH

Clécy

XX 30

XX 43

XX 59

XX 53

Falaise

XXX 1 SS

XX 21

Condé-sur-Noireau

XX 11

XX 277

XX 271

XX 89

XXXX 7 5 EBERBACH

Trun

XX 326

XX 276

XXX IISS

XXX 74

Dives

Chambois

XX 3

XX 363

XX 2

XX 9SS

XX 9 elts

XX 2 SS

XX 17 SS

XX 3

XX 331 elts

XXX 84

XXX 47

le Bourg-St-Léonard

Orne

Flers

XX 353

XX 84

XXX 10SS

XX 708 elts

Putanges

XX 116

Argentan

XX 28

XX 275 elts

XX 9 elts

XX 9 elts

XXX IISS

XX 2 Fr.

XX 90

XX 30

XX 9

Briouze

XX 3

XX 1 SS

Ecouché

Orne

Nonant-le-Pin

XX 1

XXX 12

Rânes

XXXX 3 PATTON

XXX 15

Mortrée

0   5 km
0   5 miles

BELOW A page from the official war diary of th 10ᵗʰ Brigade of the 1st Polish Armoured Division detailing its action in closing the Falaise Gap on 20 August. See translation on page 220.

			WAR DIARY or INTELLIGENCE SUMMARY (Delete heading not required).	Army Form **C. 2118.**

Instructions regarding War Diaries and Intelligence Summaries are contained in F.S. Regs., Vol. I. Monthly War Diaries will be enclosed in A.F. C.2119. If this is not available, and for Intelligence Summaries, the cover will be prepared in manuscript.

Month and Year.... Sierpien 1944.r.

Unit......10.BRYGADA KAWALERII PANCERNEJ

Commanding Officer ..PŁK.DYPL. MAJEWSKI.T.........

Place	Date	Hour	Summary of Events and Information	References to Appendices
Pole walki	20	0700	Ugrupowanie Brygady wzg. 262 obsadzone przez 1. i 2. Pułki Panc oraz 8 Baon Strzelców. 10.Pułk Drag. trzyma PŁC skraj CHAMBOIS 24.Ułanów 1.klm. od CHAMBOIS /PŁC-WSCH./.	
		0800	1.Panc. odpiera potężne natarcie czołgów wspartych wielką iloscią piechoty. /straty własne i NPLA duże/.	
		0810	24. oraz 10.Pułk Dragonów wykonują przeciwnatarcie na czołgi i piechotę NPLA ktore wyszło z rej. ST. LAMBERT SUR DIVES. Npl.wycofał się.	
		10.40	10.Drag. odpiera nacicierające /Kampfgruppen" chcące przebic się przez CHAMBOIS.	
		1050	1.Panc. odpiera 2 natarcia czołgów i piechoty. Pomimo rozkazu Dcy.Brygady nakazującego wycofanie się ze względu na ciężką sytuację pułku 1.Panc. walczy dalej i utrzymuje teren.	
		1540	10.Drag. zużył 70 % amunicji. Dowóz zaopatrzenia niemożliwy.	
		1709	2.Panc. walczy z silnym ugrupowaniem Panter i ponosi duże straty we współdziałającej piechocie.	szkic 1
		1725	Ogien art. zatrzymuje natarcie NPLA na 440568.	
		1740	Nowe natarcie czołgów NPLA na 2.Panc. z rej. 450550.	
		1805	2.Panc. dostaje rozkaz do wycofania się na las.	
		1815	2.Panc. czołgi NPLA wdarły się w pierwsze linie.	
		1850	NPL wycofał się z rej 2. anc.	
		2035	Meldunek 1.Panc. o krytycznej sytuacji.	
		2025	2. anc. otrzymał pomoc Kanadyjczyków	
		2125	1.Panc. odciążony działaniem Kanadyjczyków.	
			Załącznik - meldunki plik.	Zał. Nr. 1.
			Notatki ofic.takt.	Zał. Nr. 2.

DOWODCA BRYGADY

MAJEWSKI DOWODCA BRYGADY
płk dypl.

W.24820/1670 800,000 11/43 W. H. & S. 51-7076

THE LIBERATION OF PARIS

THE AMERICANS STRUCK OUT FOR THE SEINE BEFORE FIGHTING HAD FINISHED AT FALAISE. ON 19 AUGUST THEY CROSSED THE RIVER NEAR MANTES, AND THE BRITISH CROSSED AT VERNON FIVE DAYS LATER.

Hitler still hoped to hold Paris, but Model pointed out that the city's retention would be "a big military problem" and knew that there was little chance of holding it with the forces at his disposal.

The Paris Resistance had views of its own. Although de Gaulle sent an emissary with instructions to avoid any "premature rising", on 19 August policemen hoisted the tricoleur above the Prefecture of Police, and there was soon sporadic fighting. The military commander of Paris, Lieutenant General Dietrich von Choltitz, planned to defend the southern and western suburbs, but was told to prepare for demolition the city's public utilities, bridges and many of its most

ABOVE *A Frenchwoman exults as the tricoleur is raised in Paris.*

RIGHT *A US tank destroyer crosses the Seine by means of a pontoon bridge built by US engineers.*

PHILIPPE LECLERC

was wounded and captured in 1940. He escaped and joined de Gaulle in Britain, was sent to equatorial Africa (with a nom de guerre to protect his family), and led a column across the Sahara to join the British 8th Army in Libya. He commanded 2nd Armoured Division, the first Allied unit to enter Paris, in 1944–45, and was French representative at the Japanese surrender. Killed in a 1947 plane crash, Leclerc was posthumously created Marshal of France.

famous buildings. Choltitz was an honourable man with no appetite for this, but had a family in Germany and needed to find a solution that would neither destroy Paris nor result in "premature" surrender.

On 20 August Choltitz agreed to a short-lived truce, and a flurry of Resistance emissaries to the Allies resulted in Eisenhower's agreement that the Free French 2nd Armoured Division under Major General Philippe Leclerc, which had arrived in France on 1 August, would drive straight for Paris. When Leclerc received the order his men were still 120 miles away, but he reached Rambouillet, where he met de Gaulle, on 23 August. They agreed that Leclerc should edge eastwards to find the least-defended route into the city, and at 9.30 on the evening of 24 August his three leading tanks drew up outside the Town Hall.

BELOW *Battle in the shadow of the Arc de Triomphe. Soldiers of the French 2nd Armoured Division look out across German dead on the Champs-Elysées.*

BELOW *The Liberation of Paris. A group of German prisoners are jeered at as they are led through the streets by Free French Fighters and Gendarmes.*

On the next day there was a last burst of fighting, with moments of terrible poignancy as French soldiers died close to home, before Choltitz surrendered. On 26 August Charles de Gaulle walked ahead of his generals and a great crowd for a Te Deum at Notre Dame. There was sniping on the way, but his step never faltered.

As Paris revelled in its liberation the Allied armies hurtled across France. On 1 September Eisenhower assumed command of ground forces, but for the moment he had little impact as his divisions rolled across the battlefields of the First World War, and over the Marne and the Somme, on which Hitler briefly hoped to make a stand. The German divisions which had escaped from Normandy were still too badly bruised to fight. Although those of Army Group G, dislodged by an Allied invasion of the Riviera on 15 August, were in better shape, even Walther Model, "Führer's Fireman" though he was, could not make a stand till he neared the borders of Germany.

Montgomery had always thought in terms of crossing the Seine in D+90 days, and had indeed achieved it. He was wrong to maintain that things had gone according to plan: few campaigns do, and that in Normandy was no exception. It is unfortunate that the tensions inherent in the alliance were magnified as leaders wrote their memoirs and attracted biographers. The real truth of Normandy was that the forces of a mighty coalition had entered the continent of Europe and, mistakes notwithstanding, struck a telling blow at its occupiers. They deserve our gratitude.

BELOW *Brothers reunited. A policeman, in steel helmet, greets his brother, a member of 2nd Armoured Division, in newly liberated Paris on 25 August.*

OPPOSITE *Parisians extend welcoming hands to US troops entering the city on 25 August.*

THE LIBERATION OF PARIS

MAP KEY

— Frontline 14 August

— Frontline 19 August

— Frontline 25 August

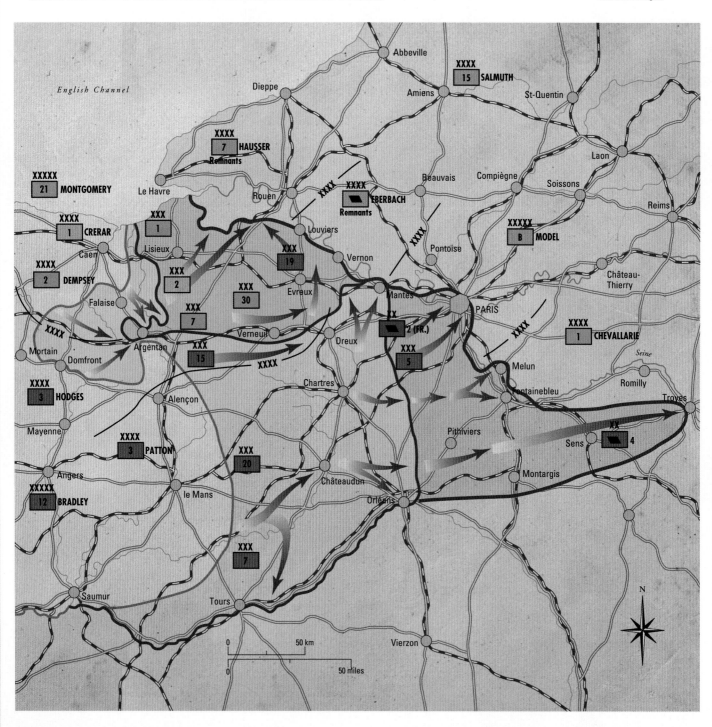

BELOW Aerial leaflet dropped by the allies on the German
troops to facilitate their safe surrender.

SAFE
CONDUCT

The German soldier who carries this safe-
conduct is using it as a sign of his genuine
wish to give himself up. He is to be dis-
armed, to be well looked after, to receive
food and medical attention as required, and
is to be removed from the danger zone as
soon as possible.

PASSIERSCHEIN

*An die britischen und amerikanischen Vorposten:
Der deutsche Soldat, der diesen Passierschein vorzeigt,
benutzt ihn als Zeichen seines ehrlichen Willens, sich
zu ergeben. Er ist zu entwaffnen. Er muss gut be-
handelt werden. Er hat Anspruch auf Verpflegung
und, wenn nötig, ärztliche Behandlung. Er wird so
bald wie möglich aus der Gefahrenzone entfernt.*

Auf Grund von Kapitel 2, Artikel 11, Ver=
tragsnummer 846 der Genfer Konvention
vom 27. Juli 1929 erhalten kriegsgefangene
Soldaten* in amerikanischen oder britischen Händen
die gleiche Verpflegung wie Soldaten des ameri=
kanischen oder britischen Heeres. Ihr Essen wird
von Köchen aus ihren eigenen Reihen auf die
Art ihres Landes zubereitet.

In Amerika oder Kanada erhalten Kriegsge=
fangene für ihre Arbeit innerhalb oder außerhalb
des Lagers pro Tag 80 cents. Die Hälfte davon
wird für die Zeit nach dem Krieg auf einer Bank
hinterlegt, die andere Hälfte in Gutscheinen aus=
gezahlt, mit denen sich der Gefangene Marketender=
waren wie Zigaretten, Süßigkeiten, alkoholfreie
Getränke und dergleichen kaufen kann.

Den Kriegsgefangenen wird Gelegenheit ge=
boten zur Abhaltung von Bildungs= und Lehr=
kursen, zur Ausübung von Sport und Spielen
und zur Veranstaltung von Konzerten, Theater=
aufführungen und Vorträgen. Sie dürfen
Zeitungen lesen und Rundfunk hören.

Postverbindung zwischen den Gefangenenlagern
und der Heimat geht über das Rote Kreuz. Sie
ist zuverlässig und verhältnismäßig schnell. Nach
Kriegsende werden die Gefangenen so bald
wie möglich nach Hause zurückgeschickt.

* Als Soldaten werden auf Grund der Haager Konvention (IV.
1907) angesehen: Alle bewaffneten Personen, die Uniform
tragen oder ein Abzeichen, das von einer Entfernung aus erkannt
werden kann.

ZG 37

TRANSLATIONS

PAGE 33

To: West Roem 1C
From: Alaric
Date: 9.6.'44
Comments: Secret

Alaric of the Arabal company reporting from England, 9th June:

Following personal contact in London on 8th June with my agents Jonny, Dick and Dorick (their reports passed on today), it is my opinion, based on the large-scale troop preparations in South-East England and East Anglia which are unconnected with present operations, that the operations could be diversionary tactics, carried out with the intention of inciting enemy reserves to attack them, in order to inflict a decisive blow at another location. In view of the continuous air raids on strategically favourable locations for this, the area for which preparations are being made could very probably be the Pas de Calais region, especially as if such an attack were to take place, the fact that the air support points are nearer would make such an enterprise easier.

RSHA, Mil. Amt., BR B no. 3435/A4 G Roem 1 H West/: V. 9.6.

[Handwritten comment] Underlines our previous opinion, in accordance with which a second blow is to be expected in another area (Belgium?)

K

PAGES 128–129

Aerial leaflet addressed to the citizens of Occupied Europe from Supreme Commander General Dwight D. Eisenhower.

General Eisenhower addresses the people of the Occupied Countries

PEOPLES OF WESTERN EUROPE:

The troops of the Allied Expeditionary Forces have landed on the coasts of France.

This landing is part of the plan devised by the United Nations, jointly with our great Russian allies, for the liberation of Europe.

I address this message to you all. Even if the first assault did not take place on your territory, the hour of your liberation approaches.

Every patriot, man or woman, young or old, has a role to play in our march toward the final victory. To the members of the Resistance movements led from the interior or from outside, I say, "Follow the instructions you have received!" To the patriots who have never been members of organized Resistance groups, I say, "Continue your auxiliary resistance, but do not endanger your lives needlessly; wait for the time when I give you the signal to rise up and strike the enemy. The day will come when I shall need your united strength." Until that day, I count upon you to submit to the harsh obligation of an impassive discipline.

FRENCH CITIZENS:

I am proud to command once again the valiant soldiers of France. Fighting side by side with their Allies, they are preparing to play their full part in the liberation of their native Homeland.

Because the first landing took place on your territory, I repeat to you, with even greater insistence, my message to the peoples of the other occupied countries of Western Europe. Follow the instructions of your leaders. A premature uprising of all the French risks preventing you, when the decisive moment comes, from serving your country even better. Do not become anxious, and remain on the alert!

As Supreme Commander of the Allied Expeditionary Forces, I have the duty and the responsibility to take all the necessary measures for the conduct of the war. I know that I can count on you to obey the orders that I shall be required to issue.

The civil administration of France must be effectively assured by the French. Each must remain at his post, unless he receives instructions to the contrary. Those who have made common cause with the enemy and have thus betrayed their country will be recalled. When France has been liberated from its oppressors, you yourselves will choose your representatives as well as the Government under whose authority you to want to live.

During the course of this campaign, whose aim is to crush the enemy once and for all, you may still have to suffer loss and destruction. But, however tragic these ordeals may be, they are part of the price that must be paid for victory. I guarantee to you that I shall do everything in my power to attenuate your ordeals. I know that I can count on your steadfastness, which is no less great today than it was in the past. The heroic exploits of the French, who have continued the fight against the Nazis and their Vichy satellites, in France, in Italy, and in the French Empire have been a model and an inspiration for us all.

This landing is just the beginning of the campaign in Western Europe. We are on the eve of great battles. I ask all men who love liberty to be with us. May nothing shake our faith – and nothing stop our attacks – TOGETHER, WE SHALL WIN.

DWIGHT D. EISENHOWER
Supreme Commander of the Allied Expeditionary Forces

PAGE 211

A page from the official war diary of the 10th Brigade of the 1st Polish Armoured Division.

UNIT: 10th Armoured Cavalry Brigade
COMMANDING OFFICER: Col.g.s. Tadeusz MAJEWSKI
MONTH AND YEAR: August 1944
DATE: 20th
PLACE: Field of battle

Hour	Summary of events and information
07.00	Brigade grouped on hill 262 held by 1st and 2nd Armoured Regiments and 8th Rifle Battalion. 10th Dragoon Regiment is holding northern periphery of Chambois. 24th Lancers Regiment one kilometre north-east of Chambois.
08.00	1st Armoured Regiment repulses formidable assault by tanks supported by a large amount of infantry (own and enemy casualties are high).
08.10	From the area St-Lambert-sur-Dives, 24th Lancers Regiment and 10th Dragoon Regiment are carrying out a counter-attack against enemy tanks and infantry. The enemy withdraws.
10.40	10th Dragoon Regiment repulses attacking "Kampfgruppen" aiming at breaking through Chambois.
10.50	1st Armoured Regiment repulses two assaults by tanks and infantry. Despite the Brigade commander's order to withdraw in the direction of the wood due to the serious situation of the regiment, it continues to fight and holds the terrain.
15.40	10th Dragoon Regiment has used up 70 per cent of its ammunition. Bringing up supplies impossible.
17.09	2nd Armoured Regiment fighting with a powerful Panther group and is sustaining heavy casualties among supporting infantry.
17.25	Artillery fire halts enemy attack on 440568.
17.40	New enemy tank assault on 2nd Armoured Regiment from area 450550.
18.05	2nd Armoured Regiment receives order to withdraw towards the wood.
18.15	Enemy tanks have broken into the first lines of 2nd Armoured Regiment.
18.50	Enemy withdraws from 2nd Armoured Regiment's area.
20.35	1st Armoured Regiment reports its critical situation.
20.25	2nd Armoured Regiment receives assistance from Canadians.
21.25	1st Armoured Regiment relieved by actions of Canadians.

Enclosures: packet of reports

Notes of the tactical officer

OC Brigade

Majewski

Col.g.s.

INDEX

(Page numbers in *italic* refer to
photographs and captions; those
in bold refer to maps; *c* signifies
chain of command)

A

Abwehr *33*
aerial leaflets *130-31, 219*
Algonquin, HMCS 102
Allied Expeditionary Force (AEF)
   8, *13*, 72
Allied Second Tactical Air Force
   (ASTAF) 16
Ambrose, Henry ("Papa") *198*
Anglo-Canadian 21st Army Group
   178
Arc de Triomphe *213*
Ardennes offensive 82, 195
Arromanches 96, 98, 99, *134, 135*
Atlantic Wall *21*
Augusta, USS 87

B

Baron and Eterville 4, 5
Barton, Major General Raymond
   O. *17*, 73
Battle of Britain *17*, 197
Battle of the Atlantic 5, 8
Bayeux, France 13, 40, 59, 72, 82,
   96, 98, *98*, 99, 105, 148
Bayeux 79th General Hospital
   162, 163
BBC 30
beach defences 16, *21, 22, 25–7,
   83*, 105
Bedell Smith, Lieutenant General
   Sir Walter 8
Berlin victory parade 124
Bernières 2, *103*, 105
Bletchley Park 49
Blumentritt, General Gunther 20,
   21, 31
Boland, Oliver *47*
Bolton, Private Robert 181
Bradley, Lieutenant General Omar
   N. 7, *8, 18c*, 87, 150, 151, 160,
   169, *169*, 171, 178, 180, 184, *185*,
   186, 192, 193, 195, 196, 206–8,
   218
breakwaters (see *also* Mulberries)
   137
Bréville, France 56, 57, 115
British Army:
   6th Airborne Division 6, 46, 52,
      56, *56, 57*, 112
   4th Airlanding Brigade 53

6th Airlanding Brigade 56
8th Armoured Brigade 96, 98,
   112
7th Armoured Division
   ("Desert Rats") 6, 22, *100*,
   124, 124, 126, 127
11th Armoured Division 143,
   145, 178, 182
22nd Armoured Brigade 126
33rd Armoured Brigade 201
79th Armoured Division *18c*,
   104, 148
2nd Army 178, 180, 182
8th Army 213
14th Army 5
21st Army Group *17*, 178, 207
9th Brigade 114
69th Brigade 98
185th Brigade 114
I Corps 102, 159
II Corps 169
VII Corps 72, 149, 184
VIII Corps 143, 145
XXX Corps 7, 73, 85, 96, 108,
   124, 143, 147, 151, 161, 171,
   183, 187, 193, 203, 210, 218
4th County of London
   Yeomanry *100*, 125, 126, *126*
Desert Rats *see* 7th
   Armoured Division
3rd Division 105, 112, 114,
   159
4th Division 72
Dorset Regiment 99
22nd Dragoon Guards 105
East Yorkshire Regiment 99,
   99, 112, 114, 115
2nd Fife and Forfar Yeomanry
   182
6th Green Howards 98
Guards Armoured Division
   178, 182
51st Highland Infantry Division
   142, *200*, 201
13th Hussars 114, *114*
18th Hussars 114, *114*
59th Infantry Division *156*,
   159
8th Infantry Regiment 73
359th Infantry Regiment 150

1st Northamptonshire
   Yeomanry 126
Nottinghamshire Yeomanry 98,
   99
Oxfordshire and
   Buckinghamshire Light Infantry
   42
9th Parachute Battalion 52
12th Parachute Battalion 56
Queen's Royal Regiment 181
Royal Artillery 117
4th Royal Dragoon Guards 99
7th Royal Dragoon Guards 99
Royal Engineers 52, 98, 105,
   117, 128, 159
Royal Hampshire Regiment 97,
   98, 99, *99*
Royal Marine Commandos 112,
   112, 113, 114, 114
3rd Royal Tank Regiment 182
15th (Scottish) Infantry Division
   143, *143*, 145, *145*, 146
1st South Lancashire
               Regiment
   112, 114, 115
1st Special Service Brigade 46,
   112, 112, 113, 115
Staffordshire Yeomanry 114
31st Tank Brigade 145, *146*
43rd Wessex Division 159
Westminster Dragoon Guards
   97, 98
Yorkshire Territorials 98
Broadhurst, Air Vice Marshal Harry
   196, 197, *197*
Brooke, Field Marshal Sir Alan 12
Brotheridge, Lieutenant Den 44

C

Caen 5, 6, 57, 98, *98*, 105, 112,
   114, 115, 124, 126, 127, 142, 143,
   146, 147, 148, 150, 156, *156, 157*,
   158, 159, *159, 160*, 161, 168,
   178, 182, 183, 192, 200, *200*, 202,
   202, 204, 207, 218
Caen Canal 42, *43, 46, 47, 49*, 114
Cagny *180, 182*, 183
Canadian Army:
   2nd Armoured Brigade *200*
   6th Canadian Armoured

Regiment 108
10th Canadian Armoured
   Regiment 108
8th Canadian Brigade *103*,
   105
I Canadian Corps 102, 159,
   201
II Canadian Corps 200, 201
Canadian 3rd Division 108
North Shore (New
   Brunswick) Regiment 105,
   105, 108, 108
1st Canadian Parachute
   Battalion 52
Queen's Own Rifles 108
Regina Rifle Regiment 105,
   108, 108, *109*
Royal Winnipeg Rifles 105,
   108, 108
South Saskatchewan Regiment
   102
Canadian Navy 102
Canham, Colonel Charles D.W. 86
Capa, Robert *83*
Chambois 208, *208*, 210
Cherbourg 6, 11, 21, 24, 59, 72,
   134, 142, 148–55, *148, 149, 150*,
   151, *152–3, 154–5*
Choltitz, Lieutenant General
   Dietrich von 151, 171, 187,
   212–13, 216
Churchill, Winston 11, *18c*, 104,
   112, 134, *137, 138*
Cintheaux 202
codenames:
   Conundrums *134*
   Hillman *see* Hillman strongpoint
   Pegasus *see* Pegasus Bridge
   Window 28
Colleville 57, 85, 87, 108, 114, 115
Collins, Major General ("Lightning
   Joe") 7, 148, 149, *149, 150*, 151,
   171, *185*, 186, 187
Combined Operations
   Headquarters 134, 137, *138–9*
Coningham, Air Marshal Sir Arthur
   16, 196, 197
construction workers *21*
Corlett, Major General Charles H.
   169, 171, 187

Corncobs 137
Cossac plan 11, *14–15*, 72
Cota, Brigadier General Norman ("Dutch") 82, *82*, 86, 87
Cotentin 58, *59*, 72, 142, 148
Courseulles 105, 161
Coutances 151, 171, 184, *186*, 187
Crepon 98, 99
Crerar, Lieutenant General Henry D. G. *18c*, *185*, 210, 218
Currie, Major David 208, *208*

D

Dempsey, Lieutenant General Miles 7, *18c*, 147, 178, 180, *180*, 184, *185*, 196, 218
Dieppe raid (19 August 1942) 11, *11*, *106*, 112, 134, 218
Dietrich, General Sepp 182
Dollmann, Colonel General Friedrich *18c*, *21*, *21*, 151, 168
DUKWs 76, 80, 86, 137, *137*
Dunkirk evacuation (1940) *16*

E

Eaker, Ira 194
Eastern Front 5, 22, 145
Eberbach, General Heinrich 168, 192, 193, 203, 207, 210, 218
Eisenhower, General Dwight D. 8, *11*, 11, 16, *17*, *18c*, *19*, 58, *58*, 68, 72, 74, *130–31*, 182, 184, 186, 196, 207, 208, 213, 216
El Alamein 180
Enigma *29*, *49*
Erskine, Major General G. W. E. J. 124, *124*, 126

F

Falaise 148, 178, 182, 192, *196*, *197*, 200, *200*, *201*, 202, *202*, 203, 206, *206*, 207, 210, 212, 218
Falaise Gap *211*
Falaise Pocket 6, 7, 145, 206–11, 210
Falley, Lieutenant General Wilhelm 60
"First Aid for Fighting Men" (Keogh) *166-7*
First US Army Group (FUSAG) 30, 150, 168
Fleury-sur-Orne *38*, 161
Forces Françaises de l'Intérieur (FFI) *36*, 40
Fort du Roule 150, *150*
Foucarville *21*, 73
Fox Green, Omaha Beach *84*
Francs-Tireurs et Partisans (FTP) 40
Free French 36, 40, *41*, 114, 213, *215*

French Resistance 30, 36–41, *36*, *37*, *40*, 212–13
FTP (Francs-Tireurs et Partisans) 40

G

Gale, Major General Richard ("Windy") 52, 56, *56*
Garbo (Juan Pujol) 28, *32*, *33*
Gaulle, General Charles de 36, 40, 212, 213, 216
German Army:
  Armed Forces Netherlands *18c*, 20
  Army Group B 16, *18c*, 20, 24, 168
  Army Group G *18c*, 20, 24, 216
  716th Coastal Defence Division 80, 85, 99, 108, 114
  LXXXIV Corps 168
  352nd Division 82
  Hitlerjugend 202, *204*
  352nd Infantry Division 73, 85, 99
  709th Infantry Division 73, 149
  intelligence map *34*, 34–5
  16th Luftwaffe Field Division 159, 182
  5th Panzer Army 192
  1st SS Panzer Corps 126, 182
  2nd SS Panzer Corps 145
  Panzer Group West 16, *18c*, 147, 168
  II Parachute Corps 168
Gerow, Major General Leonard T. ("LTG") 7, 73, 85, 94, 108, 169, 187
Gibson, Staff Sergeant Glen E. 72
Gold Beach 6–7, 96–101, *96*, *97*, 99, *100–1*, 161
Gooseberries 137, 142
Graham, Major General D. A. H. 96, 99
Guderian, General Heinz *29*

H

Hamburg, surrender of 124
Harris, Arthur 194
Hausser, General Paul 145, *145*, 151, 161, 168, 193, 218
Havard, Staff Sergeant Louie *68*
Hawkins, Sapper Cyril *116*
Hillman strongpoint 57, 114, 115
Hitler, Adolf 16, *18c*, 21–2, 30, *33*, 150, 184, 190, 192, 202, 212, 216
Hobart, Major General Sir Percy 104
Hodges, Lieutenant General Courtney H. *185*, 186, 218
Hollis, Company Sergeant Major

Stan 98, *98*
Horsa 42, *42*, 44, 47, 52, 56, 57
Howard, Major John 42, 44, *44*, 46, *46*, 47, 48, *50–1*
Howie, Major Thomas D. 169
Huebner, Major General Clarence R. 82, 85

J

Juno Beach *2–3*, 6–7, 102–11, *102–3*, *104*, 106–7, 108

K

Keller, Major General R. F. L. 102, 108
Keogh, Charles, FRCS *166*
Kieffer, Philippe 114, *114*
Kirk, Rear Admiral D. P., USN 13, 76
Kluge, Field Marshal Günther von 168, 184, 186, 190, 191, 192, *192*, 207
Kraiss, Lieutenant General Dietrich 73, 85, 99

L

Lagrune-sur-Mer 105
landing craft 5, 11, *12*, 22, 30, 68, 70, 72, 76, 80, 82, 86–7, *87*, 96, 97, 105, *112*, *118–19*, 165
Landing Craft, Tanks (LCT), dummy *30*
Le Hamel 98
Leask, Sapper Jimmy *116*
Leclerc, Major General Philippe 213, *213*
Leigh-Mallory, Air Vice Marshal Sir Trafford L. *8*, 11, 16, *17*, *18c*, 58
Les Moulins 86
Lovat, Brigadier Simon Fraser, Lord 46, *112*, *112*, *113*, *117*
Luck, Major Hans von 22, 182
Luftwaffe *18c*, 159, 182, 194

M

MacArthur, Douglas 60
Marigny *186*
Marshall, US Army Chief of Staff George C. 16, 60
medics 162–7, *162*, *163*, *164*
Mediterranean Allied Air Forces (MAAF) *17*
Merville 52, 57, 76, 115
Meyer, Kurt ("Panzer") 202, *202*, *204–5*
Millin, Piper Bill 112, *113*
Minogue, Trooper Joe 97
Model, Field Marshal Walther 208, 212, 216
Mont Fleury 98, 99

Montgomery, General Sir Bernard ("Monty") *8*, 11, *14*, 16, *17*, *18c*, 104, 112, 124, *132–3*, *164*, 169, 178, 180, 182, 184, *185*, 186, 196, 197, 207, 208, 216
Morgan, Lieutenant General F. E. 11
Morgenthau, Henry 206
Mortain 187, 190, *190*, 192, 193, 196, 218
Mountbatten, Admiral Lord Louis 134
Mulberries/Mulberry Harbour 96, 134–41, *134*, *135*, *136*, *137*, *138–41*, 142

N

Nazi Party *204–5*
"Neptune Monograph" (Commander Tank Force 124) *90–3*
Neuville 60
North Africa, Allied invasion of (November 1942) 11, 16, *17*, 114, 195
Noyers 124, 127, 147

O

O'Connor, Lieutenant General Sir Richard 143, 145, *145*, 187
Odon River 124, *127*, 145, 146, 147, 159, 161, 210
Office of Strategic Services (OSS) 36
Omaha Beach 6–7, 82–95, *82*, *84*, 87, *88–9*, *90–3*, *94–5*, 162
operations:
  Bolero 11
  Charnwood 6–7, 156–61, 161
  Cobra 6–7, 184–9, *184*, *185*, 186, 187, 190, 196
  Epsom 6–7, 142–7, *142*, *143*, 147, 150, 159
  Fortitude 30, 34–5, *34*
  Goodwood 6–7, 42, 178–83, *178*, *180*, *181*, *183*, 184, 196, 200
  Hardtack *41*
  Lüttich 6–7, 190–3, *193*
  Market Garden 59
  Neptune 5, 6, 13, 16
  Overlord 11
  Totalize 6–7, 126, 200–5, *203*
  Tractable 6–7, 126, 200–5, *203*
Oppeln-Bronikowski, Colonel von 114
Organization Todt *21*
L'Orne River 47, 56, 57, 82, 112, 114, 115, 142, 147, 182, 183, 203, 210

OSS 36
Ouistreham 13, 112, 114, *114*

P

Paris, liberation of 6, 82, 212–19,
  212–17 passim, 218, *219*
Paris Resistance (*see also* French
  Resistance) 212
Pas de Calais 11, 22, 28, *30, 31, 33,
  34, 34*
Pathfinders 52, *54–5*
Patton, General George S. 169,
  185, *185,* 186, 190, 208, 210, 218
Pegasus Bridge 42–51, *43, 44–5,
  46, 47, 50–1,* 52, 57, 76, 112, *112,
  113*
Pétain, Marshal 36
"Pilot's Flying Log Book" (RAF)
  198–9
Pluto pipeline 134–41, *134, 135*
"A Pocket Guide to France" (War
  and Navy Department) *188–9*
Pointe du Hoc 76–81, *76, 77, 78,
  80, 80, 81, 81*
Polish Army: 1st Polish Armoured
  Division 201, 208, *208, 211*
Priday, Captain Brian 44
Prosser, Private Barney H. 150
Pujol, Juan *see* Garbo

Q

Queen Red sector, Sword Beach
  112, 113
Queen White sector, Sword Beach
  116–17
Quesada, Major General Elwood
  R. ("Pete") 195, *195,* 196

R

Ramsay, Admiral Sir Bertram *8,* 11,
  16, *16*
Ranville 56, 57, 115, 161, 171, 183,
  187
Rennie, Major General T. G. 112,
  114
Resistance *see* French Resistance;
  Paris Resistance
Richter, Lieutenant General
  Wilhelm 80, 85, 99, 108, 114
Ridgway, Major General Matthew
  B. 58, 60, *60*
Robehomme 52
Roberts, HMS 143
Roberts, Major General "Pip" 178
Rochefoucauld, Duc de la *22*
Rodney, HMS 156
Rommel, Field Marshall Erwin 16,
  17, *18c,* 22, 24, 150, 168
"Rommel's Asparagus" 87
Roosevelt, President Franklin D. 11, *18c,*

Roosevelt, Quentin 72
Roosevelt, President Theodore 72
Roosevelt, Brigadier General
  Theodore, Jr 72, *72*
Royal Air Force (RAF) *42, 156,*
  168, 182, 192, 194, *195, 198–9*
  Bomber Command 28, 156
  Fighter Command 16, 17, *195,*
    197
  175 Squadron *198–9*
  Second Tactical Air Force 16,
    196, 197
Rudder, Lieutenant Colonel James
  E. 77, *77,* 80
Rundstedt, Field Marshal Gerd von
  16, 17, *18c,* 20, 24, 150, 168, 192
Russia 5, 8, 36, 126, 190, 192

S

Sadler, Sapper Fred *117*
"Safe Conduct" leaflet *219*
St-Aubin-sur-Mer 105, *105,* 115,
  161
St-Lambert-sur-Dives 208
St-Lô 6–7, 24, *98,* 142, 148, 151,
  168–77, *169, 170, 171, 172–3,
  172, 174–5, 176–7,* 178, 184,
  184, 185, 185
St-Manvieu 99, *143,* 147
Ste-Mère-Eglise 59, 60, *60,* 61,
  62–3, *62,* 73, 151, 171
Sale, Major W. H. J. 125
Samuel Chase, USS 84
Satterlee, USS 80
Schlieben, Lieutenant General
  Karl-Wilhelm von 73, 148, 149,
  150
Seine River 6, 31, 57, 58, 115, 206,
  212, *212,* 216, 218
SHAEF *see* Supreme
  Headquarters Allied
  Expeditionary Forces
Sicily, invasion of (July 1943) *12,*
  169, 201
Simonds, Lieutenant General Guy
  200, 201, *201*
Sioux, HMCS 102
Slaughter, Sergeant John R., D CO.
  83
Slim, Lieutenant General William
  ("Bill") 5
Spaatz, Carl 194
Special Operations Executive
  (SOE) 36–41
Speer, Albert 21
Stalin, Joseph 8, 112
Stars and Stripes 132–3
Supreme Headquarters Allied
  Expeditionary Forces (SHAEF) *8,*
  9, 13, 15, 172–7, *172,* 186

Svenner (Norwegian destroyer) 68
Sword Beach 6–7, 105, 112–21,
  *112, 113, 114, 115, 116–17,
  118–21,* 161
Szabo, Violette 40, *40*

T

Talybont, HMS 80
tanks:
  assault tanks (RE) 105
  Centaur 105
  Churchill *146*
  Cromwell *100–1, 126,* 178
  Duplex Drive (DD) Sherman
    swimming *30,* 72, *104,* 114
  Hobart's "Funnies" 104, *104*
  Panther 22, *178, 190*
  Sherman tanks *30,* 70, *98, 104,
    106–7, 114, 126, 126,* 182,
    182, 186
  T-34 *190*
  Tiger 22, 125, *126, 126, 128,*
    190
Taylor, Major General Maxwell D.
  58, 59, *59,* 60
Tedder, Air Chief Marshal Sir
  Arthur *8,* 11, 16, 17, *18c,* 196
Texas, USS 76
Tombola *134,* 137
Top Secret Ultra *see* Ultra
Troarn 52, 57, 183

U

Ultra 28, 192
US Air Force (USAF):
  8th Air Force 37
  9th Air Force *194*
  IX Tactical Air Command 195,
    196
US Army:
  XVIII Airborne Corps 60
  82nd Airborne Division 6, 59,
    60, 61, *62,* 64, 150
  101st Airborne Division 58,
    59, 61
  4th Armoured Division *184,*
    186
  First Army *18c,* 87, 184, *185,*
    186
  Eighth Army 60
  12th Army Group 178, *185,* 186
  V Corps 82, 87, 94, *169,* 208
  VII Corps 72, 148, 149, 184
  XV Corps *208*
  XIX Corps 169
  28th Division 82
  30th Division *190,* 192
  7th Field Artillery Battalion 86
  11th Field Artillery Battalion 86
  1st Infantry Division 85

4th Infantry Division *68,* 72, 73
9th Infantry Division *149*
29th Infantry Division 85, *169*
79th Infantry Division *148*
8th Infantry Regiment 73
115th Infantry Regiment 87
116th Infantry Regiment 82, 83,
  85, 86, 169
18th Infantry Regiment 87
Petroleum Distribution Group
  134
2nd Ranger Battalion 76, 77,
  77, 80
70th Tank Battalion 72
USAAF *191,* 192, 194, 196, 197
US Army First US Army Group
  (FUSAG) 30, 150, 168
US Army Medical Department
  (USAMD) 162
USSR 5, 8, 36, 126, 190, 192
Utah Beach 6–7, 21, 41, 59, 60,
  68–75, *68, 69, 70–1,* 72, 73, 76,
  87, *132*

V

Vaughan, Captain 44
Ver-sur-Mer 96, 98, 99
Villers-Bocage 6–7, 124–33, *124,
  125, 126,* 127

W

Wallwork, Staff Sergeant Jim 44
War Bonds 10
War of the Rails *40*
Warlimont, General Walter 22
Washington Conference (May
  1943) 11
weather maps 74–5, *74*
Western Task Force (WTF) 76
Whales 137
White, Brigadier Sir Bruce 134
Wittmann, Captain Michael 22,
  126
Wood, Wilson *132*

CREDITS

The vast majority of images reproduced in this book have been taken from the collections of the Imperial War Museums. Reference numbers for each of the photographs reproduced are listed below.

4 B 6184, 8 TR 160, 11 HU 1904, 12 A 17918, 15, 17 TR 1042 (top centre), CH 14706 (top right), CH 11943 (bottom left), 22 HU 3056, 22-23 MH 24327, 28 H 42529 (top), E MOS 1451 (bottom right), 30 H 42351 (top), 30 H 42535 (bottom), 31 H 24327, 34-35 (Heer Gen. St. d. H. Fremde Heere West, M.I. 14/841), 36 B 9376, 40 HU 16541 (top), 40 KY 24324 (bottom), 42 H 39183, 43 B 5233, 44-45 B 5288, 46 B 5234, 47 MH 24891, 52 CL 26, 54-55 H 39070, 56 B 5291 (top), H 39074 (centre), MH 2076 (bottom), 58 EA 25491, 59 EA 25509 , 60 (bottom) MH 24842, 68 EA 25902, 76 AP 25625, 81 MH 24806, 82 (centre) EA 25641, 83 OWIL 44947, 96 B 5245, 97 B 5252, 98 (centre) HU 2001, B 5685 (bottom), 100-101 B 5251, 102-103 A 23938, 103 MH 4505 (top), 105 B 5228, 106-107 MH 3097, 112 BU 1181 (top), H 11791 (right), 113 B 5103 , 114 MH 2011 (top right), B 7370 (centre), 116-117 B 5114, B 5065 (top), B 5036 (bottom), 118-121, 124 MH 7887 (right), 125 CL 344, 134 EA 5036, 135 T 54 (top), A 24360 (bottom), 136 EA 45245A, 137 A 24832 (top), MH 245 (bottom), 142 B 5957, 143, B 5963, 144-145 B 5950, 145 B 10600 (top), 146 B 5956 (top), B 5959 (bottom), 148 AP 282111, 149 OWIL 27887 (bottom), 150 EA 27890 (bottom), 152-153 PL 28033, 158 B 6800, 159 B 6897, 160 B 6794, 162 EA 25979, 163 B5482, 164 OWIL 30273 (top), EA 30750 (bottom), 168 EA 30511, 172–177 (M5/6005), (M5/6007), (M86/348), 178 B 7649, 179 CL 477, 180 B 7407 (top), 181 TP 11286E, 182 B 7760, 184 EA 3084, 185 KY 31764 (bottom), B 9473 (centre), 186 PL 31235 (bottom), 195 NYP 36636 (top), CH 13092 (bottom), 197 CH 13092 (top), NYP 36636 (bottom), 201 A 17963 (top), HU 52362 (centre), NYT 4974 (bottom), 202 (top) Dept. of Documents , German Miscellanous 153, Sweeting Collection, 206 NYP 37818, 207 HU 62168, 208 MH 4204 (top), EA 34532 (bottom), 212 EA 34532 (left), KY 482458 (right), 213 OWIL 33584 (top), EA 37079 (bottom), 216 EA 35412, 217 EA 35146

Photographs from sources outside of the collections of the Imperial War Museums:
1-3 Galerie Bilderwelt/Getty Images, 14 Papers of The Rt. Hon. Viscount Montgomery of Alamein CMG CBE and Imperial War Museums, Department of Documents (BLM72/2), 16 Keystone/Hulton Archive/Getty Images, 17 Popperfoto/Getty Images (bottom right), 17 Private Collection (bottom centre), 19 Dwight D. Eisenhower Library, Abilene, Kansas, 20 AKG-Images, 21 Bildarchiv PreuBischer Kulterbesitz, 25–27 Musée du Débarquement, Place du 6-Juin, 14117 Arromanches, Normandie, France, 29 Photo Scala, Florence/BPK, Bildagentur fuer Kunst, Kultur und Geschichte, Berlin, 32-33 The National Archives, Kew, 37 Alamy/ Photo12, 38-39 REX/Shutterstock/AP Photo, 41 Musée du Débarquement, Utah Beach, 50480 Ste-Marie-du-Mont, Normandie, France, 44 Memorial Pegasus, Avenue de Major Howard, France (left), 44 Penny Howard Bates, daughter of Major Howard D.S.O C. de G. , from his archives (bottom left), 49 The National Archives, Kew, 50–51 Penny Howard Bates, daughter of Major John Howard D.S.O., C. de G., from his archives, 53 Pictorial Press/Alamy, 58 National Archives and Records Administration, 62–67 Musée Airborne, 14 rue Eisenhower, 50480 Ste-Mère-Eglise, Normandie, France, 69 Bettmann/Getty Images, 70-71 DPA/Press Association Images, 74–75: Meteorological Office (UK), 79 Musée du Débarquement, Utah Beach, 50480 Ste-Marie-du-Mont, Normandie, France, 83 Robert Capa/Magnum Photos, 84 National Archives and Records Administration, 87 National Archives and Records Administration (bottom) & 88-89, 90–93: D-Day Museum, Portsmouth Museums & Records Service; 94–95: Musée du Débarquement, Place du 6-Juin, 14117 Arromanches, Normandie, France, 109–111: © Canadian War Museum (CWM), 112 Sgt. Wilkes/ IWM via Getty Images (centre), 113 Capt. J L Evans/ IWM via Getty Images, 126 Bildarchiv PreuBischer Kulterbesitz (centre), 126 Ullstein Bild (top), 126 Bildarchiv PreuBischer Kulterbesitz (centre), 128-129 Leonard McCombe/Picture Post/Getty Images, 130–131: Musée du Débarquement, Utah Beach,

50480 Ste-Marie-du-Mont, Normandie, France, 122–123: Papers of The Rt. Hon. Viscount Montgomery of Alamein CMG CBE and Imperial War Museums, Department of Documents, 136–141: D-Day Museum, Portsmouth Museums & Records Service (Phoenix cover and early Mulberry designs); Imperial War Museums, Department of Documents, Papers of Captain J.J. Youngs, 92/50/1 (Churchill memo), 154-155 Hulton-Deutsch Collection/CORBIS/Corbis via Getty Images, 156 Bettmann/Getty Images, 157 HIP/Topfoto
166–167 Musée du Débarquement, Place du 6-Juin, 14117 Arromanches, Normandie, France, 169 National Archives and Records Administration, 170 Frank Scherschel/The LIFE Picture Collection/Getty Images, 186 The Tank Museum, Bovington, 187 Photos12.com/Coll-DITE/ USIS (right), 188–189 Musée du Débarquement, Utah Beach, 50480 Ste-Marie-du-Mont, Normandie, France, 198–199 Janet Ambrose, 201 REX/Shutterstock/AP Photo (centre), 209 REX/Shutterstock/AP Photo, 211 The Polish Institute and Sikoriski Museum, 214-215 Bettmann/Getty Images. 219 Musée D-Day Omaha, Rte de Grandcamp, 14710 Vierville-sur-mer, Normandie, France.

Special thanks to Ray Hutchins, Memorial Pegasus, Musée du Débarquement, Musée D-Day Omaha, The National D-Day Museum for the use of their photographs.

All other badges and medals photographed by Carlton Books Ltd.

Every effort has been made to acknowledge correctly and contact the source and/or copyright holder of each picture, item of memorabilia and artwork, and Carlton Books Limited apologises for any unintentional errors which will be corrected in future editions of this book.